LGBTQ Young
Adult Fiction

ALSO BY CAREN J. TOWN

"Unsuitable" Books: Young Adult Fiction and Censorship (McFarland, 2014)

The New Southern Girl: Female Adolescence in the Works of 12 Women Authors (McFarland, 2004)

LGBTQ Young Adult Fiction

A Critical Survey, 1970s–2010s

Caren J. Town

McFarland & Company, Inc., Publishers
Jefferson, North Carolina

LIBRARY OF CONGRESS CATALOGUING-IN-PUBLICATION DATA

Names: Town, Caren J., 1957– author.
Title: LGBTQ young adult fiction : a critical survey, 1970s/2010s / Caren J. Town.
Description: Jefferson, North Carolina : McFarland & Company, Inc., Publishers, 2017. | Includes bibliographical references and index.
Identifiers: LCCN 2017023518 | ISBN 9780786496945 (softcover : acid free paper) ∞
Subjects: LCSH: Young adult fiction, American—History and criticism. | Queer theory. | Homosexuality in literature. | Lesbians in literature. | Gender identity in literature. | Adolescence in literature. | Gays' writings, American—History and criticism. | Sexual minority youth—Books and reading—United States. | Homosexuality and literature—United States.
Classification: LCC PS374.Y57 T69 2017 | DDC 813.009/9283—dc23
LC record available at https://lccn.loc.gov/2017023518

BRITISH LIBRARY CATALOGUING DATA ARE AVAILABLE

ISBN (print) 978-0-7864-9694-5
ISBN (ebook) 978-1-4766-2895-0

© 2017 Caren J. Town. All rights reserved

No part of this book may be reproduced or transmitted in any form or by any means, electronic or mechanical, including photocopying or recording, or by any information storage and retrieval system, without permission in writing from the publisher.

Front cover image © 2017 iStock

Printed in the United States of America

McFarland & Company, Inc., Publishers
  Box 611, Jefferson, North Carolina 28640
    www.mcfarlandpub.com

To Lee, Daryl, Billy, and Greg—
I wish they'd had these books
when you were teenagers.

Acknowledgments

Once again, I would not be writing this book without the support of Georgia Southern University, which provided me with academic leave, and the encouragement of my university friends and colleagues, especially those in the Department of Literature and Philosophy. I also want to acknowledge my students over the 30 years I've been teaching, particularly those in my Adolescent Literature and Teaching Literature courses, who have read many of these books with me and offered important insights about them. In addition, the Children's Literature and the American Culture associations have offered me venues for trying out some of the work in this book. Most importantly, I am indebted (in the best possible way) to my husband, Patrick J. Perkins, who has, once again, been my facilitator with the details of life, my proofreader, my conference travel buddy, and my most enthusiastic cheerleader. He has been patient with my insistence that I have to work and my distraction after I've done so. Thanks for holding down the home front—and for getting me out of the house when I needed a break.

Table of Contents

Acknowledgments	vi
Preface	1
Introduction—Queer Theory, Queer Literature, Queer YA Fiction	3
One. Getting There: LGBTQ Young Adult Literature in the 70s and 80s	23
Two. Beyond *Deliver Us from Evie*: Contemporary Lesbian Young Adult Fiction	50
Three. "But that's young gay love for you": Contemporary Gay Young Adult Fiction	78
Four. "Gender is a choice, not a life sentence": Young Adult Narratives of Trans Identities	102
Five. "Difference matters": LGBTQ Families in Young Adult Fiction	134
Six. "What a wonderful world": Utopias and Dystopias in LGBTQ Young Adult Fiction	157
Conclusion—Why Read (or Teach) These Books, and Where Do We Go from Here?	181
Chapter Notes	185
Bibliography	187
Index	195

Preface

The genesis for this project came years ago, when I was searching (often in vain) for books for my Adolescent Literature and Teaching Literature courses that represented the experiences of gay and lesbian adolescents in ways that weren't tragic or preachy, or filtered exclusively through the perspectives of straight narrators. In the early 1990s, it was difficult (if not impossible) to find such books, and students, in those days, were often reluctant to consider teaching them in the high schools and middle schools at which they would soon be working.

However, as we moved into the 21st century, things began to change, with books like David Levithan's *Boy Meets Boy* in 2003, followed by a steadily widening variety of books featuring lesbian, bisexual, and even (to a smaller degree) trans young adults who were finally not being punished for their sexualities and identities by being killed in car wrecks, having their hearts broken, or their secrets betrayed. The attitudes of my students began to change as well, as they realized that they could (and *should*) teach books that compassionately told the stories of many of their future students. However, as late as 2011, Blackburn and Clark reported that "scholarship focused on reading and becoming readers of LGBT-themed children's and young adult texts, whether in the U.S. or international school-settings, is incredibly sparse" (150). Clearly, the scholarship on this fiction had not yet caught up with its publication.

All these factors led me to want to learn more about the variety of LGBTQ[1] perspectives in literature and criticism, and so I began by taking a vertical view of the theories behind gender and sexual identity and the history of young adult literature that tackled these once-controversial subjects. I also wanted to employ a broader, more horizontal view of the literature available today for LGBTQ young adults. This book is result of those inquiries, and I hope it will be of value to others like me, who teach future middle and secondary school teachers, and to those teachers, community members, and parents who want to find out more about the kinds of books that accurately and sympathetically treat the LGBTQ experience. It is also my hope that this book will educate the wider community about these novels, as a way of preventing the censorship that still plagues the authors who write, librarians who promote, and teachers who discuss these novels. Most importantly, it will help to insure that LGBTQ young adults will have better access to books that chronicle their experience and straight (and/or questioning) students will be moved toward greater awareness and empathy.

The book has six chapters, with an introduction focusing on the debates and insights of queer theory, the relationship between theory and literature, and the connections to young adult fiction. Chapter One looks at the history of LGBTQ literature for young adults, starting with Isabelle Miller's *Patience and Sarah* and John Donovan's *I'll Get There. It Better Be Worth the Trip*, published in 1969 and ending with Carolyn Meyer's *Elliott and Win* (1986). The next two chapters discuss novels about gay and lesbian teens from the early 1990s until 2014. Following is a chapter on trans teens, both in fiction and in real life, and Chapter Five looks at LGBTQ families. The final chapter treats LGBTQ utopias and dystopias and looks at and discusses some new trends in science fiction. With the earlier novels, I tried to choose books that remain relevant today (even if some of the characters' attitudes might be somewhat dated). With books written after the turn of the century, I deliberately chose novels that treat being gay, lesbian, bi, or trans less as the primary problem of the novel and more as one aspect of the main character. With every choice, I looked for novels that were a pleasure to read and with complex characterization and interesting plot lines. Fortunately, there are now plenty of those books available, and I am confident that, unlike me, teachers in the future will not have the same difficulty finding great books on LGBTQ teens that I once did.

Table of Contents

Acknowledgments	vi
Preface	1
Introduction—Queer Theory, Queer Literature, Queer YA Fiction	3
One. Getting There: LGBTQ Young Adult Literature in the 70s and 80s	23
Two. Beyond *Deliver Us from Evie*: Contemporary Lesbian Young Adult Fiction	50
Three. "But that's young gay love for you": Contemporary Gay Young Adult Fiction	78
Four. "Gender is a choice, not a life sentence": Young Adult Narratives of Trans Identities	102
Five. "Difference matters": LGBTQ Families in Young Adult Fiction	134
Six. "What a wonderful world": Utopias and Dystopias in LGBTQ Young Adult Fiction	157
Conclusion—Why Read (or Teach) These Books, and Where Do We Go from Here?	181
Chapter Notes	185
Bibliography	187
Index	195

Preface

The genesis for this project came years ago, when I was searching (often in vain) for books for my Adolescent Literature and Teaching Literature courses that represented the experiences of gay and lesbian adolescents in ways that weren't tragic or preachy, or filtered exclusively through the perspectives of straight narrators. In the early 1990s, it was difficult (if not impossible) to find such books, and students, in those days, were often reluctant to consider teaching them in the high schools and middle schools at which they would soon be working.

However, as we moved into the 21st century, things began to change, with books like David Levithan's *Boy Meets Boy* in 2003, followed by a steadily widening variety of books featuring lesbian, bisexual, and even (to a smaller degree) trans young adults who were finally not being punished for their sexualities and identities by being killed in car wrecks, having their hearts broken, or their secrets betrayed. The attitudes of my students began to change as well, as they realized that they could (and *should*) teach books that compassionately told the stories of many of their future students. However, as late as 2011, Blackburn and Clark reported that "scholarship focused on reading and becoming readers of LGBT-themed children's and young adult texts, whether in the U.S. or international school-settings, is incredibly sparse" (150). Clearly, the scholarship on this fiction had not yet caught up with its publication.

All these factors led me to want to learn more about the variety of LGBTQ[1] perspectives in literature and criticism, and so I began by taking a vertical view of the theories behind gender and sexual identity and the history of young adult literature that tackled these once-controversial subjects. I also wanted to employ a broader, more horizontal view of the literature available today for LGBTQ young adults. This book is result of those inquiries, and I hope it will be of value to others like me, who teach future middle and secondary school teachers, and to those teach-

Preface

ers, community members, and parents who want to find out more about the kinds of books that accurately and sympathetically treat the LGBTQ experience. It is also my hope that this book will educate the wider community about these novels, as a way of preventing the censorship that still plagues the authors who write, librarians who promote, and teachers who discuss these novels. Most importantly, it will help to insure that LGBTQ young adults will have better access to books that chronicle their experience and straight (and/or questioning) students will be moved toward greater awareness and empathy.

The book has six chapters, with an introduction focusing on the debates and insights of queer theory, the relationship between theory and literature, and the connections to young adult fiction. Chapter One looks at the history of LGBTQ literature for young adults, starting with Isabelle Miller's *Patience and Sarah* and John Donovan's *I'll Get There. It Better Be Worth the Trip*, published in 1969 and ending with Carolyn Meyer's *Elliott and Win* (1986). The next two chapters discuss novels about gay and lesbian teens from the early 1990s until 2014. Following is a chapter on trans teens, both in fiction and in real life, and Chapter Five looks at LGBTQ families. The final chapter treats LGBTQ utopias and dystopias and looks at and discusses some new trends in science fiction. With the earlier novels, I tried to choose books that remain relevant today (even if some of the characters' attitudes might be somewhat dated). With books written after the turn of the century, I deliberately chose novels that treat being gay, lesbian, bi, or trans less as the primary problem of the novel and more as one aspect of the main character. With every choice, I looked for novels that were a pleasure to read and with complex characterization and interesting plot lines. Fortunately, there are now plenty of those books available, and I am confident that, unlike me, teachers in the future will not have the same difficulty finding great books on LGBTQ teens that I once did.

Introduction
Queer Theory, Queer Literature, Queer YA Fiction

> Story helps us shape and reshape life.—Kay Vandergrift, "Introduction," *Mosaics of Meaning*, ix

> [T]he world is a lonely and frightening place for kids who are growing up different. Thirty percent of teenage suicides are currently attributable to kids' unmanageable anxiety about being homosexual. How many such lives could be saved, I wonder, by giving young readers unchallenged access to books that show them they are not alone and that speak openly and nonjudgmentally about *their* life experience?—Michael Cart, "Annie.... Still on Our Minds," 127

> It's always open season on gay kids—Eve Kosofsky Sedgwick, "How to Bring Your Kids Up Gay," 140

Queer Theory: Defining Terms/Outlining History

In 1995, Michael Warner and Lauren Berlant announced in *PMLA* that "queer is hot" (343). In the two decades since then, the heat, for literary theorists and critics especially, has remained high, although, as Kathryn Kent laments in 2004, queer theory "still lacks models for the multiple ways in which deviant, perverse sexualities are formed and how they survive" (184). Debates have arisen about the employment of the word "queer," the fluidity of gender and sexuality, futurity within queer literature and culture, minority queer positioning, and, for the purposes of this book, about the relationship between queer theory, adolescence, and adolescent literature. In order to move most productively into these literary debates, it seems necessary first to outline the shape of the dis-

Introduction

cipline of queer studies and then point readers toward at least a few of the relevant debates concerning adolescence, queerness, and literature. Consequently, this introduction will begin with the definition of key terms and the identification of ongoing debates and then transition into a discussion of their relationship to current issues in young adult fiction and criticism.

As a starting place, it is important to recognize that, as historian George Chauncey points out in *Gay New York*,

> the hetero-homosexual binarism, the sexual regime now hegemonic in American culture, is a stunningly recent creation. Particularly in working-class culture, homosexual behavior per se became the primary basis for the labeling and self-identification of men as "queer" only around the middle of the twentieth century; before then, most men were so labeled only if they displayed a much broader inversion of their ascribed gender status by assuming the sexual and other cultural roles ascribed to women [13].

The sexual identities that might seem so fixed are actually a product of the mid–20th century, Chauncey insists. He also reminds us that heterosexuality, "no less than homosexuality, is a historically specific social category and identity" (26). This "stunningly recent creation" has nevertheless become reified in contemporary culture, so much so that current theorists of gender and sexuality feel the need to struggle with new terms and new ways to think about (and perhaps erase) these binaries.

In her groundbreaking 1990 book, *The Epistemology of the Closet*, Eve Kosofsky Sedgwick explores this issue. She argues that "the development of an alternative analytic axis [other than sex/gender]—call it sexuality—might well be, therefore, a particularly urgent project for gay/lesbian and antihomophobic inquiry" (32). Sedgwick, who will later consider the implications of queer theory for both LGBTQ and "straight" critics, in this instance points toward the urgent need to redefine gay and lesbian studies in a direction that recognizes the fluidity of sexual identification and practice and the importance of such a stance for literary theory and social justice. Leo Bersani enters this conversation in 1995 with *Homos*, in which he calls for "a new way of coming together" that would not involve "assimilation into already constituted communities," but instead "celebrat[es] 'the homo' in all of us" (10). As with Sedgwick, Bersani seems to be arguing for a more inclusive definition of sexuality, as opposed to the restrictive existing categories of sexual desire, identity, and/or practice.

Following Bersani and Sedgwick, Theresa De Lauretis reminds readers that "the sexual remains within the social as an unmasterable, uncontainable excess, a force of conflict, disaggregation, unbinding" (256). The overflowing nature of sexuality, she says, can lead to productive conflict and the breaking down of barriers. Other theorists tend to agree with De Lauretis. Bert Archer, in *The End of Gay: And the Death of Heterosexuality* (2006), provocatively argues that "sexual attraction is as slippery and sloppy as the bodily fluids it produces. Fitting it into slots serves only to hem us in and dry us up" (229). Annette Schlicter agrees: "[H]eterosexuality—like all sexual identities," she argues, "is an unstable, incoherent category" (546). The important things to recognize in all of these theorists' arguments are the ways in which instability and incoherence can be seen as valuable and necessary. This becomes especially important when considering LGBTQ literature for young adults, whose sexuality is especially "slippery" and "unstable" as they attempt to define themselves emotionally and sexually.

In response to all this slipperiness of gender and sexual identity, theorists and critics (as well as political activists and regular folks) have come to embrace the word "queer" as both an identity and a critical practice. As Michael Warner says in his introduction to *Fear of a Queer Planet*, "The preference for 'queer' ... rejects a minoritizing logic of toleration or simple political interest-representation in favor of a more thorough resistance to regimes of the normal" (xxvi). By this he means that traditional identity categories such as gay, lesbian, or straight must now give way to a questioning of the "normal" in favor of the "queer." Warner continues: "Queer politics has not just replaced older modes of lesbian and gay identity; it has come to exist alongside those older modes, opening up new possibilities and problems whose relation to more familiar problems is not always clear" (xxviii). Although this could be seen as unsettling, or at the very least uncertain, it does suggest that old and new ways of thinking about sexuality might eventually be combined. This creates exciting challenges for the literary theorist and critic, as well as for the writer of fiction for adults and adolescents.

Calvin Thomas, in his 2000 book on queer theory and heterosexuality, articulates this flexibility well: "However we perform (and whomever we perform with), the extent to which our actions and performances are 'critically queer' may be the extent to which we promote connections—erotic and political, with others and with the world—that

Introduction

indeed seem possible only if identity and identity politics are allowed to be put at risk" (32). Those who read the world and those who read literature must find new ways to be "critically queer," even if those ways of reading might be personally unsettling and challenging. Nevertheless, the connections that might be created could be exciting—aesthetically as well as theoretically.

More recently, Sarah Ahmed discusses queerness in terms of spatial orientation in her *Queer Phenomenology* (2006). "If orientation is a matter of how we reside in space," Ahmed says, "then sexual orientation might also be a matter of residence; of how we inhabit spaces as well as 'who' or 'what' we inhabit spaces with" (1). Practicing non-normative sexualities, she says, "involves a personal and social commitment to living in an oblique world, or in a world that has an oblique angle in relation to that which is given" (161). Finally, she argues, "[t]o make things queer is certainly to disturb the order of things" (161). Certainly, the works discussed in this book do "disturb the order" of the heteronormative and often homophobic world of young adult literature.

Gender as Performance

"Gender" has become as contested a term as homo/heterosexuality and queer. Perhaps the first theorist to interrogate this issue (and to elaborate and complicate her position over time) is Judith Butler. Early on, she argues that "gender proves to be performative—that is, constituting the identity it is purported to be" (25). This has implications, of course, for feminist and queer theory, but it is also of special relevance to adolescent literary theory, where adolescence can be seen as the quintessential time of performance, of trying on various ways of being, which would of course include various sexualities and kinds of sexual desire. Both hetero- and homosexuality are performances, or as Butler puts it in her groundbreaking *Gender Trouble* (1990), "gay is to straight *not* as copy is to original, but, rather, as copy is to copy" (31). She continues this argument: "[I]f gender is something that one becomes—but can never be—then gender is itself a kind of becoming or activity, and that gender ought not to be conceived as a noun or a substantial thing or a static cultural marker, but rather as an incessant and repeated action of some sort" (112). This idea of gender as verb—as action—rather than as noun—as static—is vital for the ways in which LGBTQ literature contributes to changing notions about gender and sexuality.

Butler also acknowledges the relationship between sexuality and the State, an issue that concerns adolescents (and the writers of adolescent fiction) as well. She says, "[T]he body is not a 'being,' but a variable boundary, a surface whose permeability is politically regulated, a signifying practice within a cultural field of gender hierarchy and compulsory heterosexuality" (139). That is, within the contemporary capitalist heteronormative state, "male" exists in a hierarchy to "female" and "heterosexuality" to "homosexuality." Typically, crossing borders is not allowed. However, Butler argues that gender "ought not to be construed as a stable identity or locus of agency from which various acts follow; rather, gender is an identity tenuously constituted in time, instituted in an exterior space through a *stylized repetition of acts*" (140). These "stylized repetitions of acts" through which we perform gender—and through which our gender at any particular moment is recognized by others—are the shifting ground of our bodily identities—and therefore should not be subject to State control.

In *Bodies That Matter* (1993), Butler expands her argument, saying that it is necessary to include language that identifies gender and sexuality and to "claim" those words "to refute homophobic deployments of them in law, public policy, on the street, in 'private' life" (229). Thus, if we declare ourselves using words such as "lesbian," "gay," "straight," and/or "queer," we avoid appropriation of those words by others who use them homophobically or, on the other hand, to valorize the categories in some way.

Importantly, she also suggests that we are not entirely in control of our gender "assignments," which are "never quite carried out according to expectations, whose addressee never quite inhabits the ideal s/he is compelled to approximate." In addition, she says, "this embodying is a repeated process. And one might construe repetitions as precisely that which *undermines* the conceit of voluntarist mastery designated by the subject in language" (231). Again, I think this is relevant to adolescent development and to the depiction of adolescence in fiction. Young adults may believe that they control their gendered performances (and the reception of those performances), but it is highly likely that neither their representations nor the reception of them can be regulated.

Rosi Braidotti continues this discussion by describing a "non-uni-

Introduction

tary vision of the subject. A subject which is definitely not one, but rather multi-layered, interactive and complex" (43). Drawing on the work of Luce Irigaray and Gilles Deleuze and Félix Guattari, Braidotti argues that the body is to be understood as "neither a biological nor a sociological category, but rather as a point of overlap between the physical, the symbolic and the material social conditions" (44). The body can be seen as "an interface, a threshold, a field of intersecting material and symbolic forces. It is a surface where multiple codes (race, sex, class, age, etc.) are inscribed; it's a cultural construction that capitalizes on the energies of a heterogeneous, discontinuous and unconscious nature" (44). This idea of body as "threshold" is particularly useful when describing the adolescent body on the threshold of adulthood. She names this the "nomadic" self, "a subjectivity 'beyond gender' in the sense of being dispersed, not binary; multiple, not dualistic; interconnected, not dialectical; and in a constant flux, not fixed" (50). Here, Braidotti takes this gender instability of Butler and extends it to *any* definition of self: "What is crucial to becoming-Nomad is undoing the oppositional dualism majority/minority and arousing an affirmative passion for and desire for the transformative flows that destabilize all identities" (52). Particularly relevant to works in the study about lesbian young adults, she claims that lesbians "are caught in the same historical contradictions as everyone else; they are simultaneously within and without the majority. The lesbian faces the task of assembling disorganized, monstrously hybrid disruptive bodies, while being simultaneously within the system she is trying to subvert" (53). Authors attempting to represent these "monstrously hybrid disruptive bodies" have an especially challenging task.

Social scientists have come to agree with Butler and Braidotti's constructions of gender fluidity and shifting sexuality identity. R.W. Connell and James Messerschmidt, for example, report that "masculinity is not a fixed entity embedded in the body or personality traits of individuals. Masculinities are configurations of practice that are accomplished in social action and, therefore, can differ according to the gender relations in a particular social setting" (836). Connell and Messerschmidt's "configurations of practice" sounds very much like Butler's "stylized repetition of acts" and Braidotti's "becoming-Nomad," although the focus here is more strictly on masculinity, rather than femininity or sexual desires and practices. Still, Connell and Messerschmidt conclude that "not only the essentialist concept of masculinity but also, more generally, the trait approach to gender needs to be thoroughly transcended" (847). This is interesting for narratives of adolescent development, as YA writers in particular often use specific traits (physical prowess, emotionality, sociality, aggression) as a shorthand way to define characters. This research, as well as Butler's and Braidotti's work, suggests that writers, especially for adolescents, should rethink this "trait approach to gender."

Such a focus, which has come to be known as Masculinity Studies, has had much to say in recent years on the topic of shifting definitions of gender and sexuality. Michael Kimmel, for example, discusses the relationship between homophobia and masculinity. "Homophobia," he says, "is the fear that other men will unmask us, emasculate us, reveal to us and the world that we do not measure up, that we are not real men" (24). This fear, he continues, "keeps men exaggerating all the traditional rules of masculinity, including sexual predation with women. Homophobia and sexism go hand in hand" (6). He argues that thinking of masculinity as a "defensive effort to prevent being emasculated" may help to explain a "paradox in which men have virtually all the power and yet do not feel powerful" (28). Finally, Kimmel concludes that "masculinity has become a relentless test by which we prove to other men, to women, and ultimately to ourselves, that we have successfully mastered the part" (30). Once again, Butler's concept of the performativity of gender informs this reading of the relationship between masculinity and homophobia. Men, worried that they are not appearing masculine, that they are not playing their parts, fear and attack those men who most challenge masculine roles. How this homophobic defense of masculinity plays out in young adult fiction will be a primary focus of the chapters in the study addressing gay (and trans) young adult fiction.

As Kimmel discusses the relationship between masculine identity and homophobia, Terry Castle, in her *The Apparitional Lesbian: Female Homosexuality and Modern Culture* (1992), discusses a similar relationship between lesbianism and literature/culture. Lesbianism in much film and literary history, she says, "is reduced to a ghost effect: to ambiguity and taboo. It cannot be perceived, except apparitionally" (31). She continues:

> One might think of lesbianism as the "repressed idea" at the heart of patriarchal culture. By its very nature (and in this respect it differs significantly from male homosexuality) lesbianism poses as an ineluctable challenge to the politi-

Introduction

cal, economic, and sexual authority of men over women. It implies a whole new social order, characterized—at the very least—by a profound indifference to masculine charisma [61-62].

Lesbianism, according to Castle, presents a challenge to masculinity because of its "profound indifference" to it. In a lesbian world, men might cease to be recognized, to be seen, so therefore lesbianism must remain as a "ghost effect." However, works that make male homosexuality and lesbianism visible, while perhaps initially unsettling, might work to complicate and expand our attitudes about our own identities. This can be seen clearly in the more recent LGBTQ young adult narratives.

Continuing this discussion of gender and identity, Paul Morrison, in his *The Explanation for Everything: Essays on Sexual Subjectivity* (2001), comments on the "curious asymmetry" that while men are able to clearly ascertain whether or not they are gay, "no lesbian, no matter how homosexual her bonds, must ever be received as irredeemably lesbian. Gender trumps sexuality. A lesbian is, after all, a woman and a woman is defined by her sexual availability to men" (5-6). To be a "woman," then, is to be the object of *male* sexual desire, not to desire other women. Again, Morrison, like Castel, Kimmel, Butler, and Braidotti, sees gender as something that is defined relationally, in connections, and in actions, a praxis rather than a fixed identity. This notion of gender (and sexuality) as practice is explored in many of the adolescent novels discussed in later chapters.

Queer Theory and Futurity

Another area of queer theory of particular interest to theorists of adolescent literature is the constellation of discussions (and sometimes arguments) about nostalgia and images of the future in LGBTQ culture. In his book *Foundlings: Lesbian and Gay Historical Emotion Before Stonewall* (2001), Christopher Nealon initiates this conversation on time, identity, and the future and also returns to the arguments begun by Butler. He argues:

[It is possible to] think of sexuality as a mode of address, as a set of relations, lived and imagined, that are perpetually cast out ahead of our "real," present-tense personhood, as a kind of navigation, or proleptic sketch of historical futures.... [These might be called] huddled temporalities, allergic to the present tense and couched in allegories of coming-of-age or aging or becoming historical, a mid-century example of what we now call "performativity" [180–81].

This idea of "huddled temporalities" has much in common with the performative nature of gender in Butler, Archer, Kimmel, and the others mentioned earlier. It involves a way of telling one's life story by creating a new past and looking toward an imagined future, while remaining "allergic" to the present. His argument has resonance for adolescents, who are always trying to reimagine an origin story that more congenially aligns with their sense of self and are always looking forward to a future in which they are completely self-determining. What adolescent, locked in heated battle with his parents, doesn't wish to be adopted, a "foundling, with a secret (and much more congenial) lineage?"

This, however, is only one aspect of the discussion of the past, present, and future. Lee Edelman, in his explosive *No Future* (2004), gives his now-famous shot over the bow in the sexuality wars:

> On every side, our enjoyment of liberty is eclipsed by the lengthening shadow of a Child whose freedom to develop undisturbed by encounters, or even by the threat of potential encounters, with an "otherness" of which its parents, its church, or the state do not approve, uncompromised by any possible access to what is painted as alien desire, terroristically holds us all in check and determines that political discourse conform to the logic of a narrative wherein history unfolds as the future envisioned for a Child who must never grow up [21].

What Edelman calls "reproductive futurism," the political injunction to think about children and their futures, "impose[s] an ideological limit on political discourse as such, preserving in the process the absolute privilege of heteronormativity by rendering unthinkable, by casting outside the political domain, the possibility of a queer resistance to this organizing principle of communal relations" (2). The child, or rather a future that involves children, he argues, creates a heteronormative vision of the world that excludes those who don't plan to reproduce. As a result, he says, "the queer must insist on disturbing on queering, social organizations as such—on disturbing, therefore, and on queering ourselves and our investment in such organizations. For queerness can never define an identity; it can only ever disturb one" (17). "Queerness" must turn its back on the "Child"; it must always undermine and not reproduce old ways of being.

Needless to say, this oppositional politics generated much discussion

Introduction

of the possibilities for a future for queerness—and for those identified as queer. Judith Halberstam, in *Queer Time* (2005), has an early response: "[P]art of what has made queer compelling as a form of self-description in the past decade or so," Halberstam says, "has to do with the way it has the potential to open up new life narratives and alternative relations to time and space" (1–2). Instead of there being no future for queerness, she argues, "queer subcultures produce alternative temporalities by allowing their participants to believe that their futures can be imagined according to logics that lie outside of those paradigmatic markers of life experience—namely, birth, marriage, reproduction, and death" (2). She sees the postmodern moment as "simultaneously a crisis and an opportunity—a crisis in the stability of form and meaning, and an opportunity to rethink the practice of cultural production, its hierarchies and power dynamics, its tendency to resist or capitulate" (6). Instead of a politics of disruption, Halberstam offers a politics of opportunity—opportunity to rewrite "life narratives" and imagine a new future for the queer person, something that YA novelists in this study are already attempting to do.

In *Feeling Backward: Loss and the Politics of Queer History* (2007), Heather Love suggests that "backwardness" might provide a satisfying alternative to reproductive futurism. Many queer people "feel backward," she says, and "backwardness has been taken up as a key feature of queer culture.... Over the last century, queers have embraced backwardness in many forms; in celebrations of perversion, in defiant refusal to grow up, in explorations of haunting and memory, and in stubborn attachments to lost objects" (7). She continues:

> Rather than disavowing the history of marginalization and abjection, I suggest that we embrace it, exploring the ways it continues to structure queer experience in the present. Modern homosexual identity is formed out of and in relation to the experience of social damage. Paying attention to what was difficult in the past may tell us how far we have come, but that is not all it will tell us; it also makes visible the damage that we live with in the present [29].

What interests Love is "trying to imagine a future apart from the reproductive imperative, optimism, and the promise of redemption. A backward future, perhaps" (147). The question facing queer people, she says, is "how to make a future backward enough that even the most reluctant among us might want to live there" (163). This idea of a "backward future," paradoxical as it might sound, has affinities with much of the work that contemporary LGBTQ writers for young adults are trying to create—novels that look forward to a future free from homophobia and rigid identity categories, while at the same time attempting to evoke (for adult readers) the nostalgia for a lost childhood.

Michael Snediker goes even further than Love in *Queer Optimism: Lyric Personhood and Other Felicitous Persuasions* (2009), suggesting that nostalgia be replaced by happiness. "[W]hat if happiness weren't merely, self-reflexively happy, but interesting?" he asks. "Queer Optimism cannot guarantee what such happiness would look like, how such a happiness would feel. And while it does not promise a road to an Emerald City, it avails a new terrain of critical inquiry, which seems a felicity in its own right" (30). This question of what it would be like to be queer and to be happy is one that YA novelists are actively engaged in constructing.[1]

Queer Sexualities in Adolescent Literature

Almost every argument about sexuality and its relationship to cultural production begins with Michel Foucault. Especially relevant to a discussion of queer adolescent literature is a quotation from his landmark *History of Sexuality, Vol. I*. In it, Foucault says that "the sex of children and adolescents has become, since the eighteenth century, an important area of contention around which innumerable institutional devices and discursive strategies have been deployed" (30). He continues, saying that "in appearance, we are dealing with a barrier system; but in fact, all around the child, indefinite *lines of penetration* were disposed in terms of the surveillance and curtailment of childhood sexuality" (42). Thus, childhood sexuality is a taboo subject, and yet at the same time there has been much energy expended in policing and monitoring it. This "surveillance and curtailment" has also been applied to cultural products, such as novels, which attempt to address sexuality in children and young adults.

In his 2010 essay "Is the Rectum a Grave?" Leo Bersani also comments on the often fraught relationship between the child and adult sexuality. He argues:

> Adult sexuality is split in two: at once redeemed by its retroactive metamorphosis into the purity of an asexual childhood, and yet preserved in its most sinister forms by being projected onto the image of the criminal seducer of

Introduction

> children. "Purity" is crucial here: behind the brutalities against gays, against women, and, in the denial of their very nature and autonomy, against children lies the pastoralizing, the idealizing, the redemptive project I have been speaking of. More exactly, the brutality is identical to the idealization [29].

The more that children (and their innocence) are idolized, Bersani says, the greater the oppression of those who are perceived as a threat to that innocence. Literature and other forms of art that seek to lift the veil on childhood can also be perceived as a part of that threat, and this has come to light in the numerous censorship battles that have been fought over the representation of the gay, lesbian, or trans child in young adult literature.

Michael Warner talks about the particular problems faced by LGBTQ children in *The Trouble with Normal* (1990). "Almost all children grow up in families that think of themselves and all their members as heterosexual," Warner says, "and for some children this produces a profound and nameless estrangement, a sense of inner secrets and hidden shame" (8). Queer children, he adds, "bear a special burden of disclosure. No wonder so much of gay culture seems marked by a primal encounter with shame" (8). However, the good news is that "[s]ex dos not need to be primordial in order to be legitimate. Civilization doesn't just repress our original sexuality; it makes new kinds of sexuality" (11). Certainly, these "new kinds of sexuality" can—and are—represented in fiction.

Continuing this discussion in their introduction to *Curiouser: On the Queerness of Children* (2004), Steven Bruhm and Natasha Hurley say that "people panic when [children's] sexuality takes on a life outside the sanctioned scripts of child's play. And nowhere is this panic more explosive than in the field of the *queer* child, the child whose play confirms neither the comfortable stories of child (a)sexuality nor the supposedly blissful promises of adult heteronormativity" (ix). Thus, sexuality—and especially queer sexualities—in children and in children's and young adult literature is an especially contested area of representation. However, as David Bergman reminds readers, it is vitally important for the LGBTQ child to find literary examples. As he says, "the child who will become gay conceives his sexual self in isolation. I cannot think of another minority that is without cultural support in childhood" (5). Still, Kenneth Kidd asserts in his 2011 essay in *PMLA* that "if children's literature has heteronormative tendencies, which it assuredly does, it also homes all sorts of queerness" ("Queer Theory" 185), and Kathryn

Bond Stockton argues persuasively that "the silences surrounding the queerness of children happen to be broken—loquaciously broken and broken almost only—by fictional forms" (2). Thus the responsibility for breaking the silences (especially about non-heteronormative sexualities) falls disproportionally on the shoulders of writers of children's and young adult fiction.

Not surprisingly, though, arguments for how fiction can best represent these conflicted and shifting sexualities and gender identities are all over the map. Heather Love rightly claims that "the history of Western representation is littered with the corpses of gender and sexual deviants" (1), and this is certainly true of much early LGBTQ young adult fiction as well. However, Christopher Butler argues that although we "are circumscribed in our emotions and desiring responses by our development, or ability to imagine ourselves into other people's situations, and most particularly by our moral presuppositions," it is possible that the arts "may well be a very deep and involving way of changing them. They certainly seem to teach many people about sex, and often in advance of their direct experience of it" (44). Literature is the source of information for many people whose experiences haven't been validated by the culture, but it can also reinforce stereotyping and, in the case of LGBTQ issues, can normalize—in the name of realism—homophobia and violence against LGBTQ individuals.

Bert Archer affirms the first part of this position for American gays and lesbians, saying that books such as *The Well of Loneliness*, *Rubyfruit Jungle*, *A Boy's Own Story*, and *Tales of the City* "have been the most instrumental factors in the creation of our sense of gay. These stories become the means through which gay men and women come to know each other, through which they communicate, and into which they fold their own perceptions of themselves and their pasts" (222). This argues strongly for the need to create LGBTQ young adult fiction, as well as more "adult" works. In his 1991 book, *Gaiety Transfigured*, David Bergman agrees, saying that literary representation "has been of greater importance for gay communities than for any other ethnic, national, or religious group" (9). However, this "reliance on literature has not, however, always been helpful. Even literature written by homosexuals has often presented gay life as a depressing, marginal, and unfulfilling experience dominated by violence, drugs, alcoholism, poverty, and prostitution" (7). Only when LGBTQ YA fiction, for example, shows gay,

Introduction

lesbian, bi, and trans kids living exciting, hopeful lives will it be most valuable for its readers.

Several critics have directly addressed the role that adolescent fiction might play. YA author Nancy Garden says that "gay and lesbian kids need to read about people like themselves, just as kids in other minorities do. They need to read about ordinary people who are gay and lesbian, and, also like kids from other minorities, they need to read about the artists, athletes, performers, educators, political figures, and other notables who have come from our community" ("Foreword" xii). Both ordinary and famous LGBTQ people should be represented in fiction for young adults. Bestselling YA novelists Suzanne Collins insists that "books, all books, that young adults read have power. Their power rests in their ability to sway and to change the reader in so many ways, not the least of these is morally" (181). Writers of LGBTQ fiction for young adults should keep in mind their powers of moral suasion as well as the potentially-transformative effect on their young and impressionable readers.

To a considerable degree, young adult writers and critics have responded to the challenge, albeit rather slowly. As far back as 1977, the American Library Association's Gay Task Force and Committee on Children's and YA Literature published their "Guidelines for Treatment of Gay Themes in Children's and Young adult Literature," in which they argued that "young gay women and men can and should be portrayed as heroes as simply as their non-gay counterparts with no emphasis on the sexual component of their identities." If their sexuality is part of the plot, however, they said that "gay adolescents must be shown coping adequately with the social pressures that they will realistically encounter." Gay minor characters "should be included as a natural part of all kinds of situations, not they themselves being 'the situation.'" In addition, "there ought to be more, and more realistic, portrayals of affection and falling in love for gay teenagers" (qtd. in Cuseo 491–93). Unfortunately, it would be many decades before LGBTQ young adult fiction would rise to meet those standards.

For example, in his 1992 book on LGBTQ fiction for young adults, Allan Cuseo studied 69 novels between 1969 and 1982, and he found that, in general, YA literature "reflects society's impression of the homosexual as an individual it is permissible to harass" (85). Minor characters who are homosexual, he says, serve, unfortunately, as one aspect of a sordid societal setting, engaging in behaviors not approved by the heterosexual mainstream, and their sexual orientation is usually the basis for their outcast status. Their world is one of illegal activities, promiscuity, and aberrant behavior. YA literature, Cuseo says, is filled "with violent acts against the homosexual" (205), and homosexuality "is to be more feared than suicide" (247). There is one bright note: homosexual characters from minority cultures "are portrayed as positive models and as significant in the lives of the other characters with whom they interact" (287). However, in all 69 novels, there is "no homosexual character who is an ordinary individual, an individual whose orientation does not provide the concern of the story" (394). These novels "reinforce society's stereotypes and cast the homosexual as a defiant, an outcast, and as a stigmatized individual" (409). The good news, though, is that this started to change very dramatically after the time period Cuseo studied.

Jan Goodman's "Out of the Closet, But Paying the Price: Lesbian and Gay Characters in Children's Literature" (1983) supports Cuseo's conclusions. Her study of 15 YA works from 1969 to 1983 revealed that it is "physically dangerous to be gay." In almost half of the YA works she studied, gay adolescents continue to be victims of violence and tragedy, and implied "punishment" for being gay (13). Life for LGBTQ young people in fiction, she argues, is "bleak," "lonely," and filled with "severe hardships and misfortunes" (13). These novels also make the case that LGBTQ people should not be around children (13), traumatic experiences in the past makes someone homosexual (14), and "gay men want to be women and lesbians want to be men" (14). Instead, Goodman insists, "young and older children alike should read positive and diverse portrayals of gay people as main characters and as members of the general community" (15).

Although things are not yet perfect, progress in the direction of creating diverse and positive LGBTQ characters in young adult fiction has certainly been made. For example, in a study (begun in 1992 and ending in 1996) of 193 books for young adults addressing GLBTQ issues, Marjorie Lobban and Laura Clyde concluded that there has been "a trend away from the treatment of homosexuality as a major issue, towards acceptance of homosexuality as part of the normal social environment" (xv). However, homosexuality and its effects on characters, they demonstrated, remain "central concerns" (xvi). In 1995, Nancy St. Clair noted a historical movement from "books that depict homosexuality as a tragic flaw" to

Introduction

novels that represent adolescent homosexuality as "increasingly complex and decreasingly moralistic" to works that treat "sexual identity as something to be explored and come to grips with" (41). Still, she notes that novels from the late 1980s and early 1990, have moved GLBTQ characters "off center stage," and their stories are often told "from the perspective of a heterosexual" (42). She concludes, as does Goodman, that there was still a need to provide GLBTQ students "with the same resources as we do other minority students" (43).

From her exhaustive 1998 study of 300 LGBTQ young adult novels, "From Queer to Gay and Back Again," Christine Jenkins sees progress since the publication of John Donovan's 1969 *I'll Get There. It Better Be Worth the Trip*, which she and many others cite as "the first YA novel to specifically address homosexuality in the lives of young adults" (299). Jenkins comments that the "most notable trend was a shift in the book's narrative distance—a move away from protagonists dealing with their own same-sex attractions/orientation and toward heterosexual protagonists dealing with gay/lesbian seconder characters, most commonly sibling, friend, uncle, or teacher" (301). While she lauds the increasing number of LGBTQ characters of color, Jenkins notes that the majority of characters remain middle class, and gay male characters outnumber lesbians three to one (302). Jenkins also wonders why this literature is "so tenaciously conservative" (305) and worries that "portrayals of gay and lesbian characters as targets, scapegoats, and victims will continue to be an element in future YA novels" (309). She laments that there is no wider gay community represented in these novels (309–10) and that "remaining closeted is the price gay men and lesbians pay for a place in the mainstream and 'a place at the table'" (314). Finally, although she praises M.E. Kerr's *Deliver Us from Evie* for its queer main character (324), she concludes:

> With a few exceptions, it appears that it is not yet possible for a mainstream young adult novel with gay/lesbian content to take any vantage point except that of the mainstream, and gay/lesbian characters continue to be portrayed as outsiders who live (often somewhat precariously) within the heterosexual mainstream but who will never really be "one of us" [320].

Fortunately, this has changed—although perhaps not fully enough—in the past decade.

Continuing her work, Jenkins' and Michael Cart's landmark 2006 study of LGBTQ literature, *The Heart Has Its Reasons*, reports that

Queer Theory, Queer Literature, Queer YA Fiction

LGBTQ young adult literature "has begun to move—as have many of the individual titles that comprise it—toward assimilation, moving, that is, from being an isolated or 'ghettoized' subgenre to becoming a more integrated part of the total body of young adult literature" (128). They also note that the treatment of LGBTQ young people "has become more expansive and, as a result, readers now get to observe the increasing opportunities for assimilation that occur after the dramatic moment of coming out" (165). This is key: LGBTQ young adult protagonists and secondary characters can now have a life beyond coming out.

Looking toward the future for LGBTQ YA literature, the authors stress the need for more books featuring characters of color, lesbian and bisexual and transgender characters, and characters with same-sex parents. Also, since gays and lesbians do go to the same schools and hang out together (and even become friends), they should both be represented in novels (165). In addition, more works, they argue, need to feature homosexual characters for whom sexuality is "simply a given and who are dealing with other issues and challenges—emotional, intellectual, physical, social, developmental, etc. that are a part of teens' lives" (166). It is also time, they say, to "abandon the traditional and too-easy equality of homosexuality with violent death" (166). Most importantly, "like the rest of young adult literature," Cart and Jenkins conclude, LGBTQ YA literature "must continue to come of age *as literature*" (166). Fortunately, the most recent writers of fiction about LGBTQ young adults have begun to rise to this challenge.

Clearly, though, there is still much work left to be done. In his 2009 essay on gay adolescent novels, Thomas Crisp says that even though a number of YA novels depict gay males in "positive" ways, they "still often rely on heteronormative or heterosexual assumptions." Many gay adolescent novels, Crisp argues, "use homophobia as the foil against which characters with non-normative sexual identities struggle in order to find happiness as a monogamous couple." Also the fact that gay characters are represented "with either stereotypically 'feminine' or 'masculine' traits limit the extent to which such books constitute a departure from heteronormative traditions" (335–36). He stresses that the emphasis on homophobia in these novels actually "repeat[s] and thereby strengthen homophobia" (339). As of 2009, he says, "there has not yet been any book that really inscribes queerness" (344). Crisp concludes that "it may feel rewarding to look at the range of ways in which gay males have

Introduction

started to 'appear' in literature, but it is important to remain cognizant of the ways in which authors and publishers work to create—and readers attempt to confront, embrace, or reject—depictions that feel 'affirmatively' queer" (346). Writing in 2011, Tison Pugh agrees: "Gay fiction for children and adolescents provides a necessary alternative to a literary landscape that often overlooks homosexuality, yet ironically, antigay ideology triumphs even within many of these texts when they depict homosexuality as a problem to be overcome rather than as an identity to be celebrated" (162). This may be changing, however, in the novels appearing most recently.

Unfortunately, even if the kinds of books that Pugh, Crisp, and Jenkins desire do exist, it's possible that many young people would never have access to them, especially in public schools. In their 2005 essay, Mollie Blackburn and J. F. Buckley note that U.S. public high schools are "generally heterosexist, often homophobic institutions that tend to foster an irrational fear of lesbian, gay, bisexual, transgender and questioning people," and English language arts curricula in U.S. public high schools "either ignore or reject the connection between same-sex desire and literature" (202). The authors surveyed 600 secondary high schools in the United States. Out of the that 212 that responded, only 18 (8.4 percent) said that they use texts, films, or other materials addressing same-sex desire in their English language arts curriculum (205). "[T]eachers are failing their adolescent students" (205), Blackburn and Buckley insist, and they want to encourage them to "construct images of the possible" (206) for all their students.

All is not gloom and doom, however. YA novelist David Levithan argues in *Library Journal* that 2004 was "a pivotal point for lesbian, gay, bisexual, and transgender (LGBT) literature for teens. After many, many years of fear, threat, hesitation, self-loathing, and (in the case of all these) defiance, a crucial time has been entered where courage has the potential to win the day" (44). He calls for "courage … on many levels"—from authors, to publishers, readers, and librarians—because "it's not just literature at stake; it's lives" (45). Levithan has continued to write with courage, completing several LGBTQ novels for teens since his groundbreaking *Boy Meets Boy* appeared in 2004. In addition, his work as an editor for Scholastic Press has opened the door for a wider and wider variety of LGBTQ fiction for young adults.

Also writing in 2004, Terry Norton and Jonathan Vare argue that while LGBTQ young adult literature has changed for the better since Donovan's novel in 1969, it is still necessary for writers "to subvert unflattering images and provide more hopeful depictions for an audience still vulnerable to overt and covert homophobia" (65). Literature "may not eliminate homophobia nor alleviate the risks stemming from it," they say, but "well-written books may help subvert the culture of silence still current in many school environments and offer a supportive framework for self-understanding by gay and lesbian teens" (69). Nancy Garden agrees, saying that LGBTQ young people need books about themselves "even more now than they did back in Stonewall days and earlier. And straight kids need them also, for such books are a route to their understanding of who their gay peers really are" (23). This argument may be the strongest one against censorship: straight teens can learn empathy for those unlike themselves through fiction.

Critics and theorists of LGBTQ young adult fiction have a role to play as well. In his introduction to the 2011 *Children's Literature Association Quarterly*'s special issue on Lesbian/Gay Literature for Children and Young Adults, Kenneth Kidd comments that "not only has homophobia replaced homosexuality as the designated social problem addressed in [LGBTQ] novels, but some of the more recent titles also explore sexual identity in unconventional ways" (114). He argues that the challenge for critics and theorists in this area is to "acknowledge that while bodies and attractions are real and should not be trivialized, representations transform as well as profile those realities, and are at once stable and shifting. What is often the most interesting about literary texts, after all, is not how they fit certain categories, but how they complicate and/or evade them" (115). The goal, for fiction and for theory, then, is to transform as well as record. LGBTQ teens—and their straight classmates and friends—need a literature (and an understanding of that literature) that is transformative on an individual and a social level.

With this in mind, it may be useful at the end of this chapter to invoke Rita Felski's call for a new kind of criticism in her landmark *The Limits of Critique* (2015). Felski asks, "Why even as we extol multiplicity, difference, hybridity—is the affective range of criticism so limited? Why are we so articulate about our adversaries and so excruciatingly tongue-tied about our loves?" (13). Critics have become so wary of sentimentalizing the works they analyze that they have neglected to celebrate them appropriately. Criticism, she argues, "can be respectful, even rev-

Introduction

erential, in tone, with the critic adopting the role of a disciple or follower, aspiring to go beyond the text in the service of the text" (57).

What is needed, Felski says, "is a politics of relation rather than negation, of mediation rather than co-option, of alliance and assembly rather than alienated critique" (147). In this matter, reading becomes "a matter of attaching, collating, negotiating, assembling—of forging links between things that were previously unconnected … *a coproduction between actors that brings new things to light rather than an endless rumination on a text's hidden meaning or representational failure*" (173–74, author's emphasis). Such criticism values, Felski says, not just the power of works of literature "to estrange and disorient but also their ability to recontextualize what we know and to reorient and refresh perception. It seeks, in short, to strengthen rather than diminish its object—less in a spirit of reverence than in one of generosity and unabashed curiosity" (182). Finally, she argues, "serious thinking calls for a judicious decrease rather than an increase of distance—a willingness to acknowledge and more fully engage our attachments" (192). Seen in this light, critics need to move closer, emotionally, to the works they admire.

This approach has relevance for the study of young adult fiction, especially those novels that explore traditionally-taboo desires and the fears they invoke in others. Critics should embrace works which demonstrate acceptance and encourage empathy and which show readers the complexities of sexual and gender identity. They should also strongly resist censorship of such potentially-controversial novels, acting as advocates for their young readers and demonstrating the ways in which these texts can make the world of young adults safer and more inclusive for those who have traditionally stood on the margins or inside the closets. Writers can't do this alone: they need the help of teachers, and community leaders, and literary critics to get these books into the hands of the children who already know they need them—and, perhaps more importantly, into the hearts and minds of those who don't yet know.

ONE

Getting There
LGBTQ Young Adult Literature in the 70s and 80s

> Your future is bleak if you are gay. If lesbian and gay characters are lucky enough to survive, they are likely to face severe hardships and misfortunes—Jan Goodman, "Out of the Closet, But Paying the Price," 13

> [S]o what if happy endings didn't exist? Happy moments did—Sandra Scoppettone, *All Happy Endings Are Alike*, 178

In his monograph focusing on 69 YA novels from 1969 to 1982, Allan Cuseo concludes that "the realistic novel which attempted to discuss homosexuality had a slow and often difficult birth" (2). He also notes that "there is no homosexual character who is an ordinary individual, an individual whose orientation does not provide the concern of the story" (94). As a result of Her exhaustive analysis of LGBTQ works from the early 1970s to the late 1990s, Christine Jenkins agrees: "gay and lesbian characters have come out to loved ones and then waited stoically for the homophobic abuse to cease and the relationship to be restored" ("From Queer" 312). Honest or over-wrought, passionate or melodramatic, she says, "social conscience" portrayals of gay/straight relationships continue to be standard fare in YA literature (313). According to these novels, remaining closeted is the price gay men and lesbians pay for a place in the mainstream and "a place at the table" (314). The "overwhelming tendency" is to tell these stories "from a mainstream heterosexual perspective" (315), she adds. Among the patterns that emerge from these novels, Jenkins notes, is a consistently oppositional relationship between traditional families of parents and children and the gay/lesbian community (321). This bleak landscape was the norm in LGBTQ young adult fiction from its beginnings in the late 1960s until the middle of the 1990s.

A study of 14 YA books from 1969 to 1883 by Jan Goodman reveals that at that time it was "still physically dangerous to be gay. In almost half of the YA works, gay adolescents continue to be victims of violence and tragedy, and implied 'punishment' for being gay" (13). Part of the reason for this dismal picture could be, as Eric Tribunella argues in *Melancholy and Maturation*:

> Mature adults are heteronormatively gendered. One of the key things a child must grow up into is a man or a woman, so to be a mature adult means to identify unambiguously as one or the other and to enact clearly conventional manhood or womanhood. To be heteronormatively gendered also means that one takes another heteronormatively gendered person of the other sex as one's sexual and romantic object, or at least to demonstrate an interest in doing so. Similarly, it means that one should procreate or demonstrate a willingness or ability to procreate. Either way, this outcome should seem likely or inevitable [xxii].

Thus, to be same-sex attracted means to remain, essentially, a child. The growth and development which is standard fare in young adult fiction was therefore not allowed to the LGBTQ child. Thomas Crisp concurs, arguing that although many YA novels featuring gay characters appear "affirmative" and give voice and representation to gay males, "because they so heavily rely on heteronormative constructions of romance, sex, sexuality, and the world more broadly, they often actually work to continue the invisibility of gay males by filtering queer existence and distancing readers" (345). Gay and lesbian characters, then, remained either childlike or absent from fiction directed toward adolescents during this time period.

However, I would agree with Nancy St. Clair that the decade from the mid-70s through the mid-80s also saw the publication of works "in which with representations of adolescent homosexuality becomes increasingly complex and decreasingly moralistic" (40–41). I would also argue that these complexities were present from the start of LGBTQ literature intended for (or often read by) young adults—from John Donovan's and Isabel Miller's groundbreaking novels in 1969 through the works of Rosa Guy, M.E. Kerr, Sandra Scoppotone, Nancy Garden, Clayton Bess, and Carolyn Meyer. The ways in which these authors laid the groundwork for later authors such as Francesca Lia Block, David Levithan, Brett Hartinger, Ellen Wittlinger, Jacqueline Woodson, and many, many others should be acknowledged, not just for the ways in which they provided negative examples or stereotypes that needed to be broken in later years, but for how they created sometimes self-assured, often brave, occasionally defiant, but always complicated LGBTQ characters and situations. As Nancy Garden tells Anne Horning in 2007, "I think today's gay literature is very healthy" (251), and such a state of health began with this earliest fiction. "Many of today's LGBTQ teens eschew labels altogether or have developed more fluid or inclusive ones for themselves," Garden says, "many feel that it's 'no big deal' to be gay or lesbian, bi or trans or questioning, or some combination of other-than-strictly-heterosexual" (252). It could be argued that fiction from the 70s and 80s laid the groundwork for this confidence and fluidity.

The first of these novels was Isabel Miller's *Patience and Sarah* (1969). Under her pen name (which is an anagram of "lesbia" and her mother's maiden name), Alma Routsong initially self-published the lesbian historical romance. According to novelist Emma Donoghue's introduction to the 2005 Arsenal Pulp Press edition, the novel is "a profoundly feminist work that questions but also celebrates and eroticizes difference in gender roles" (10). Donoghue correctly notes that "[g]ender itself must be made new in this novel of transformation" (11–12). As well as rewriting notions of gender, the novel is also rewriting history, telling the story of characters "negotiating the complex dynamics of the early nineteenth-century rural family, and finding breathing room for that original creation, the female couple" (12) and chronicling their attempt "to find privacy and autonomy in the psychological wilderness of a patriarchal society" (15). Finally, Donoghue says, "Routsong was inventing a history rather than teaching a known one, which helps give the novel its vigour and zest" (17). There is no doubt that *Patience and Sarah* changed the direction of lesbian fiction and opened up a potential market of young readers for such works.

Elisabeth Deran, Routsong/Miller's romantic partner while she was writing *Patience and Sarah*, said that the author "devoured every lesbian book she could find, all of them either 'tragedies' with the heroine committing suicide, or 'happy endings' where the heroine finds a man who rescues her from her erroneous ways. She definitely had no wish to contribute to such a genre" (209). This comment makes it clear that Routsong/Miller was consciously attempting to rewrite the genre from the lesbian pulp fiction available in the 1950s and early 60s. In an introduction to his 1972 interview with Routsong/Miller, Jonathan Katz calls the novel (along with *The Well of Loneliness*) part of "a literary-political genre—the Lesbian fiction-defense" (434), a work of resistance to prevailing homophobia at the time. Routsong/Miller tells Katz that the book was rejected by several publishers, although she doubts they "had any moral objections to the subject," just concerns that it wouldn't sell (436). She also says that the novel is "very threatening to straight women, and closeted Gay women. If they say they like it, people with think they're Gay" (436). By the time the book is reissued in 2005, however, few of these concerns remain, in large part because of the groundwork this novel laid.

Writing in *Critical Inquiry*, Catharine Stimpson calls *Patience and Sarah* "among the first of the more hopeful lesbian novels" (375) and refers to it as "gentle, kindly" (375). Anne Herrman is more interested in the ways this "ur-text of current lesbian fictions" employs "crossdressing plots" (n.p.). The novel, she says, "negotiates the contradiction between femininity as a middle-class construct and an iconography of the lesbian feminist as 'butch'" (n.p.). Unlike *The Well of Loneliness*, Herrman argues, in this novel "the butch ... does not abandon the femme to a better butch, that is, a real man, by feigning infidelity. Instead, she discards the clothes that signify the role in order to avoid not the pathology of inversion but, rather, a politically incorrect lesbianism" (n.p.). Both Stimpson and Herrman agree that *Patience and Sarah* creates a new kind of lesbian novel, one that is both hopeful and gender-bending.

In a memoir of her lifelong reading experience, Suzanne Juhasz says the novel is still considered by many women of her generation (she came of age in the 1960s) as the "quintessential lesbian romance," one that "celebrates the resonance and strength of mutuality in female love and identity" (213). In this novel, Juhasz says, "coming out ... is the achievement and assertion of female identity and power" (214). Bonnie Zimmerman agrees about the novel's importance. *Patience and Sarah*, she says, "came into the world quietly and would not have had its current significance had it not been for the political and social events transforming western societies during the 1960s and 1970s. Lesbian life and literature was never the same after this time" (10). Clearly, for many women in that turbulent but exciting period, *Patience and Sarah* affirmed both lesbian identity and female solidarity.

It is important to mention here that like many (eventual) YA writers, Routson/Miller likely didn't intend her novel to be read exclusively by a young adult audience. However, it has been taken up by young readers since its publication, it is referenced in other young adult novels, such as *Annie on My Mind*, and contemporary readers on Goodreads insist that all queer kids should read it. Also, the characters, while technically adults, still live at home as the novel begins and are under the jurisdiction of father (in Sarah's case) and brother (Patience). Both men try to dictate the young women's life choices, forcing them, in typical adolescent fashion, to rebel and then, when defeated, to lie. The dependent position of the women clearly has analogies to the lives of adolescents.

The novel opens with Patience living with her conventional brother and sister-in-law—and stresses their desire that she acclimate herself to the role of babysitter and household drudge. If they can't kill her, Patience thinks, the "[n]ext best was to make me want to die, but I had enough spite in me to want to live, usually" (25). Clearly, Patience has enough stubbornness to resist traditional expectations for women. She also had the advantage of a father who, although now dead, supported her artistic ambitions and other "eccentricities," and she rightly notes that "if one of your folks will back you up, you don't get broken" (29). Nevertheless, Patience has had a hard time with 19th-century gender expectations, beginning with her first days, when her father worried how "someone with all that go could stand to be a woman" (29) and named her "Patience" to try to curb some of that energy. Juhasz says that Patience is "smart, talented, funny, *different*" (214), but she is also missing the love and support (at least among the living) that she will seek in Sarah (215).

Sarah first appears delivering wood to Patience's house, and Martha quickly lets Patience know that Sarah is not considered socially acceptable. This goads Patience into inviting Sarah into her home and, while admiring her abilities, also wanting to take care of her. "Surely a few small codlings wouldn't spoil [Sarah] or undermine her capable ways," she thinks (32). As Juhasz points out, Patience's first "strong" acts in the novel are to light a fire, help Sarah to warm up, and safely shelter her cattle. Sarah offers something important to Patience as well: her admiration of Patience's paintings, which causes Patience to realize that she'd been "lonesome" since the loss of her father, the only family member to encourage her artistic endeavors (32–33).

In what Bonnie Zimmerman calls "an important step in her assertion of herself as an artist and a lesbian," Patience notices that the fire she has built for Sarah is actually yellow not red, as it is more typically represented in art. In doing so, Patience "disentangles the fiction of fire by attending to how it appears to her" and therefore reads it differently, Zimmerman argues. In a similar way "patriarchal culture 'reads' the text of lesbian life and names it deviant or depraved." Lesbian writers like Routsong/Miller reveal this limiting fantasy, Zimmerman says, but they are also "tempted to enshrine another reading, equally static and potentially entrapping. In attempting to say *this* is a lesbian identity, *this* is what it means to be a lesbian, we simply call fire yellow instead of red. Rather than reveal the truth about lesbians, we fabricate new myths for old without acknowledging that our stories are exactly that—stories" (25). However, *Patience and Sarah* does its best to resist this temptation to limit the lesbian experience—to make it simply yellow rather than red.

For example, Miller plays with stereotypical gender roles, as an attempt to reveal the complexities of lesbian self-presentation. Sarah tells Patience (like Pa in the *Little House on the Prairie* books) that she wants to "live nice, and free, and snug" (34), and Patience decides that there's plenty of time to teach the masculine Sarah "that it's better to be a real woman and an imitation man, and that when someone chooses a woman to go away with it's because a woman is what's preferred" (39). Although Patience admires Sarah's skill with tools and with a gun, she is attracted to her because she is a woman, *not* a man. Still, she imagines herself in a "wifely" role, thinking she is "going with Sarah to feel her and hold her head against me when she was sad and knead her shoulder when it ached" (42). This gets her to wondering "if what makes men walk so lordlike and speak so masterfully is having the love of women. If that was it, Sarah and I would make lords of each other" (49–50). Here, Routsong/Miller shows that it matters less whether "women" behave like "men" and more whether they "make lords" (or ladies) of each other.

Zimmerman agrees: "Patience knows that her attraction to Sarah is lesbian, not pseudo-heterosexual" (49). Routsong/Miller told her interviewer Katz that "one of the jokes in the book is that although Sarah dresses like a man, she's not butch, she's not male-identified. Men's clothes are not male identification; they're freedom" (441). In both her interview and in her novel, Routsong/Miller seeks to complicate gender identity and practice. Victoria Flanagan says that *Patience and Sarah* uses "cross-dressing as a unique and effective strategy through which to interrogate gender stereotypes" (xv), and, in addition, the cross-dressing in the novel "serves to subvert and undermine the very question of what it means to be a man or a woman, gay or straight" (16). This is clearly what is happening in the novel: Patience dresses like a woman but pursues her artistic dreams like a man; Sarah dresses like a man but wants physical intimacy like a woman.

Not surprisingly, the women's challenge to the heteronormative status quo is soon noticed by their families, with disastrous results. Their plan to build a life together is thwarted when Sarah, naïvely, tells her younger sister that she is in love with Patience and plans to run away with her. Sarah's father decides to keep her prisoner in the cabin and beats her every time she tries to go to Patience—as a way of trying to break her will. "It is a sin to raise a girl to be a man," Patience thinks about Sarah, "believing in strength and courage and candor. We can't prevail that way" (63). Patience realizes that women cannot stand up to the force and power of men. Eventually, Sarah confronts Patience, who denies her love for Sarah (in part to save Sarah from being beaten to death by her father and in part to save face in her own family). During the chaos, Patience, not surprisingly, feels "a rage against men," not because they could go to college, or work at their chosen profession, or escape from the physical costs of childbearing, but "because when they love a woman they may be with her, and all society will protect their possession of her" (67). As Juhasz says, "Lesbian love cannot be condoned by society. To feel it, to express it, are acts of defiance that become integrally associated with what this love is. Likewise, suppressing, hiding, and fearing it come to define the experience as well" (219). What Sarah wants most is to have her love for Patience supported by their families, something they seem unable to do.

After her rejection by Patience, who feels defeated and trapped, Sarah decides to assume a male identity and go out on her own. She wants to teach her younger sister to shoot, so she can help out the family in Sarah's absence, but her father refuses, fearing she might want to be a "boy" as well. "Did learning to shoot cause that?" Sarah wonders. "I expect it could've. It made me feel I could take care of myself, and not be beholden, and love who my feeling went to" (72). Sarah's gun, Zimmerman says, is "a classic phallic symbol that in this context signifies potency and activity, not masculinity. Sarah possesses the power of doing and acting that is reserved for men in a patriarchal society" (48). The gun, of course, didn't "turn" Sarah into a lesbian, but it may have helped her feel confident enough to attempt the kind of life she wanted.

On the road, Sarah starts to realize, to her great disappointment, that she will only ever look like a boy, never a man. "I began to see how boys aren't much better off than women," Sarah thinks. "Men are the ones who get their way and run the world" (80). She also discovers, however, that she "didn't like to fight. I never really knew for sure till then how much I had the feelings of a woman, and not only that but I rated a woman's feelings higher" (93). As Zimmerman says, "Sarah learns about womanhood not from Patience, but from her own [mostly negative] experience passing as a male in the outside world.... Sarah returns to Patience no longer a boy, but a lesbian" (49). Sarah finds out she can't be (or even appear to be) a man, but she can be a woman who loves women (and doesn't particularly like to fight). She also realizes that she must come home to Patience.

After Sarah returns, Patience thinks, optimistically, that they can be lovers "who will never behave dishonorably in each other's sight, and invincible. Let the world either kills us or grow accustomed to us; here we stand" (116). Still, they try to keep their relationship an open secret, until Martha finds the two lovers embracing. And then, strangely, Martha chastises Patience for being with someone "*not even in the family!*" Patience says that she's "astonished" by Martha's admission. Shortly afterward it becomes clear what Martha had in mind: "It could've been so sweet, working and helping each other here. It was what I thought about. It was what I thought would be. Edward and you and me together" (133). Homosocial (or perhaps even homosexual) attraction, apparently, is everywhere in this novel, albeit mostly hidden, and may be the cause of much of the anxiety over Patience and Sarah's relationship.

After much resistance, the two women find support from Sarah's mother and Patience's brother. After Sarah's mother assures them her father will "say nothing" about Sarah leaving with Patience in the spring, Patience thinks, "Women are not so very powerless after all. He will say nothing. She should make up her mind more often" (138). As they board the ship for New York City, her brother gives them his blessing (143). Sarah thinks, however, that he might be "too fond" of thinking of them together (145). Clearly, Routsong/Miller is making an allusion to the attraction heterosexual men have for lesbian sexuality, which could be seen as another blurring of the lines of sexual attraction, which here, leads to greater empathy (combined with a bit of discomfort) instead of anger and violence.

Still, things are not altogether rosy. As Sarah tries to take the bags to the ship, she is admonished by Patience not to act like a man. Patience recognizes it is "folly," asking Sarah to act like a lady in public when "it's because you are not a lady that there is hope for us" (142). Patience is attracted to Sarah precisely because she is a masculine woman, and *not* a lady. Sarah doesn't conform quickly enough, though, and because she doesn't know that "ladies" do not respond to strange men with frank and open conversion, she is assaulted by a man and must be saved by Patience's haughty "ladylike" demeanor. Sarah has to act less "like a man," and Patience has to assert her feminine power in order for them to pass through the world of heterosexual men unremarked and undamaged. In spite of this, Sarah sees some advantage to traditional gender roles, especially those that call for wives to submit to the will of their husbands. Sarah wants to talk Patience into settling in Greene County, instead of going to Genesee, as they had planned. She starts to see that "there was a lot to be said for a way where there's no backtalk and everybody's place is set" (173). In their lives, on the other hand, each of the partners contributes to the discussion of their future, which can make for much "backtalk" and confusion.

Eventually, however, they do buy the land in Greene County, and, after some travail, get their house and garden ready, and Patience observes that "now we were planted, to see what grew of us" (196). Herrmann points out that "in the final scene Sarah builds the bed on their homestead and Patience paints the picture to hang above it, thus reinforcing the division of labor that began in gender and class differences even as the sartorial signifiers of those differences have been discarded" (n.p.). However, this is still not (heterosexual) happily ever after. Juhasz expresses it well: At the end of the novel the lesbian romance fantasy is fulfilled. Mutual recognition generates mutual empathy, which develops into a maturity of interactive strengths and qualities: 'gender-free' as far as culture constructs gender; deeply womanly, as lesbian identify constructs the woman" (227). "As far as culture constructs," this novel transcends gender stereotypes and creates a new image of domesticity.

Zimmerman notes that the ending of *Patience and Sarah* is "not surprising" given that in "lesbian mythology, when a woman loves another woman, she breaks a fundamental rule of patriarchal society and puts herself beyond the pale" (61). On their farm, the women's relationship "convey[s] the message that lesbian love ought to be fully and openly a part of nature, rather than covert and illicit" (81). She continues that the "original (and superior) title of *Patience and Sarah—A Place for Us—* captures this longing for a home that provides the self-sufficient lovers refuge from patriarchal society" (84). Alma Routsong/Isabel Miller has created a place for lesbian relationships, although one that his far removed from "civilized" society. Nevertheless, this novel will provide the model for much lesbian fiction to come and will appear (as will become evident in later chapters) as an iconic text for the lives of later lesbian young adult characters. The first of its kind, hopeful and innovative, *Patience and Sarah* remains a powerful voice in LGBTQ adolescent fiction.

John Donovan's 1969 *I'll Get There. It Better Be Worth the Trip* could be seen as a companion to *Patience and Sarah* for gay young adults. Although, as Cuseo says, it "did not begin a plethora of works with homosexual characters," it did, nevertheless, "initiate a steady expansion of literary exploration of the subject" (3). It also represents the first book to show gay adolescents who aren't tragic or tortured by their same-sex attraction. In the 40th Anniversary Edition of the novel, young adult writer Brett Hartinger says that Donovan "didn't just write a terrific, surprisingly timeless book. He founded a genre" (203). "Almost every person spends his or her teen years navigating the treacherous waters of identity formation, but unlike gay kids," Hartinger says, "most heterosexuals don't do it completely alone: they don't do it in a world where plenty of adults and other authority figures are telling them blatant lies about who they are; and if they make a mistake, the stakes usually aren't nearly as high" (205). Hartinger adds that there are no simplistic answers in the novel. "The book ends on a hopeful but ambiguous note. Wherever the 'there' of the title is, protagonist Davy hasn't arrived yet. How could he? It wasn't possible in the world of 1969, not for a thirteen-year-old boy" (209). With this "simple emotional truth," however, Donovan "was still far ahead of his contemporaries" (209). Hartinger concludes that while today's readers aren't as likely to read stories whether a character's homosexuality is the primary conflict, the fact that "gay teens no longer begin their own stories completely alone [is] in large part because of John and all the books he inspired" (213).

One. Getting There

Young adult writer Martin Wilson, also writing in this edition, said reading the novel was a "joyous occasion" (217) that led him to realize that the long-out-of-print book was a work of art dealing with "homosexuality in a convincing and compelling way" (217). To those who criticize the novel for not having Davy affirm his homosexuality, Wilson says, "Davy is on a journey, and by the end of the novel he has grown and matured in countless ways. But he's still a kid. He has a ways to go…. He'll get there one day—whatever 'there' is" (219). In her foreword to this edition, Donovan's niece (and YA novelist herself) Stacy Donovan says that Davy is "tender" and "deep," and he is also "lost, not fake" (vii). Kathleen T. Horning, director of the cooperative Children's Book Center at the University of Wisconsin–Madison, calls the book was "downright revolutionary" (221), although she notes it was "widely and positively reviewed" in professional library journals when it appeared (225).

Other critics, however, are less sanguine in their comments, pointing out that the novel "falls into the same trap many early gay teen novels did, which was to punish the main character with a car accident leading to death or serious injury" (225). They also complain that the novel suggests "that being gay is just a passing phrase" (225), and focuses on Davy's guilt after his homosexual encounter. Talking about four novels, including Donovan's, Hankel and Cunningham conclude that "being gay has no lasting significance and/or costs someone a terrible price. Not one plot has a happy ending in which the protagonists meet hostile pressures successfully and go on to find fulfillment and a supportive relationship based on love and respect. For gay adolescents the negative impact of these novels cannot be minimized" (532–33). This seems too dire, however. It is true that there isn't exactly a "happy ending" to *I'll Get There*, but both the ending and title indicate that the very young protagonist is on his way toward a brighter future—whenever that might be.

As the novel opens, 13-year-old Davy, with his dachshund Fred, moves in with his alcoholic mother after his beloved grandmother (and caretaker) dies. His father, who has remarried, is distant but kindly. The main plot point arises when meets Douglas Altschuler at his new private school, and they have a brief romance. Two thirds of the way through the book, the two boys kiss after roughhousing with the dog, but then Davy quickly assures himself that he and Altschuler "don't have to worry about being queer or anything like that" (150) and insists that there is nothing about which to feel guilty (158). Still, he worries, telling himself that "it's not dirty, or anything like that" (161).

Shortly after the kiss, Davy's mother finds them "spread out tighter on the floor of her living room" with their arms "stretched across each other's back" (166) after they'd sampled her whiskey. Davy's mother, worried that "unnatural" happened between the two boys (169), arranges for Davy to talk to his father. Drunk as usual, she takes Fred out while Davy has a talk with his father. Davy tells him, "I'm not queer or anything," and his father says that "a lot of boys play around in a lot of ways when they are growing up and I shouldn't get involved in some special way of life which will close off other ways of life to me" (173). He also tells him that people who want others to be just like them are "dangerous" (174), condemning those people who try to make him conform to their notions of identity, rather than Davy. During their talk, Fred is hit by a car, and Davy blames himself and his affair with Altschuler (180).

Later, the boys fight in the locker room shower when Davy tells Altschuler that "all that queering around" led to Fred's death (185). When they reconcile, Altschuler says that if Davy thinks kissing boys is "dirty or something like that, I wouldn't do it again. If I were you" (197), and in the end they agree to "respect each other" (199). Horning suggests that this ending, which has been attacked by some critics, "is wonderfully vague and open to interpretation.... Donovan has brilliantly constructed the novel so that it offers one message (it's just a phase) to the audience who needs that message in order to find the book acceptable, and another 'be true to yourself' for those who needed to find ... recognition and relief" (237). What the novel does is show that homosexual behavior needn't be punished, while at the same time suggesting that one's sexual preferences do not have to be fixed at 13. It should come as no surprise, then, that this novel is seen as opening the door to a new kind of LGBTQ fiction for young adults.

Rosa Guy's *Ruby* (1976) is one of the earliest intentionally adolescent novels to include lesbianism (Lee 158, note).[1] According to Marjorie Lobban and Laura A. Clyde, the novel's prose is "lyrical and the book is distinguished by emotional honesty and its complex, credible characters" (60). Nancy St. Clair calls *Ruby* a "significant" novel, given its positive approach to same-sex experimentation (40–41). In her annotated bibliography of lesbian and gay fiction Francis Ann Day offers qualified praise, mentioning the novel's "finely drawn, complex characters; poetic,

One. Getting There

stylized language; and emotional honesty." However, she says, "the abelism and lookism in the portrayal of the teacher [Miss Gottlieb, who is also racist and generally mean] are inexcusable, even for a book that was written in the early 1970s" (33). Nancy Garden tells an interviewer that *Ruby* represents "an important and daring first—I think it was also the first teen novel focused on gay characters of color" (250). There is no doubt that Ruby also represents a significant moment in the depiction of lesbian adolescent characters of color.

Ruby is 18 when the novel begins, but, much like younger adolescents, is lonely and restricted in her movements and contact with other people by her overprotective Jamaican father, Calvin. She falls in love with Daphne Duprey, a high school classmate. Ruby describes the object of her affection:

> Daphne of the smooth, tan skin. Daphne of the heavy, angry black eyebrows that were so fantastically right in combination with her gray eyes. Daphne of the thick, well-formed lips, the large white teeth. Feminine Daphne with her thick crisply curly, black shoulder-length hair. Boyish Daphne with her thick neck, her colorful silk skirts, her tweeds [15].

Daphne is clearly a young woman of color with "crispy curly" black hair and "tan skin." When Daphne kisses her, Ruby thinks "she had found herself, a likeness to herself, a response to her needs, her age, an answer to her loneliness" (55). Her father forces her away from Daphne, but Ruby thinks that "the issue is not obedience or disobedience," it is "the needs of my body ... of my mind" (173). In spite of their attraction, Daphne breaks up with Ruby, saying that she's "going straight" (216). Ruby tries to jump out a window, but her father stops her, and father and daughter reconcile, both of them in tears (220). At this point, her father realizes that he would rather have her attracted to girls and alive than obedient, straight, and dead.

At the end of the novel, a boy, Orlando, who was an earlier love interest of Ruby's, comes by, and Ruby tells her sister that she may see him tomorrow. Although it appears that Ruby is reconsidering (or at least revising or expanding) her sexual attractions at the end of the novel, her intense affection for Daphne—and the ways their relationship helped her mature and move toward independence—isn't erased by the conclusion. She also learns to reach out to others—in particular her father and sister—for the emotional support she clearly has needed all her life. Like Patience and Sarah, Ruby is trying to find her place in the world and, like Davy, she is accepting the complexities of her sexual and emotional attractions. She is not yet established in the world (although she is much older than Davy), but she does seem more able at the end of the novel to "get there."

I'll Love You When You're More Like Me (1977), by M.E. Kerr, is an earlier version of the lesbian young adult novel she will write later (and possibly better) in *Deliver Me from Evie* (1985). According to Virginia Wilder, who reviewed the book, "both straight and gay friendships are described, [but] the future promises a sex life only to the straight" (qtd. in Lobban and Clyde 85). Unfortunately, this seems to be the case. The novel is told through two straight first-person narrators, Wallace "Wally" Witherspoon, Jr., whose family owns a funeral parlor (which he doesn't want to inherit), and Sabra St. Amour, a teenaged soap opera actress. Predictably, Wally falls for Sabra.

The gay character in the novel is Charlie, Wally's best friend. Charlie is open about his sexuality, which, as he puts it, leads to his "ostracism and disgrace" (38). The humorous tone of the novel undercuts the reality the homophobia of the era, but, overall, Charlie seems fairly well adjusted and not, at least in the time frame of the novel, a victim of bullying or isolation. He feels free to share his life story with Charlie. Although Charlie and Wally agree not to unload their emotional problems on each other, they "never paid any attention to their pact" and frequently debriefed each other about their love affairs (real and imagined) (38).

Wally's father also treats Charlie with respect. Although he has "an assortment of names" for him (thankfully—or perhaps strategically—not mentioned in the novel), he always speaks to him courteously and "almost convivial[ly]. After all, everybody's going to die someday," he reasons, "why throw business to Annan funeral Home?" (39). It appears that good business sense trumps homophobia. The more negative reactions of other adults don't seem to bother Charlie much. He remembers how a recently-deceased teacher mocked his somewhat feminine walk, and he tells her body to "rest in peace" (45), a sign of his relative imperviousness to her insult but also an assertion of his triumph over her (by outlasting her). His sardonic comment also hints at the ways in which those who express their homophobia are not at peace while alive.

In spite of his confidence and his general openness, "Charlie was always trying to be someone in Seaville besides The Resident Fairy"

(65). Sabra says that Charlie "came out of the closet without even a hanger trailing after him" (88). This makes it difficult for him to find work, however, and he worries about how he might make a living. Harriet (Wally's ill-matched girlfriend) tells Charlie that "it is a real pity that you chose to make yourself conspicuous." Charlie says "I don't mind being conspicuous.... I mind being poor" (77). Again, the issue here seems less about identity or about self-esteem and more about economics.

In fact, all three main characters suffer from their inability to fit into their surroundings. Sabra repeats a line from her soap opera, "I'll love you when you're more like me," that she believes defines people's attitudes toward her. Wally says, "That's really what my father is saying to me underneath it all," and Charlie replies, "It's what the whole world is saying to me" (113). None of the characters seem destined to become "more like" their communities. At the end of the novel, Charlie decides to go into the funeral business with Wally's father, Wally gets ready to go to college, and Sabra goes back to the soap opera. No one has a romance at the end, but each of the characters appears ready to begin their futures. This early novel may not have blazed the same trails as *Patience and Sarah*, *Ruby*, or *I'll Get There*, but its light tone and apparently happy ending for the three protagonists suggests a path for future novels that chronicle the LGBTQ young adult experience.

Published a year after Kerr's novel Sandra Scoppettone's *All Happy Endings Are Alike* (1978) is often cited as an early lesbian YA novel, but unfortunately it is one that reinforces stereotypical images of young lesbians as doomed, destined to be unhappy, in denial, or lacking a caring community. However, the novel has supportive parents (either initially or eventually) and what can only be seen as a happy ending. This novel, along with Nancy Garden's *Annie on My Mind* (1982), which will be discussed later in this chapter, are part of a group of works that Vanessa Lee says create lesbian identities with varying degrees of "depth, endurance, and scope" (152). In most of these novels, Lee argues, "female characters in these texts discover their homosexuality beginning with a 'queer,' unnamable feeling" (155) and the relationship between the two protagonists "is occasionally joyful, but predominantly torturous as the girls deal with judgmental family members and a violent community." She continues: "The sexual nature of love often brings about feelings of fear and guilt, about sex in general and about the public condemnation of homosexuality in particular" (155). Nancy Garden says, on the other hand, that this book is a deviation from "the few books that focused on relationships between teens that were more clearly acknowledged as homosexual, those relationships were almost always seen as developmental stages, or they ended with a breakup or death" (250). Sandra Scoppettone's novel, she says, was a "real breakthrough book" for its clearly lesbian protagonist and its "hopeful" ending (251).

The novel introduces readers to Jaret Tyler and Peggy Danziger, high school seniors in Gardener's Point, "a hundred miles from New York City" (7). Perhaps the most interesting adult character, compared to the parents in earlier novels, is Jaret's mother, a 70s feminist who struggles to come to terms with her daughter's lesbianism. When Jaret tells her mother Kay about her attraction to Peggy, her mother asks, somewhat surprisingly, "Why?" Jaret "had expected all kinds of questions but never 'Why?' What did that even mean? It really bugged her" (11). Even though she is trying to be understanding, Kay reveals her suspicion that homosexuality is a choice, or, even worse, simply another way for adolescents to annoy their parents. Jaret admonishes her mother: "I know you probably think this is a phase but I think you should know that I'm sure it's not" (15). Unlike in *Ruby*, Jaret's attraction for women will not pass with oncoming adulthood. Jaret also tells her mother, who often puts down men and thinks her feminism might have influenced her daughter's sexuality, "it doesn't matter what you say or don't say [about men]. I am the way I am" (48). Thus, from the beginning of the novel, sexuality is established as integral to identity, unchanging and unaffected by outside influences. This, of course, is progress from earlier novels that saw same-sex attraction as a passing phase on the way toward "true and adult" heterosexuality.

In addition, the novel insists on connections between all adolescents, gay and straight. Kay thinks about her own romantic and sexual past, which she didn't share with her mother, and wonders if Jaret's feelings for Peggy were the same as hers had been (72). This moment of identification and empathy doesn't last long, though, and she starts blaming herself and her husband for their daughter's same-sex attraction. Still, she wonders, "why the need to put it in those terms? She knew it was because she still had one foot in the fifties and a lesbian lifestyle was not what she'd had in mind for her daughter, it was not something Kay could fully accept as normal, no matter how liberated she might be"

(74). Kay doesn't think lesbianism is "dirty or disgusting or bad," or she says she doesn't, but she does think lesbianism is "a way of life that could only make Jaret unhappy, even thought it was more acceptable now than when she'd been Jaret's age" (75). At this point in the novel, Kay worries about how miserable her lesbianism will make her daughter in the adult world, but she is also concerned about the effects of such ostracism, wondering "did lesbians kill themselves anymore?" when she remembers a girl in college she had teased who had then committed suicide (75). Clearly, Jaret's mother has some learning yet to do.

Unlike Jaret's mother, Peggy's sister Claire, clearly disapproves, especially when she finds the girls (rather innocently at this point) entwined on Peggy's bed. Peggy thinks, "It didn't matter that they felt right about their love, Claire represented society and her constant put-downs had an undermining effect" (28). Claire, who the narrator says is unattractive and unpopular with boys, thinks about her sister and Jaret, who are both good looking, that they'd "had everything and still they persisted in this demented thing. It made Claire dizzy with frustration" (38). This jealousy, although (probably) without the accompanying homoeroticism, recalls Martha's response in *Patience and Sarah*. Both women long for romance and sexual fulfillment and resent others who have found it, and they feel they can indulge their anger because the relationships are not socially sanctioned. Jaret's brother Chris, on the other hand, feels "strange" when he thinks about Jaret and Peggy being lovers, but he quickly realizes that his sister is happier with Peggy. In spite of this understanding, he nevertheless bows to social conventions. He tells his friends that his sister has a college boyfriend (to explain her not dating boys) and insists that he doesn't "want to know about" her lesbianism (55).

The pressure from her sister leads Peggy to worry about her widowed and grieving father finding out about her relationship with Jaret, and she decides to break up with her. Left alone in their isolated romantic spot after Peggy goes on an ill-fated date with a boy, Jaret is raped and beaten by a friend of Chris' who is jealous because she won't pay any attention to him. After he finds out about the rape, and before he knows it was his friend, Chris thinks that the rape might make his sister permanently hate men and that he intends to "make mincemeat out of him" (126). As Lee has pointed out, most lesbian relationships in literature lead to violence, especially after the secret has come to light.

Jaret reports the rape, and, as a result, both fathers find out about their daughters' relationship. Predictably, Jaret's father responds better, telling her that no one "could be against a happy relationship" (160). He nevertheless worries about what to do about Jaret's rape and her lesbianism, while his wife tells him that they are going to continue loving their daughter (153). Kay also has abandoned her concern that Jaret might not have children: "[A]nyone can be a grandmother," she says, "but not anybody can be the mother of a brave, independent lesbian who's also a lawyer" (175). Jaret's family, at least, has decided that their daughter is their daughter, regardless of her sexuality.

Peggy's father is more troubled. He realizes that "knowledge of their relationship had been with him for some time. He simply hadn't allowed it to surface" (157). He's unhappy for her and worried about his career [he's a doctor], and then thinks that he is a "phony liberal," who is "[a]lways preaching live and let live; always railing against forces that would deny *anyone's* civil rights." He wonders, "Was this all that it really amounted to, all this huffing and puffing? That it was all right for others to be homosexual but not his own" (158). In spite of this newfound insight, he concludes that Jaret must be a "temporary substitution" for Peggy's lost mother and that with a few sessions with a psychiatrist would result in Peggy's being "straightened out" and "herself again before she started college" (158). When they talk, he tells her he is afraid for her: "I want you to be happy—have a normal life.... [L]ife is tough enough without stacking the deck" (166). This response is fairly typical in early LGBTQ young adult novels: parents worry about how difficult homosexuality will make their children's lives and cast about for ways of making the "problem" go away.

In general, this discussion of various family and community members' reactions to the girls' love affair indicates, as Lee says, that sex "is not the source of the tension in these coming out stories. Rather, the girl's verbal and physical articulations become meaningful with the threat of public knowledge" (156). In other words, nothing really happens between the two young women until others know about their relationship. Lee continues: "the girls in each of these texts are punished once they reach a level of sexuality activity ... the ultimate punishment for transgressors is a forced coming out" (156). Once the girls are physically intimate, either a violent conflict and/or a public shaming results. In this case, the drama surrounding the rape and subsequent trial, and the "forced coming out" leads the girls to separate more decisively.

However, toward the end of the novel, Peggy returns to Jaret, telling her that although she may not know exactly what she wants to be in life, she knows, for now at least, with whom she's in love. The last lines of the book are: "they held each other tightly knowing the future held many surprises, that nothing was guaranteed" (178). In spite of the violent sexual assault and the disapproval of some community and family members, this novel remains an important milestone in lesbian and gay young adult fiction, in large part because the lovers refuse to fit into "prescribed roles," either as women or as lesbians.

Like Scoppotone's novel, Nancy Garden's *Annie on My Mind* (1982) is concerned with the connection between identity and sexual attraction. The novel, Nancy St. Clair says, "examines what reality is for two young women coming to grips with their sexuality and trying to find models around which to structure their lives" (42). Day says that in this "groundbreaking" book, "two engaging young women fall in love, struggle with both internalized and external prejudice, and ultimately triumph over the forces that threaten to keep them apart. The body of adolescent literature waited a long time for this tender, bittersweet lesbian love story, which is still considered one of the best in the field" (29). Although it is technically not "the first young adult novel with a happy ending for characters in a lesbian romance," as Gavrielle Owen calls it (674), or "the first YA novel to portray lesbians in a positive light (112), as Gillis and Simpson put it, it has become one of the most widely read and appreciated.

Garden tells interviewer Kathleen T. Horning that she wanted to write a new version of Radclyffe Hall's classic lesbian text *The Well of Loneliness* (1928). At the end of that novel, she says, "there's an impassioned plea for justice and understanding, and that made me vow to someday write about book about my people with a happy ending " (43). *Annie* was also inspired by Garden's "desire to tell the truth about gay people—that we're not sick or evil; that we can and do fall in love and lead happy, healthy, productive lives" (247). Nevertheless, the hardest part of writing the book, she says, was "[r]emembering to concentrate on telling a story instead of standing up on a soapbox and lecturing to my readers!" (254). In *Annie on My Mind*, she has succeeded in writing a captivating story—and making a larger point about sexual desire and love—without lecturing to her young audience.

The novel starts with Eliza "Liza" Winthrop writing a letter (which she declares she won't send) to her former lover, Annie Kenyon, after they have both left for college. In this letter, Liza indicates that she hasn't communicated with Annie since they separated in the summer. The novel then goes back to the beginning of their relationship when Liza is 17 and is a senior at financially troubled Foster Academy and meets Annie, a public school senior, at the American Wing of the Metropolitan Museum of Art in New York City. When she looks Annie, Liza thinks, "for a moment or two I don't think I could have told anyone my name, let alone where I was. Nothing like that had ever happened to me before, and I think—I know—it scared me" (13). Not surprisingly, after such a meeting, Liza has the "feeling something important had happened" (15). Shortly afterward, they go on a picnic to The Cloisters, and Liza notices the tapestry of the unicorn, "disillusioned, so lonely and caged," which "always makes [her] shiver" (56). Clearly, Annie and Liza, although joyously falling in love, also identify with the trapped unicorn, unable to be what they want to be in the society that attempts to constrain them.

Not surprisingly, the girls have a difficult road ahead. Although Liza feels "so close" to Annie that she can't understand why they have "two separate bodies, two separate skins" (91), she nevertheless experiences "a war inside," with voices telling her that her attraction to Annie is "wrong and bad and sinful," that "[n]othing has ever felt so right and natural and true and good," that things were happening too fast, and that she "wanted to stop thinking altogether and fling [her] arms around Annie and hold her forever" (93). In spite of these multi-faceted concerns and impulses, Liza realizes that she is calmer around Annie (102) and that she has always been attracted to and preferentially enjoyed the company of women (105).

These realizations don't help the two young women ease into the physical side of their relationship, however. As they circle around whether or not to consummate their relationship, Annie tells Liza, "I don't want to be afraid of this, of—of the physical part of loving you. But you're making me afraid, and guilty, because you seem to think it's wrong, or dirty, or something—maybe you did all along, I don't know" (121). Liza realizes she has to come to terms with her attraction to Annie or lose her, and she tells herself, "*You're in love with another girl, Liza Winthrop, and you know that means you're probably gay. But you don't know a thing about what that means*" (italics in the original). She looks up homosexuality in the encyclopedia, but there's no mention of the

One. Getting There

word "love," and then Annie tells her to read that now iconic text, *Patience and Sarah* (143). In what will become a typical scenario in later LGBTQ fiction, the girls also check books out of the library and buy magazines, and Liza says that she feels as if she "were meeting parts of myself in the gay people [she] read about" (144). As Lee says: "These intertextual references suggest that reading lesbian texts is political because it offers a point of lesbian identification and community" (158). Young lesbian women reading this book can see that others have wrestled with these same challenges and pleasures.

This community is strengthened by two of Liza's teachers, Ms. Widmer and Ms. Stevenson, a lesbian couple, who, although closeted at work, "in their house they were like a couple of old shoes, each with its own special lumps and bumps and cracks, but nonetheless a pair that fit with ease into the same shoe box" (132). When the girls agree to cat sit for the two women, they realize that their teachers are lesbians, "like us" (152). Not surprisingly, they find *Patience and Sarah* on their bookshelf as well (153). However, Annie says that she doesn't want to hide the "best part" of herself as the older women have had to do (154).

The girls start spending time at the teachers' house, where they are eventually discovered by one of Liza's "friends" and the school secretary. The teachers are outed and forced to leave the school. Liza has to come out to her family (although Annie doesn't because she doesn't go to the same school), and she is suspended and threatened with expulsion. Her family has what can only be described as mixed reactions. Liza's mother says that she "knows what it's like to have no close friends and then suddenly to have one—it happened to me, too, when I was a little younger than you" (187), although she claims it was "experimenting" and "normal" (188). Like the father in *Happy Endings*, Liza's dad tells her that he's "never thought gay people can be very happy—no children, for one thing, no real family life" (191). Her brother Chad asks if she has to "be like that," and when Liza tells him that she is "like that," he hugs her but then cries in his room (196).

Things do turn around for Liza, however. She is eventually allowed back in school, and she even retains her position as student council president in a new election. On her first day back, her brother wishes her luck and, much like the brother in *Happy Endings*, offers to punch someone if need be (215). Her friend Walt tells her that he's "not going to desert a friend just because of a little—sex problem or anything," and he says "it's just like any other handicap" (217). This dismaying response, even though it was meant to be sympathetic, is not typical, however. For the most part, the response at Liza's school is positive: "for every kid who was rotten—and there were really only a few—there were at least two" who were ordinarily friendly (218–19), Liza notices with relief.

Although it is not unexpected, given the time period, the two teachers are stoic about their firing. Ms. Stevenson tells the girls that lots of people experience unfairness and that what matters is "the truth of loving, of two people finding each other" (229). She adds, "I can't lie to you and say that losing our jobs like this is easy. It isn't but the point is that it'll be okay; we'll be okay. And we want to know that you will be, too" (230). In another sign of the times, the girls learn that Ms. Stevenson was kicked out of the army for being gay and had trouble getting into college as a result (230). "Don't let ignorance win," Ms. Stephenson says. "Let love" (232). Unsurprisingly, the novel has been criticized for the ways in which the teachers become scapegoats for the residual homophobia in the culture, but Gardner says that she didn't have them protest being fired because "they just wanted to reconstruct their lives quietly, do some of the other things they'd always wanted to do, and live together in peace" (255). This is not an unusual response in the 1980s, given the various kinds of legislation arrayed against the LGBTQ community.

After these dramatic events, the novel returns to the frame narrative and ends with Liza finally calling Annie, their making plans to meet for Christmas break, and declaring that they love each other (234). As with the other novels discussed previously, this is an upbeat but nevertheless ambiguous ending, which befits the adolescent literature genre. Adolescence is a period of growth and development that doesn't finish upon graduation from high school. Annie and Liza have reconciled, but their future remains (necessarily) vague. Like Ruby, Daphne, Altschuler, Davy, Peggy, Jaret, Wally, Charlie, and, to a certain extent, even Patience and Sarah, the adult lives of these young women is uncertain.

A less well-known book than *Annie*, Clayton Bess' *Big Man and the Burn-Out* (1985) nevertheless offers an interesting treatment of homosexuality—this time a teacher. As Lobban and Clyde say, Mr. Goodban's sexuality "is not discussed and it is not an issue in the book. Rather, it is simply a fact there in the background; some teachers are heterosexual, others are not, and that is the way the world is" (11). There has been little critical commentary about this relatively obscure novel, although reviews taken from Bess's website cite the novel as "a sensitive story for younger teens ... a story of coming of age, of friendship, and of nurturing" (*Booklist*), "a gem of a book that is incandescent and fragile with its loving, caring people who are unable to express their emotions" (*Voice of Youth Advocates*), and "a unique young adult account which departs from traditional formula to offer a realistic protagonist, insights on rural life, and a mixture of issues" (*Midwest Book Review*). According to Amazon's page for the book, the *School Library Journal* review by Deborah M. Locke called it a "badly flawed book," with unconvincing characters and dialog that threatens to become parodic. Still, the novel should be examined for its treatment of the relationship between student and teacher, as well as its sensitive discussions of homosexual/homosocial bonds.

The novel starts with protagonist Jess, who lives with his grandmother and step-grandfather, finding a goose egg and deciding to incubate it with his grandmother's chicken eggs. Jess hates school, although he likes his English teacher Mr. Goodban, who Jess thinks is "kind of handsome and looked like he should be a race car driver or a detective or a decathlon star or something instead of a teacher" (18). Mr. Goodban keeps his personal life private, but Jess imagines the kind of woman he might be married to, in fairly specific detail and assumes that she and Mr. Goodban have "a wonderful life" (18). When Mr. Goodban lends Jess a copy of Jack London's short stories, Jess notices the inscription "To Bill, with deep admiration and love, V.," and he decides the giver must be "a beautiful and noble Englishwoman" (50). Jess' infatuation with his handsome teacher (and his imagined love life) is derailed when he gets into a fight at school, and Jess thinks Mr. Goodban has "turn[ed] against him" (57) for causing the ruckus. Shortly after, Jess has a dream where Mr. Goodban is calling him endearing names.

After a complicated series of events that involve a plagiarized paper and a panicked visit to Mr. Goodban's house, Mr. Goodban and his "friend" Vic, who first appears as "a barechested man in a pair of cut-offs" (141) give Jess a ride home in his "sporty little Toyota that never had a particle of dust on it." When the men meet Jess's grandparents, his grandmother "didn't know just what to make of these two men. They talked so pretty and she talked so plain. It made her tongue-tied" (148). Nevertheless, they invite Mr. Goodban and Vic to stay for dinner. Much of the description (of Vic in particular) is a coded indicator of homosexuality, from the cut-off shorts, to the clean car, to the "pretty" talking, but Jess' grandparents seem oblivious (as does Jess at this point). At the end of the dinner, Mr. Goodban gives Jess the copy of *The Sea Wolf* with the inscription "For Jess, For Good, Bill Goodban," and Jess is "so disappointed that he could only stare at it. There wasn't any of the stuff he imagined might be there, about respect, or admiration, or about how Jess was his favorite student, or anything." Jess goes to bed that night "feeling miserable and alone" (158). Clearly, his crush has not reciprocated his affections, and Jess is disappointed, although he might not have been able to see his attraction for his teacher as clearly as do readers.

The novel then shifts to Jess' friendship with an older boy, Meechum, which can be seen as a substitute for his unrequited love for Mr. Goodban. At one point, the young men go skinny dipping, and when Jess gets an erection, Meechum says, "You know what we can do?" "Jess is frozen, looking into Meechum's eyes and thinking, 'At this moment anything was possible.'" His grandmother interrupts with "What are you doing over there?" and tells the boys to "get decent this minute!" (184). Jess and his grandmother fight about her interference, and his grandmother slaps him. Hannah talks to her husband Sid and says while she didn't quite know what they had done or were about to do, the boys were "ready for it" (186). Sid tells her to remember when she was that age, "full of fire to know the answers." If she didn't feel that, he says, "more's the pity for you, Hannah, if the Lord never gave that time of youth to you. But I remember it. It was a good time. A time for playin' and for explorin'. And for rememberin.'" Hannah worries it's not just play, and Sid says, "Well, then, Hannah, that's who the boy is then. And if that's who he is, and what he is, then you'd better get used to it" or risk losing him as well (186–87). Sid has become the voice of tolerance in the novel, and readers sense that he will guide both Jess and his wife toward acceptance and growth.

Hannah and Jess reconcile at the end, and Sid opines that they all are "going to make it" (197). At the end of this novel, the gay teacher hasn't been forced to resign, and Jess and Meechum still seem to be friends. Granted, the homosexuality is mostly implied rather than explicit, but it also seen as more than simply benign. The relationship between Mr. Goodban and his partner is affectionate and not damaging to his career (although it is a secret), the attraction between Meechum and Jess is seen as natural exploration, and the focus of the novel remains on friendship and family.

Carolyn Meyer's *Elliott and Win* (1986), the last of the early LGBTQ books to be discussed in this chapter, focuses (like *Big Man*) on the homosexuality of a secondary adult character and not on the primary adolescent protagonist. Lobban and Clyde say that the novel's "persistent theme" is "that friendship and acceptance are the most important things in life" (117). Also with *Big Man*, there is very little extant criticism on the novel, and it appears not to have been reissued since its 1986 release. Amazon's page for the book indicates that *Publishers Weekly* says that the author "invests the characters with the humanity that makes them memorable, and *School Library Journal* says that the book is "an emotionally powerful examination of individuality in the face of peer judgments." Unlike *Big Man*, though, homosexuality is much more directly addressed.

Fourteen-year-old Winston Kelly, abandoned by his father and somewhat neglected by his hardworking mother, is saddled with a "Los Amigos" buddy, Elliott Deerfield, a gourmet cook, geologist, jump roper, bandana wearer, confirmed bachelor, and opera lover whom Win's "friend" Paul Crowser suspects is gay. Paul warns him that if he hangs around "with a faggot, people are going to start thinking you're a faggot too" (27). In the course of their relationship, Elliott teaches Win how to cook, enjoy opera, and appreciate photography. As a result of his experiences with Elliott, Win is able to tell Paul, "You think everybody who's different is a faggot. And I'm telling you cooking doesn't have anything to do with being gay or straight or anything else. Liking to cook is about liking food. It's not about sex" (72). He asks Paul, "You afraid of catching queerness, Paul? Something that floats around like salmonella in the tuna fish?" (72). Win resolves to "show Paul that there was nothing weird, queer, or faggotish [nice neologism] about eating good food, and nothing weird, queer, or faggotish about cooking it either" by cooking him a meal, but then he decides that he resents Paul for the sexist things he's been saying about Win's love interest Heather (90–91).

Although he dismisses Paul's view of homosexuality as contagion, when Elliott hugs Win goodbye as he's leaving for a business trip, Win, who hasn't been hugged by anyone "for a long time" except his mother, thinks it "felt good," but then he worries "that maybe liking Elliott to hug me meant there was something wrong with me" (117). While Elliott is gone, Win starts to emulate him, putting *Huckleberry Finn* next to his place as he eats an Elliott-inspired meal (124). Homophobe Paul comes back from visiting his dad, who he finds out is gay, a twist in the plot that sympathetic reviewers found "too pat" and a "poorly executed contrivance" (Amazon page). Paul tells Win about his father and starts to cry (153). This kind of comeuppance for Paul is really unnecessary for the overall message of the book and is really its only flaw.

The significant plot conflict comes when Win and Heather decide to have an Elliott-style gourmet meal in the "blockhouse," a cinder-block shed in a vacant lot where Elliott and Paul used to meet. They are attacked by several older boys, and Heather is raped. Win, who has been held down by the boys, is unable to help her. Afterward, Heather's parents won't let Win see her, and they make plans to move away.

At the end of the novel, Elliott and Win take a camping trip, where Win painfully reveals that he was too weak and scared to help Heather. Win decides that over the summer, he has learned that "Elliott wasn't crazy. Unusual, yes. Individual, yes. Crazy, no" (188). In the last scene of the novel, the two are settling down in the tent, when Win's "best friend began to snore" (193). Like *Big Man*, *Elliott and Win* shows young boys in relationships with gay men that are not sexual or predatory and treats the emerging sexuality of the two main characters with sensitivity and subtlety. These two early novels nevertheless suggest that homosexuality can be successfully integrated into "mainstream" society and that children are not in danger from contact with adult gay men. In fact, both Win and Jess learn important lessons about love, about masculinity, and about family from their contact with Mr. Goodban and Elliott.

These eight novels indicate that the 70s and 80s were not the wasteland for LGBTQ young adult fiction many critics assume them to be. Obviously, there are several LGBTQ novels for adolescents where the gay and lesbian characters are assaulted in various and sundry ways, but the novels discussed here suggest that there is another side to the picture of adolescent literature with LGBTQ content in the 70s and 80s. The landscape of early GLBTQ young adult fiction didn't consist of John Donovan, then a vast wasteland, then Nancy Garden, then another wasteland until the 1990s. Writers such as these were working on representing LGBTQ adolescents, and the gay and lesbian adult figures in their lives in compassionate, funny, and sophisticated ways.

Most importantly, works like these represent the groundwork on

One. Getting There

which writers such as Francesca Lia Block and Ellen Wittlinger would begin building in the 1990s and David Levithan and Brent Hartinger would continue in the 2000s. Without *Patience and Sarah, I'll Get There. It Better Be Worth the Trip, Ruby, Annie on My Mind* and the other novels discussed here, and publishers willing to go out on a limb to see them into print, wonderful works such as *Weetzie Bat, Boy Meets Boy, Hard Love* and, more recently, *Dante and Aristotle Discover the Secrets of the Universe* and *Fat Angie* (among many, many others) might never have been published. Without these pioneers, young readers who are same-sex attracted, or trans, or questioning, wouldn't find themselves reflected in the fiction they read today and would have come to believe that their feelings and experiences are not "normal," or worse, that they deserve to be harassed, ostracized, and/or abused.

Two

Beyond *Deliver Us from Evie*
Contemporary Lesbian Young Adult Fiction

> Lesbian desire is everywhere, even as it may be nowhere. Put bluntly, we lack any general agreement about what constitutes a lesbian—Martha Vincinus, "'They Wonder to Which Sex I Belong,'" 468

> [The lesbian novel] has helped shape a lesbian consciousness, community, and culture from the movement's beginning—Bonnie Zimmerman, *The Safe Sea of Women*, 2

Bonnie Zimmerman's 1990 *A Safe Sea of Women* defines the lesbian novel as one that "has a central, not marginal, lesbian character, one who understands herself to be a lesbian," contains "mostly lesbian characters," and centers on "lesbian histories." A lesbian novel also "places love between women, including sexual passion, at the center of its story" and locates men "firmly at the margins" (15). Lesbian novels, she continues, are read by lesbians "in order to affirm lesbian existence" (15). She acknowledges that while these novels "create a mythology for the lesbian community," they also "can be both inspirational and stifling," limiting readers' ideas of what it means to be a part of a lesbian community (16). As she puts it so well: "[M]ost lesbian novels require good lesbians, bad men, and happy endings" (20). In spite of their tendency to stereotype both their male and female characters, these novels attempt to "express what lesbians feel to be true and important" about themselves (26). This insightful definition highlights the central tension that can be seen in lesbian novels for younger audiences as well: the desire to inspire and create community, while not restricting definitions of what it might mean to be a "good" young lesbian.

Vanessa Lee's 1998 study of lesbian young adult novels found "texts that position lesbianism as a threat or a problem," texts that "focu[s] on the formation of lesbian identities," and texts that "interrogate received wisdom about lesbianism and lesbian identity" (152). Since 1998, YA lesbian novels have mostly moved away from considering lesbianism as a threat and more toward examining the various ways in which young women become aware of, act on, and talk about their same-sex attractions. Coming out remains a focus, as does questioning often-restrictive or damaging stereotypes, but newer lesbian YA fiction also works to normalize lesbian desire for young adult audiences and to integrate young lesbian characters into both homogenous and heterogeneous communities.

It could be argued that M.E. Kerr's *Deliver Us from Evie* (1994) perfectly represents this transition between the "lesbianism as threat or problem" and the more contemporary acceptance (or at least acknowledgment) of lesbian desire. This novel, which I discuss at length in my book on censorship and young adult fiction, has a young lesbian character (not the main character but the sibling of the narrator) whose lesbianism initially presents a problem for her family and their wider community. However, Evie is also a strong advocate for her butch identity and for her same-sex attraction. Unlike many of the early LGBTQ young adult novels discussed in the previous chapter, she neither renounces nor reconsiders her lesbianism at the end of the novel, nor does she or any of her family members (or her pets) die. The novel ends with Evie's parents reconciled to her relationship with her female partner and encouraging the girls to come visit.

Dawn Thompson says that *Evie* "engages the sympathy of heterosexual readers and leads them toward empathy, introduces a surprisingly sophisticated analysis of the relationship between gender and sexuality, and provides some effective lessons on reading for young readers." It also "engages with the gay and lesbian literary tradition, recalling and revising Radclyffe Hall's *The Well of Loneliness*." In spite of these groundbreaking qualities, however, the novel also shows "the appalling lack of change in dominant attitudes toward homosexuality" and raises questions about "the workings and effects of internalized homophobia" (283). Thus this groundbreaking novel, in Thompson's view, looks forward to new lesbian young adult fiction and backward toward the repression and judgment of the past.

In an article published a year after Thompson's, however, Michele Abate disagrees, saying that Evie "is devoid of the shame and self-loathing so commonly found in queer characters of the past" (232) and argues that lesbians like Evie "may still encounter oppression, but they can also lead happy, fulfilling, and, most importantly, openly queer lives" (234). Evie, according to Abate, "repeatedly announces and asserts her own queer identity. In doing so, she demonstrates that the butch stereotype is not merely a leftover legacy from the 1950s but an important lived form of contemporary lesbian gender identity and sexual expression" (243). Clearly, *Deliver Us from Evie* is poised at the brink of change, and critics are undecided about whether it leaps the chasm or falls into the abyss.

There is no such quandary with Stacey Donovan's *Dive* (1996), which falls into Lee's category of novels that "interrogate received wisdom" about lesbianism. She also carries on a family tradition of LGBTQ fiction for young adults. Donovan is the niece of John Donovan, writer of what has come to be regarded as the first gay YA novel, *I'll Get There. It Better Be Worth the Trip* (1969), which was discussed in the previous chapter. *Dive*, however, is a much more postmodern novel than the one written by her uncle. Lee says that *Dive* "portrays adolescence as complicated and does not presume that this state is knowable or honestly representable." It also shows lesbianism "as part of a larger cultural landscape" (152) and presents "fractured and less identity-bound versions of both adolescence and lesbianism" (156). In addition, "lesbianism is not the central element of this text, and intimacy between adolescent girls is articulated as a negotiation, rather than a definition, of sexual identities" (156). Both adolescence and lesbianism are seen as more of a negotiation, a shifting part of identity but not the sole identity. It is also a well-written and enjoyable novel. As Lobban and Clyde put it, "The writing is cool, precise and lyrical, while the emotions portrayed have genuine warmth and integrity" (36).

As the novel opens, main character Virginia's dog, Lucky, has been hit by a car (the driver leaves the scene of the accident), in what might be seen as a veiled reference to the dog in her uncle's book, except in this novel the death occurs at the beginning instead of the end. Perhaps the message here is that the death of a pet is not a punishment for homosexuality but an apparently random act that must be uncovered as the novel proceeds. Shortly after this first scene, readers learn that Virginia's father is sick with a rare and fatal blood disorder, and her mother is overwhelmed by the situation (and distant with her children). Told in the first person, this novel uses humor, pathos, and a complex extended metaphor about diving to make its points about love, loss, and life.

In a trope common to many contemporary YA lesbian novels, a new girl comes to school, coolly dressed and reading Rimbaud, and when Virginia sees her, "the bad taste in my mouth disappears. My mouthful of unanswered questions vanishes. There's never been anything like this woozy, wonderful breath. Let the wind in" ("What Is and Is Not"). This scene lyrically describes lesbian desire in a way that makes it accessible to both straight and gay readers, as it also naturalizes that desire. Her name is Jane, and she makes Virginia think of Romeo's paean to Juliet's beauty ("And Think It Were Not Night"), which equates same- and opposite-sex desire.

The novel is in no hurry to develop the romance, however. Eighty percent of the way through the novel, Jane and Virginia finally go to a secluded spot by a pond, and Virginia thinks she'd like Jane to lie closer: "Inside me would be good. If only we could get rid of these clumsy bodies and dissolve into each other. The way water disappears into sand" ("Welcome Hurry"). Jane kisses her, and "her entire body and everything I wonder about in her seems to roll onto my lips as she kisses me. Then she kisses me again. It's beyond dissolving" ("Welcome Hurry"). Virginia doesn't know what to call what she feels for Jane, but it's stronger than what she once felt for a boy, although not that different, really. She wants to tell the truth about this experience: "If I can't make somebody understand what I feel, I'll disintegrate into the air. My eyes will close. My mouth will shut. My life will vanish. I'm too young to die" ("Just by Being There"). Her attraction must be acknowledged for it (and her) to be real, and it seems that Jane feels the same way: "She holds me just as tightly as I hold her as we reel in the grip of this new spell we're under. The laughter, like wind, finally stops" ("Just by Being There"). They kiss in the middle of the road, and Virginia thinks that she doesn't care who sees, and she wonders if she loves Jane ("Just by Being There"). Although this is a private scene, the implication is that their love will soon become public. Significantly, unlike in earlier novels, the physical encounter is not observed by hostile others, nor is it punished by parents or peers.

This combination of fear and desire is linked to a time when Virginia's father took her to the ocean. He told her to dive into a wave, but she didn't want to let go of his hand: "The white waves crashed around us, brutal and spitting. And what fools we were, rushing to meet them!

I must've opened my mouth in horror, or to say something, because suddenly it was full of salt, burning, when my father yelled, 'Dive!' and let go of my hand" ("When the Wave Comes"). The message is obviously that one has to dive into life, regardless of the danger—that sometimes it is impossible to hold on. This is true with love, with desire, and with sorrow. While her father is dying, she can't be with Jane because "stuff is being dragged out of me," and at the same time she wonders if she will kiss her again ("Roaring"). When she sees Jane again at the end of the novel, Virginia tells herself, "Dive, I think to myself, or sink" ("Rush").

Dive she does, thinking "how simple it is, how natural. I know how to touch without ever having touched I know without knowing.... My hands ached with joy, wanting to linger around her lips, my arms ache from holding her so tightly, my chest aches, as if I am underwater, as if I have dived into a pool and rise, laggardly, unbreathing, to the surface" ("Rush"). This scene is not one of unmediated pleasure, however. Virginia wonders about why people think two girls having sex is wrong, including herself, but she also thinks it is "the most natural thing in the world." She also worries about whether it is love, since they haven't mentioned the word. "I guess that's where the danger is. In the things that aren't mentioned" ("Danger"). Both love and shame, desire and taboo, are "the things that aren't mentioned."

At the end of the novel, Virginia finds out who hit her dog, and she forgives them, it appears, because she now understands both love and loss. At her father's wake, she decides she will tell someone about Jane. She thinks that "surrounded by all those people, and the endlessness of everything I already remember, I am on fire. Unbelievably dreamy with hopes. And I wish I could feel this way forever" ("Dive"). The novel ends with some ambiguity about where Jane and Virginia's relationship will go from here, but the tone is optimistic and the implication is that Virginia's same-sex attraction will soon become public.

Lee says that *Dive* "offers an ambitious postmodern portrayal of adolescent lesbianism." Donovan, she argues, "presents complex adolescent sexuality and how it cannot be cleanly extracted from the rest of a person's identity in order to be examined or depicted. To do it right, in a postmodern sense, you have to show the whole messy picture, and it will not always fit into a nice narrative form" (157). Virginia's dog (who, unlike Fred in *I'll Get There*, survives his accident), her friendships, her family dynamics, her memories and loss of her father, and her uncertainty about her sexuality all contribute to this complicated and nuanced portrait of a young lesbian. It also shows the ways in which contemporary lesbian young adult fiction is moving away from a focus on same-sex desire as a problem to the more generalized problems all young love engenders.

Like *Dive*, Ellen Wittlinger's *Hard Love* (1999) is a postmodern book, unwilling to commit to fixed notions about identity or literary genres. It also resembles Kerr's *Deliver Us from Evie*, in that the straight (at least as far as he can tell at this point) male main character tells the story. However, this isn't the story of a lesbian sister but of the narrator's inappropriate (or at least doomed) love for a lesbian, who is an important, but secondary, character. Like *Evie*, and unlike much earlier fiction about lesbian teens, the lesbian is not "turned" from her same-sex attraction by the love of a good man. Day says that *Hard Love* is "an absorbing book about loss, love, trust, family, transformation and, interestingly, authorship" (57).

Indeed it is (in part) about budding authors—and their budding sexualities. John "Gio" Galardi, Jr., is the author of a zine, *Bananafish*, and he is in love with Marisol Guzman, creator of the zine *Escape Velocity*. Marisol is clear about her sexuality, declaring that "the truth is bioluminescent" and that she never lies (although this comes into question later in the novel). "Do you know what 'coming out' really means?" she asks John, whom she has nicknamed Gio. "It means you stop lying. You tell the truth even if it's painful, especially if it's painful" (Ch. 2).

In Marisol's zine, she tells the story of her coming out: "When I opened the closet door my mother assured me I could always count on her support, but she cried for days with the bathroom door locked. She was mourning expectation, I think: dresses and a wedding, boyfriends and babies, things she was looking forward to. (One of those things even I had been looking forward to. I still am.)" (Ch. 4). Marisol believes that being lesbian doesn't mean that she can't have a wedding or a baby, clearly an optimistic view (at least about the wedding) in 1998. Parents, even the most accepting, also seem willing to believe that same-sex attraction might be a passing phase. When Gio/John talks to Marisol's mother on the phone, he thinks that it is sad that she was "grabbing onto me like a life raft. Here she was marching in the Gay Pride parade, flying the PFLAG flag, but still hoping to find out there'd been a little mistake about what Marisol mean by 'coming out'" (Ch. 10). The difference here is that Marisol's mother, while she might still entertain fantasies about potential boyfriends, is nevertheless supportive of Marisol's sexuality.

Marisol's father is much less accepting. "It's been more than a year now," Marisol says, "and my father has never discussed my lesbianism with me, but he speaks to me again and pretends nothing has changed" (Ch. 4). Marisol says she resents her parents, even though they could have been much worse: "One denies and one embraces. My father wears a blindfold, and my mother wants to out-gay me: I barely know what it means to be homosexual myself, and she's racing ahead of me, reading all the literature, consulting experts, wanting to 'explore my feelings.' I don't want to explore my lesbianism with my mother, at least not now" (Ch. 4). This is a response that will become more familiar in later LGBTQ YA fiction, young characters who refuse to be categorized by their parents and society. In fact, John/Gio's nickname is also indicative of the young adult who refuses to be locked into any particular identity.

These flowing categories and sense of gender/sexuality as performance comes up again when Marisol tells John/Gio about her first girlfriend, who tells Marisol that she's not sure if she's really a lesbian. "She decided she really preferred the straight and narrow," Marisol says. "Like homosexuality was just this *outfit* she was trying on, and it didn't quite fit. I never saw her again after that night" (Ch. 6). It might be possible, though, that same-sex attraction could very well be an "outfit" that one (especially a young person) tries on, sees if it will fit, and discards if it doesn't. Interestingly, during this time, John/Gio starts a correspondence with Diana, who also writes a zine. John/Gio, who claims that he doesn't know what kind of person attracts him, is now "trying on" heterosexuality. It isn't a perfect fit, though. Perhaps foolishly, John/Gio asks Marisol to the prom, and they talk about other girls in the school who would be more appropriate dates, and John demurs, in part because they are ordinary, straight girls. Marisol tells John/Gio he's "radically confused" (Ch. 8).

They go to the prom, and John/Gio fools himself that some of her cryptic comments about their friendship mean that she is secretly in love with him and tries to kiss her. She rebuffs him and tells a friend that John/Gio knows this "but doesn't want to believe" (Ch. 12). John tells her that she "should have shown up looking like that," meaning looking so beautiful (Ch. 12). John's heterosexuality has allowed him to be fooled by Marisol's appearance. Because she is physically attractive to him, he assumes, wrongly, that she must be *attracted* to him as well. Needless to say, Marisol sets him straight (so to speak). This passage highlights the complexity of desire—the ways it is indicated and received.

In the culminating event of the novel, Diana invites John/Gio to a zine writers' conference in Provincetown, and Marisol comes along, planning to prove to John/Gio that she is truly is a lesbian. When they get there, John/Gio wonders whether Diana might be lesbian as well. "There weren't any obvious signs" (Ch. 14). It may be that John/Gio is just not reading the signs Marisol believes were quite obvious. At the conference, "Marisol couldn't wait to surround herself with other gay people, to show me how gay she could be once she'd ditched me. She wanted me to see her lesbianess in action. (Lesbianity?) It was the last thing I wanted to do" (Ch. 14). It's interesting here that John is trying to coin a word for the state of being lesbian, for the identity, while at the same time he recognizes that it is, in large part, shown "in action."

Leaving the workshop early, Marisol decides to go to New York City with her newfound lesbian friends, and she and John/Gio part on friendly terms. She thanks him for telling her she is beautiful, and he thanks her for breaking down barriers between him and other people. "Hey, I love you too, Gio," she says. "As much as I can" (Ch. 15). The novel ends with John/Gio preparing to meet the new day and the participants in the workshop, including Diana. John/Gio is "very anxious, more than a little scared, susceptible now to anything that might happen" (Ch. 15). It also seems clear that John/Gio is ready to "join" the world of heterosexual romance, at least for now. Although the novel ends with a restoration of heterosexuality and the lesbians move off stage, it also shows that neither Marisol nor John/Gio are damaged by their encounters with crossed signals and non-normative desires, and the novel does *not* end with a straight kiss at the prom.

Listed on the front cover as the "companion book" to *Hard Love*, Wittlinger's *Love and Lies: Marisol's Story* (2008) provides a clear example of how lesbian YA fiction changed from 1998 to 2008. Earlier novels usually featured straight main characters and/or narrators who struggled with lesbian friends or relatives, while those in the early part of the 2000s shifted to same-sex-attracted main characters.[1] Now telling her own story, Marisol Guzman has graduated from high school and is living with her gay friend Birdie (who had a relatively small role in the earlier book) in an apartment in Cambridge. She is writing a novel, taking a class in creative writing, working in a coffee shop, and deferring her acceptance to Stanford for a year. Her friend from *Hard Love*, John "Gio" Galardi, Jr., who narrated the first book, is (conveniently) also taking the class. The class is taught by the beautiful Olivia Frost, who is charismatic, full of wisdom about writing, and soon to be the object of Marisol's affection.

In the midst of this, Marisol meets high school senior Lee O'Brien, who has left home in Indiana to live with her sister in Boston after she came out as a lesbian and things became difficult at home. When she first meets Lee, Marisol tells her, "Welcome home" (14), which hints at the kind of lesbian community several scholars of the genre had called for in the 1990s. Lee immediately develops a crush on Marisol, which is unrequited, as Marisol only has eyes for Olivia, and the romantic love triangle is complete.

In a discussion that explores the flexibility of sexual attraction, Birdie tells Marisol that his boyfriend Damon says he's bi, and Marisol says that he "can't quite get the old closet door open." Birdie retorts that the closet metaphor is "getting tired." "Old homos have that closet issue," he says, "but we've grown past it." Marisol teases him about that comment, and he replies that Damon "doesn't want homosexuality to define him," and he adds, "there's nothing wrong with that" (55). Marisol begins to see his point, thinking that one doesn't always "want to lead with your sexuality" (56). This conversation is a sign of the increasing awareness in literature and in literary theory of the fluidity of sexual desire and identity. It also resonates with young adults of all sorts, who are often not ready to be defined—or even to define themselves—by already existing identity categories.

Relatively quickly, at least compared to the slow pace of John/Gio's "romance" with Marisol and Virginia and Jane's relationship in *Dive*, Marisol and Olivia sleep together, and Birdie is excited to hear that "not only have you finally vanquished your virginity, but you did it with a totally hot chick" (132). The more explicitly sexual nature of the book might also be explained by the age of this protagonist. However, the sexual component immediately creates problems. Worried about what Olivia might say about her first assignment, Marisol starts to realize there might be reasons "not to date your teacher," and when Olivia instead praises it effusively, she feels "sleazy," because she can't be sure if she can trust Olivia's judgment (136). In addition, Olivia soon becomes possessive and controlling. Gio says that Marisol is a "more interesting person, and, frankly, a deeper person than [Olivia] is" (143). Marisol cannot see this at this point, maintaining what readers are coming to see is a doomed (and possibly damaging) relationship with Olivia.

Marisol, Gio, Birdie, Lee, and Damon decide to go to Provincetown (which was also the setting for the most dramatic part of *Hard Love*). In Provincetown, which is filled with "throngs of gorgeous bodies, all tanned and muscled and homosexual," Marisol feels "that the world was really mine" in a way she doesn't feel anywhere else (182). However, there are a variety of troubles in paradise. Initially, Birdie worries that having Gio along might cause problems, given his lingering attachment to Marisol. When Birdie insists that, even though he knows Marisol is a lesbian, he is still attracted to her. Marisol thinks, "Wouldn't it be great if we all had a sex switch that we could turn off and on? So that you could hang out with somebody you liked as a friend and there would be no hurt feelings or sexual misunderstandings?" (173). This is indeed the problem in many of the LGBTQ young adult novels (or perhaps in all novels). However, the drama is complicated here because of heteronormative assumptions many characters make and the wider romantic possibilities that open up when same-sex attracted characters are introduced.

To further complicate things, Gio tells Marisol that Lee is crazy about Marisol and wonders why she wants to be with Olivia instead of Lee, who would be a more age-appropriate partner. "There's something wrong with her. Olivia," Birdy says. "I mean, I know she's smart and sexy and everything, but something isn't right. I don't know—I just don't *trust* her" (176). This proves to be prophetic when Olivia shows up unexpectedly and creates a jealous scene when she sees Marisol dancing with Gio and assumes (falsely) that there is a mutual romantic attachment between them. "There is nothing I despise more than a woman who pretends to be a lesbian," Olivia says, "but then the minute a man shows up, she's suddenly straight as a ruler" (190). This is ironic, given that Marisol is resolutely lesbian and was burned in a previous relationship by a woman who was uncertain about her sexuality. This scene also reverses the dance sequence in *Hard Love*, with the jealous partner not being John/Gio but Olivia. To make matters worse, Lee is upset by all this drama and unhappy that Marisol doesn't care for her, and she suddenly leaves Provincetown and returns to Illinois.

These events lead Marisol to reconsider her relationship with Olivia. Toward the end of the novel, Marisol finds out that Olivia hasn't finished (or even *started*) a novel, as she claimed and that she plagiarized all the quotes about writing she used in her class from famous authors. Lee's older sister with whom Lee has gone to stay) also recognizes Olivia (perhaps a bit too conveniently) as someone who was expelled from their college for plagiarism, and who had a pattern of getting intensely involved with inappropriate people and then punishing them when they didn't remain under her complete control. After learning the truth about Olivia, Marisol contacts Lee, who says she wants to stay in Illinois. This novel ends not with a happy reunion of Lee and Marisol, but with Marisol settling down (alone) to write: "The day was not over yet. Or the week. Or the semester. Or the year. Things could change. And I had work to do" (245). Like Gio in *Hard Love*, Marisol recognizes the value of her creative work and will postpone any definitive action on her sexual and romantic desires. This pattern of being willing to sit with an uncertain future, both emotionally and professionally, is a hallmark of contemporary LGBTQ adolescent fiction, and it, in fact, typical of all young adult novels.

Following the lead of Kerr, Donovan, and Wittlinger, other writers of young adult fiction begin featuring lesbian characters, both as protagonists as well as secondary characters. Julia Watt's *Finding H.F.* and Sara Ryan's *Empress of the World* (2001), Bonnie Shimko's *Letters in the Attic* (2002), Lauren Myracle's *Kissing Kate* and Wittlinger's *Heart on My Sleeve* (2003), Maureen Johnson's *The Bermudez Triangle* (2004), Catherine Murdock's *Dairy Queen* (2006), and E. E. Charlton-Trujillo's *Fat Angie* (2013) all explore aspects of lesbian identity and community in interesting and groundbreaking ways.

In Watts' *Finding H.F.*, Heavenly Faith (H.F.) Simms is 16 when the novel opens. Her mother is out of the picture, and H.F. is being raised by her grandmother, who H.F. thinks would "[p]ray and try to get me 'cured'" if she knew that she was a lesbian. "She'd never understand it, and neither would most people in Morgan, Kentucky," H.F. says, "which ain't exactly San Francisco, if you know what I mean" (3). This is clearly not a place she will find a lesbian community. H.F. says the popular kids in her high school know that she's different: "Different on the inside. Like lions on nature shows that sniff out which gazelle is ripest for the picking, those people can sniff out different—and it's a smell they hate"

Two. Beyond Deliver Us from Evie

(5). Still, she recognizes that "sissy boys" like her friend Bo, "the only boy flute player in all of Kentucky" (7), "always have it harder than the tomboys. If you're a boyish girl, other girls just snub you, but if you're a girlish boy, other boys beat the living hell out of you" (5). This comment captures an interesting dichotomy that has girls being "allowed" to be masculine, but boys being punished for displaying feminine characteristics.

In a plot element that is common to earlier YA lesbian novels like *Deliver Us from Evie*, H.F. falls for a rich girl, Wendy, and when they have a sleepover, Wendy kisses her, and they fool around. Afterward, Wendy says that she doesn't "like girls that way" (54). Her grandmother (who doesn't yet know that H.F. is lesbian) thinks that the class differences pushed them apart, that "there are lines you don't cross." H.F. agrees in part and says that "the hardest lines to remember not to cross are the lines you can't see" (55). H.F. also wishes that she could "just naturally be what other people want you to be" (60). This is similar to Marisol wishing she could have an on/off switch for her sexual attraction, but it also highlights the ways in which sexuality intersects with social class dynamics.

When she finds out that her grandmother has been keeping her mother's address from her, H.F. and Bo decide to take a road trip from Kentucky to Florida to meet her mother, and in leaving Kentucky they begin to get a sense of the wider LGBTQ community. In Atlanta, they meet three young lesbians who are currently homeless. One comes from a wealthy family who threw her out when she came out to them (96). This section of the novel underscores the reality for many LGBTQ teens: if they are open about their sexuality or gender identity they are often kicked out of the family home or coerced into (appearing to) change.

The girls and Bo are taken in by "Preacher Dave," a gay man who helps out younger LGBTQ kids. He takes them to what Bo calls "a church for queers," which surprises them and suggests that not all religions demonize homosexuality (109). When Bo and the two older men sing together, H.F. thinks that "for the first time, he's in good company" (112). Bo is also heartened by the fact that Dave and his partner have been together for many years. In addition, Dave tells Bo that life will "get easier" (120) after adolescence. This scene recalls the "It Gets Better" campaign by Dan Savage, which uses social media to send the hopeful message to young LGBTQ kids that an adult life—when you can control your friends and your lovers—will be much easier. Bo has found that multi-generational community of gay men that will sustain him in later life and inspire him to hold it together until he gets there.

Bo and H.F. finally get to Florida, and they go into the ocean naked. "I feel like we're a new kind of Adam and Eve," H.F. thinks. "We already ate the fruit from the Tree of Knowledge, and instead of being punished for it, we learned that the world is big and full of opportunities, and that love is always good. Girls can love girls if they want to, boys can love boys if they want to, and a girl and a boy can love each other as dear friends and nothing more or less. We are naked, and we are not ashamed" (127). In an interesting reinterpretation of Biblical imagery (which is used by fundamentalist Christians to support heterosexual marriage and demonize homosexuality), Watts takes her characters back to Eden and imagines a new kind of accepting world for them.

In spite of this liberating moment at the beach, the visit with H.F.'s mother is a colossal disappointment, and the two young people return home to Kentucky. Reminiscent of the uncertainties of characters in novels previously discussed, Wendy tells H.F. that she isn't sure about her feelings for her. "I don't know if I really like girls ... or if I just like you," she says (144). H.F. apologizes to Wendy, too, understanding now that she had loved her "so worshipfully that I had turned her into a perfect goddess instead of a regular person, with doubts and fears" (148). Wendy's mother leaves a copy of *Patience and Sarah* (that now-archetypal YA lesbian text) for Wendy to read. "It was good," H.F. says, amusingly, "kind of like *Little Dykes on the Prairie*" (149). At this point in the historical trajectory of lesbian YA fiction, *Patience and Sarah* iconic function has become a mild joke, not simply the liberating and transgressive book it once was. Things are looking up for Bo as well, who is making plans to go to school in Atlanta, on a scholarship arranged by Dave. Both Bo and H.F., it seems, will be allowed to be queer and to be happy, even in rural Kentucky.

H.F. summarizes her experiences at the end of the novel with more Biblical language: "the world was getting mean, just like it was for Noah, so we climbed into Bo's Ford Escort just like Noah did in his ark, and we took a little trip." They didn't pack their car with people but that "gathered up our good people along the way" (151). She continues, linking her newfound sense of gay and lesbian community with her local and religious community:

Two. Beyond Deliver Us from Evie

> Memaw would say I was blaspheming if she knew I was comparing something in the Bible with my own experience of being queer, but I think the way I do because of who I am: a teenage dyke from small-town Kentucky, raised by her memaw on Bible stories and old-timey hymns. And to me, the rainbow sign God put up in the sky for Noah sad pretty much the same thing as the sign I saw at the gay bookstore, at the church, and in the faces and hearts of the rainbow of people who are my gay family. "Here you were, thinking it was the end of the world, when it turns out it was only the beginning" [151].

H.F. is a self-anointed "queer" and "dyke," but she is also a small-town girl raised on "Bible stories." Just as the rainbow has been appropriated by gay culture (much to the chagrin of many Protestant religious fundamentalists), H.F. has used all the experiences of her Christian past to recreate a self that his both lesbian and Kentuckian.

Sara Ryan's novel *Empress of the World* is set in a place that is very different from rural Kentucky: genius camp, or more precisely, the Siegel Institute summer Program for Gifted Youth. Blackburn and Buckley say the novel "goes beyond disrupting stereotypical notions of what it means to be lesbian or gay, as few young adults novels do" (207), although it, like many of the novels in this chapter raises questions about the fluidity of sexual attraction, especially for young people who have had little (if any) sexual experience. It is as much about finding likeminded friends, dealing with divorce, choosing one's career, finding a personal style, and the value of coke and vending machine snacks as it is about lesbianism. Moreover, its references to Orf's *Carmina Burana* underscore (pun intended) the changeability of fortune, especially in matters of love.

At camp, main character Nicola "Nic" Lancaster is studying archeology during her eight-week summer session, honing her artistic, compositional, and observational skills, occasionally playing the oboe, and also falling in love with Battle Hall Davies, a dancer who is taking a world history course. Almost 16, Nic is also getting to know other quirky and precocious kids at the camp who, at least in their immediate circle, are enthusiastically supportive of Nic and Battle's relationship. In one of their late-night dorm room conversations during their tentative courtship, Battle makes a reference to "people like us," and Nic feels herself "heat up, not in an embarrassed way, but in the way you fell when you walk into a room when you've been out in the cold for hours" (46–47). Still, Nic thinks she isn't exactly the same kind of person as Battle. When she recalls her previous year in school, she remembers a classmate calling her a "thespian lesbian," but she isn't sure that she could be same-sex attracted when she spent much of that year trying to attract the attentions of a boy (66). In fact, all the kids in Nic and Battle's circle—gay, straight, bisexual, and uncertain—seem confused about who they are and what they want to be (and who they want to be with).

At one point, their mutual friend Katrina tells Nic that she doesn't like feeling like a third wheel with Nic and Battle, and Nic tells her that she isn't sure if Battle even cares for her. "I thought you two were having this secret dyke thing behind my back, and you didn't want me to know. I thought you thought I was this fucking homophobe or something," Katrina says (83). Katrina is far more upset about being kept out of the loop and considered a homophobe than she is about Nic and Battle's (almost) relationship. Shortly after that, another friend, Isaac, makes a passing, casual reference to his aunt and her girlfriend, suggesting a wider lesbian community to which Nic may be able to go for advice and stories (102), much as H.F. and Bo did in *Finding H.F.*

In her diary, Nic considers whether she is lesbian or bisexual (109). She also wonders about people calling her a "dyke," wondering if she looks different or is doing anything to call attention to her sexuality. However, she admits that when she and Battle are in public "something happens that keeps us from doing anything but holding hands, like magnets that repel each other if they get too close" (115–16). They eventually go out to the forest and have sex, after drinking some wine, which "makes it easier." She comments: "Everything we've been awkward about, all those steps we haven't taken yet, all of it gets blurry and soft until all that's left is sensations: cool night air on skin, hands and mouths moving over each other, the scent of pine mixed with lavender, the sound of breath" (131). This evocation of the senses sounds very much like the romantic scene in *Dive*. Talking to Katrina later, Nic insists that she is bisexual, rather than lesbian, because she has liked boys, and that Katrina shouldn't label her. "Why are *you* so obsessed with *not* being one?" Katrina asks. "I believe that the appropriate word is *denial*" (139). As with Wittlinger's novels, the main characters resist having their sexualities definitively labeled.

Toward the end of the novel, Nic gives Battle a present, a puppet she calls Empress of the World (a complicated reference to Battle's shaving her head, missing her older brother, and hating her domineering parents). Battle gets upset that Nic, as she says, is trying to "explain" her (143), and the two girls break off their relationship. After their breakup,

Nic sees Battle kissing a boy, and Nic even has a brief kiss with Isaac. Nic thinks about finding someone else to take her mind off of Battle, but she isn't sure if she should be looking for a boy or a girl (176). In her diary, Nic says her summer has turned into "some idiotic soap opera mess," although she acknowledges, in a nod to earlier, more tragic, YA LGBTQ fiction, that "no soap operas would have a love affair between girls as a storyline, unless one of us died tragically in a car crash, and then the other one was comforted in her grief by some charming young man" (184–85). Eventually, Nic and Battle reconcile, and they have one last romantic evening, although they are soon going to be separated when they leave camp. "I want a happy ending, dammit," Nic says to Battle. "It's not an ending," Battle replies. "We're not even in college yet, for God's sake" (212). Like many young adult novels, the trajectories of their lives are not entirely clear yet, no matter how much they might want them to be.

The companion book to *Empress of the World*, *The Rules for Hearts* (2007) takes place the summer before Battle Hall Davies goes to Reed College. She comes to stay with her brother, Nick, who is living with a theater troupe in Portland. She falls in love with Meryl Davenport, who is a swimming instructor and resident of the same house. In a reference to the previous novel, she says her summers at Siegel Summer Institute for Gifted and Talented Youth "expanded [her] horizons a lot more than Mom and Dad had bargained for" (24). However, her failed relationship in that book with Nicola "Nic" Lancaster "turned [her] into an oyster" (37). At this point her parents know that she's a lesbian, although they "weren't thrilled to learn that I like girls, you know, that way. Mom kept talking about how she was afraid my life would be so hard, 'living that lifestyle'" (73). Although the main character's sexuality isn't the main focus of the novel, the lingering concerns (and prejudices) of parents look backward to earlier LGBTQ adolescent fiction.

Battle and Meryl have sex on a camping trip, but Meryl is worried Battle will want to jump into a relationship, and she is also concerned about them being housemates (156). They get together one more time, and then Battle calls it off because she's going to college. Meryl says that she doesn't "always want things to turn to sex.... But I don't know what to do when they don't," implying that she isn't very good at relationships or breakups. Battle remembers telling Nic "that words don't always work," and she concludes, "Some things don't change" (210). It is significant here that the younger person in the relationship is the one with more control and insight, unlike the Marisol's situation in *Love and Lies*.

Battle discovers that Nick has gambling debts and has been stealing to pay them and, even worse for the other tenants, *not* paying the household bills (which were his responsibility). Battle eventually talks him into calling their parents, from whom he's been estranged since he left home years before. At the end, Battle is getting ready to head off to college. She has a dog, which she rescued as a stray, and the last image of the book is Lucky "fling[ing] himself forward, running like leashes have never been invented, like his ridiculous little legs can carry him anywhere" (222). Battle, too, is "running like leashes have never been invented" toward her future. In a move that recalls the pets both *I'll Get There* and *Dive*, Battle is linked with her dog (who has the same name as the one in Donovan's novel) in her excitement to start her new life.

Unlike the older girls in the previously discussed novels, Lizzy McMann in Shimko's *Letters in the Attic* is a very mature 12-year-old. Also unlike the other novels discussed so far, it is set not in the present but in the Kennedy Era. As the novel opens, Lizzy's father Manny leaves them, and mother and daughter go to stay with her kind grandfather and bitter, mean grandmother. "This is a prison sentence without a trial," Lizzy thinks, but she insists that she won't let her grandmother "ruin" her, as she did her mother. Seeing Manny bully her mother, she has resolved not to let anyone do that to her: "It's going to take a lot more than a mean old woman to conquer me," Lizzy thinks. "Bring her on" (44). Already, Lizzy is showing herself to be both tough and resilient.

She isn't, however, completely invulnerable. In a way similar to many of the other budding romances in these novels, Lizzy falls in love with Eva Singer, "an eighth grader who looks like Natalie Wood" and who is "so pretty that I think the other girls are too jealous to be around her" (53). When her hand touches Eva's "the deepest most private part of my body becomes the Fourth of July full of sparklers and firecrackers and I want this feeling, whatever it is, to go on forever" (56). Eva is "the girl who has awakened an excitement in me that's been asleep just under the surface. An excitement so strong and wild that I didn't know such a thing was possible" (63). For lesbian, gay, and straight teens, this romantic sparkle will likely seem very familiar.

Lizzy reads some of her mother's letters in the attic (hence the title), and she discovers that her biological father is the P.E. teacher, Mr. Brand.

Mr. Brand is a homophobe, however, which Lizzy finds out from his daughter Madeline. This news feels to her like "a punch in the stomach" (82), and Lizzie senses that if her father thinks she's "a freak" then it must be true. "I'm someone to stay away from, to make fun of—a leper" (83), she thinks. Eventually, Mr. Brand is conveniently discovered to be a child molester and is sent to jail. At this point, Mr. Stephens, the kind and gentle school English teacher, starts to fall for Lizzy's mother. In this novel, the homophobes, not the homosexuals, are punished.

For reasons more related to the impending arrival of a new sibling and not to her lesbianism, Eva tries to commit suicide by cutting her wrists, in part because she's afraid that her parents will no longer love her after they have their new baby. After she visits Eva in the hospital (she's going to survive), Lizzy has a dream that she and Eva "are angels in heaven dressed all in white with huge fluffy wings. We both have bandages on our wrists. She kisses my wounds, then I kiss her full on the mouth. This wakes me up and I have the same amazing feeling down deep inside that I had the day we met" (118). They don't resume their relationship, though, at this point, and although Lizzy feels that she "might burst wide open because of the love" she feels for Eva (128). On a skiing trip, Lizzy sees Eva with a boy, and she's "so overcome with jealousy that my insides turn on me" (133). This back and forth continues for many pages, with Lizzy even going out on a date with a boy (which does not turn out well).

At the end of the novel, Eva seems more attracted to boys, and Lizzy decides that she might be willing to come out to her mother (194). Although at first glance this might seem a return to earlier YA lesbian novels, where the teen characters try out same-sex attraction and abandon it. However, Eva still considers herself a lesbian at the end of the novel and is willing to share that knowledge with her mother, who, after her own difficult romantic experiences, might be a sympathetic audience. Lizzy's romance, while it didn't continue as long as she might have liked, nevertheless left her relatively unscathed and ready for whatever new adventures might await.

Unlike in *Letters*, Myracle's main character in *Kissing Kate* has known her future love interest for a long time. When she first meets Kate in 7th-grade gym class, Lissa thinks that she is "small and blond and pretty, and she had a laugh like an open present. Compared to me, she was a goddess" (6). However, their relationship stays platonic until

16-year-old Kate and Lissa kiss at a drunken party. After the kiss, she realizes that she feels something for Kate that is "stronger than maybe I'd admitted," although she worries that maybe she is, in a childish way, confusing friendship for love (42). Still, Lissa notices that her "heart whammed in my chest and sweat pricked my armpits" when she thinks she's going to see Kate (61).

When her little sister jokingly calls a friend a "lesbo," Lissa thinks that she hates the word. She also wonders if being gay is wrong. "[I]t was one thing for someone else to be gay," she thinks. "It was something else entirely if that person was me" (84–85), and shortly after she prays that she's not (87). This labeling of an identity is something than many lesbian teens (especially in novels written since the 1990s) resist, not solely because of negative societal pressure—or internalized homophobia—but also because they seem to want to think of themselves primarily as teenagers in love, not just as lesbians.

A subplot has Lissa becoming friends with a flakey co-worker Ariel. Lissa goes out to eat with Ariel and a male friend Finn, and during the meal, she feels her "heaviness, without my realizing, had begun to lift" (107). Lissa tells Ariel that she might be gay (183). Ariel says, "God. It shouldn't be so hard to talk about this stuff. All I'm saying is maybe you're gay or maybe you're not. Maybe you're bi. Or maybe it's totally a Kate thing. Maybe you'd want to be with her whether she was a girl or a boy." Lissa isn't sure if that makes things better or worse (184). Lissa and Ariel go to a bookstore in Little Five Points to see Ariel's lesbian cousin, Jessica, who, invites the girls back, in case Lissa needs to talk (191). As Cart and Jenkins (among others) have noted, this is a distinctive feature of more recent LGBTQ YA fiction—the introduction of an extended and multigenerational LGBTQ community.

As do many of the girls in the novels discussed in this chapter, Lissa also goes to the internet to find out about lesbianism. She finds the grim statistics about suicide among the LGBTQ teen population, but she also discovers an online magazine called *Prism* with work by LGBTQ kids. One poem gives her "a breath-catching feeling inside, anxious and fully of longing" (159). Interpersonal and online communities give her both a sense of belonging and legitimization of her desires.

While Lissa is coming to understand and accept her same-sex attractions, Kate keeps resisting their relationship, telling Lissa that lesbianism is "just not normal" (141) and that she's "not a fucking dyke, all

Two. Beyond Deliver Us from Evie

right?" (180). These conversations about what's "normal" is an important part of YA fiction for LGBTQ adolescents, as they try to find new ways of defining what's normal for them. At the end of the novel, Lissa has dream in which she conquers her fears, and Ariel says that these were her fears about people wanting to turn her into someone she's not. The last sentence has Lissa leaning into Ariel's friendly "embrace" (198). Neither Kate and Lissa (nor Lissa and Ariel) are a couple at the end of the novel, but Lissa has learned more about who she is and who her friends are, and she appears to have lost her worries about being accepted for who she is.

The only epistolary novel in this chapter, Wittlinger's *Heart on My Sleeve* is told in emails, text messages, postcards, and letters to and from camp. While this novel isn't focalized from the perspective of lesbian characters, it is interesting for the wide variety of (mostly sympathetic) responses to the main character's sister coming out. The lesbian romance is presented as parallel to the straight romances, with all their teenage impulsiveness and angst. The format allows readers to see how the various characters evolve in their relationships with each other and with their understanding of lesbian issues. There is also an older gay couple in the novel (in New York City, not surprisingly), but they play a very minor role.

Main character Chloe falls for Julian, when she meets him at freshman pre-orientation at the college they plan to attend in the fall. They go their separate ways for the summer (Julian to prepare for classical singing contests and working at a Chinese restaurant, Chloe to work as a camp counselor and song writer), and they enthusiastically correspond. Chloe's older sister Genevieve has gone to New York City to work as an intern in a theater, and she comes out as gay, first to her sister, then to her parents. Meanwhile, there are a number of other teen romances building and breaking. Eventually, Julian and Chloe meet again, and neither lives up to the fantasies their correspondence has generated.

When she comes out, Genevieve tells Chloe that when she went to college she stopped going out with guys because it seemed "hopeless." "I'd sort of decided that I didn't want to be a lesbian," she says, "but I obviously wasn't straight, so I just wouldn't be with anybody." This plan worked until she met her current lover, Alice, with whom she moves to New York for the summer. Chloe has some initial trouble with

Genevieve's announcement, telling her that it "does freak me out a little." She also worries that she won't have a husband or kids. "I feel like you won't be you anymore" (76–77). These concerns soon fade, however.

The girls' parents ask Chloe if anything they did caused her sister's lesbianism and if it is "likely to be a stage" her sister is passing through (87). Chloe tells her sister, half-jokingly, that her parents "think if you let your hair grow out, this will all go away" (91). Chloe tells her parents that people are born gay and that her sister is now happy (101) and wisely remarks to her sister, "I guess when you start knowing people who are gay, you stop caring so much about the differences [between hetero and homosexual couples]" (137). This, too, is fairly typical of many more recent LGBTQ young adult novels, where either the gay character or the straight advocate sets parents (and other retrograde adults) "straight" about homosexuality.

The only completely negative response comes when Chloe tells Bill, the camp director, about Genevieve, and he says that wouldn't have hired her, if he had known. Chloe tells her sister that she feels "betrayed" by his response (138). Other friends are "weirded out" by the news (143), although Julian seems to be making some progress, when he writes to Chloe that "some people are afraid of homosexuality. When you think about it, it's stupid, but most of us are sort of suspicious of people who seem different from us. How do you change that?" (145). At the end of the novel, Genevieve and Alice break up, and she and her mother have a heart-to-heart conversation. Genevieve's life isn't destroyed, she doesn't drop out of school, and she seems to be more engaged with the campus lesbian community. Chloe and Julian part amicably, both excited about the directions they've chosen for their lives.

Set in a time frame similar to *Heart on My Sleeve*, Johnson's *The Bermudez Triangle* starts the summer before senior year, an optimal time for a young-adult novel about discovery and growth, as the characters have a school year to figure out who they are—and who they aren't—before they head out to college to act on those discoveries. Main characters Nina Bermudez (straight), Avery Dekker (probably bisexual), and Melanie "Mel" Forest (lesbian) have been best friends since grade school. It is not accidental, of course, that Johnson chooses to represent several aspects of female sexuality in her three main characters.

Mel is in the process of slowly coming to terms with her same-sex attraction. She thinks it "would have been nice, after all, if she could have explained why she never went out with guys more than once or why they never made much of an impression on her. She knew the reason, though she'd never put words to it" (35). For years the signs had been there, but Mel had chosen not to interpret them (44). It is significant that she waits until her senior year to consciously define herself, not because she's afraid, necessarily, but because there didn't really seem much point to it—until she falls for Avery.

When Mel and Avery buy friendship bands, Avery begins to notice that others are aware (and approving) of their relationship. When the woman who is selling the bands smiles at them, Avery feels "a wave of recognition." The woman, she believes, is "giving her a coded message of affirmation" (63). This affirmation doesn't extend to their friend Nina, however, who, when she discovers Mel and Avery kissing in the dressing room on a shopping trip, is upset. Nina worries that she, too, might be gay. "Unconsciously, she had been setting herself up for this all along [by having a long-distance boyfriend] because she must have known that deep down, she was *a total and complete lesbian*, part of a lifelong lesbian trio" (111). Strangely, Nina is both resentful that she is excluded from the couple and fearful that she will be included in their "lesbian trio."

Avery doesn't want to mix with the other lesbians at her school because "she liked keeping her relationship with Mel a complete secret. She wanted to be the only one who knew what it was like to be with Mel—to be able to look at her and know that Mel was all hers, and she was all Mel's, and no one else with all their posturing had *any idea* what that meant" (121–22). She also worries about jumping in too quickly into a serious relation with Mel. She worries that the old joke about lesbians and U-Hauls might be true: "What if Mel wanted to get married and have a commitment ceremony and play Ani DiFranco and k.d. lang songs and have cats as bridesmaids?" (205). Consequently, Avery and Mel break up, and Mel goes to talk to Nina. "'I didn't really get it at first,' Mel says. 'I thought I just really liked certain people. And then I realized that I *really* liked certain people. And then I noticed they were all girls'" (225). While Avery is worried about fixing her identity as a lesbian, Mel is coming to realize that she is exclusively same-sex attracted.

In the only overt reference to cultural homophobia in the novel, Mel is harassed for being a lesbian by drunken guys at the restaurant. After the harassment, Mel experiences "a deep feeling of disgust and shame spread all over her, making her body cold and turning her stomach.... Never in her life had she felt so useless and small" (270). This seems mostly a passing glance at the discrimination and harassment that LGBTQ people still experience, though, and the bulk of the novel is focused on the off-again-on-again relationship between the two girls.

Mel and Avery's relationship is accidentally revealed to the girls' parents by Nina, and this shows a more damaging aspect of homophobia. The parents have a meeting, and Mel's mother says that she doesn't "want this for Mel. When she's older, she'll regret all the things she could have had—a husband, kids. She'll see that people treat her differently, and she won't like it" (324). Mel's father said that his ex-wife does "have a point." "It's going to make things harder," he says. Mel says that "faking the rest of my life would be harder"; her father considers that and then tells her that he's going to love her "no matter what" (330). These kinds of parental concerns have been seen in novels since *Deliver Us from Evie*, although the parents in these later works accept the news much more quickly. Consistent with earlier novels, though, they worry about the difficulties associated with a non-traditional lifestyle and whether or not they will have grandchildren. It will be interesting to see how the representations of parents will change once same-sex marriage starts to make its way into YA fiction.

At the end of the novel, the three girls reconcile, and Mel and Nina go to New York City during a snowstorm to support Avery at her audition for a music conservatory. The novel ends with the girls "tightly holding on to one another for support on the slick sidewalk" (370). Clearly, the road ahead will be "slick," and they will need each other's friendship to keep them moving forward. Mel has (although inadvertently) come out to her parents and asserted her lesbianism, Nina has come to accept her friend's differences, and Avery appears to be postponing further identity crises to concentrate on her music. As with all YA novels, all the characters' problems have not been solved, but the ending is hopeful.

Murdock's *Dairy Queen* accepts the challenge to create images of female masculinity advocated by Judith Halberstam. Instead of having "the tomboy instincts of millions of girls ... remodeled into compliant forms of femininity" (194), Halberstam wants to argue for "gender proliferation and what we might call the deregulation of masculinity, or the extension of masculinity to nonmale bodies" (201). Like *Deliver Us from*

Two. Beyond Deliver Us from Evie

Evie, this novel takes place on a family farm, this time a Wisconsin dairy farm, and both the protagonist and her best friend do not look or behave in stereotypically feminine ways. Also like that novel, the main character is straight, although this time she is the love interest, not the sibling, of the gay character.

Protagonist D.J. Schwenk has to take over the day-to-day running of the farm after her father is injured and her older brothers go off to college. Conflicts arise with D. J.'s uncommunicative Midwestern family and her clearly unhappy mother and father. D.J. is also flunking English and may not graduate because she has been too busy with the farm to attend to classes. While hanging out in the local movie theater parking lot (a common activity for rural teens all over the country) with her best friend Amber, some obnoxious boys from a rival high school give her the name "Dairy Queen," most likely implying something about her sexuality—although it is a strange inversion of the concept of the "queen," which is usually applied to gay males. Later that night, Amber (for reasons that will become clear later) starts to talk about all the gay people she recognizes in their little town of Red Bend, WI. The narrator disagrees, thinking that unlike in New York or Los Angeles, Wisconsin "doesn't have any gay people. Or if it did, they all left" (33). Clearly, D.J. is going to need some lessons in demographics and empathy over the course of this novel, which she will get.

Shortly after this conversation, the handsome quarterback on her high school's rival team, Brian Nelson, comes to her farm to get in shape, help out, and, eventually, be coached by D.J., as part of his coach's plan to toughen him up for the upcoming season. Of course, they fight, come to respect each other, and then make out. This is a fairly typical boy-meets-girl plot (and the stuff of almost every romantic comedy), with the male and female lead initially hating each other and then having a relationship. However, *Dairy Queen* complicates this formula by having Brian never take D.J. seriously as a girlfriend, as she's a self-described big girl who should be dating football backs and ends and not a skinny cheerleader who dates quarterbacks. D.J.'s masculine characteristics—her skill at farm work, her football knowledge, her large size—render her (in Brian's mind) unacceptable girlfriend material.

As if this is not complicated enough, midway through the book, D.J. finds out that Amber is in love with her, and D.J.'s response is long and convoluted:

> Amber was … one of those people. Jeez. I don't say "those people" like it's a bad thing. But those words—lesbian, homosexual, gay—they're like medical words. Like cancer. I didn't want to think of Amber having cancer. I know, you die from cancer and you don't die from being gay, unless you have AIDS, which I've never heard of anyone in Wisconsin having. I know I sound like a stupid hick moron, but I bet it would be a shock to you too, if you found out your best friend was in love with you and thought of the two of you as some sort of couple without you even having a single clue. Which I guess really does make me a moron [170].

In this passage, D.J. works through several of the common stereotypes about lesbianism, eventually ending up simply being embarrassed about being unable to recognize her friend's attraction for her (170). She is somewhat "weirded out" by Amber's admission (the exact response several characters in previous novels have had), but she's more angry that she kept it a secret from her. Perhaps because of her anger (and maybe a bit because of her discomfort), D.J. starts avoiding Amber, partially because she's absorbed in her relationship with Brian.

After finding out she enjoys coaching Brian, D.J. decides to try out for the football team, which doesn't please her father, although (in true Midwestern fashion) he never tells her why; they simply stop speaking. When she makes the team and is heading off the field at halftime, an opposing player comes up to her and gives her "butt a squeeze and said 'dyke' under his breath" (244). D.J. appreciates the slur, though, because it helps her to understand the harassment that Amber has experienced. In additional her anger at herself for not being a very good friend to Amber is turned into rage at the opposite team, which leads to making a touchdown, and helping her team to win the game against their rivals. After the game, she sees Amber with another girl, and D.J. notices that Amber "looked happy. I guess I hadn't seen her like that. Ever, really" (261). This moment of misdirected homophobia leads to the empathy that will help her understand the world from Amber's point of view (and to win the game).

At the end of the novel D.J. reconciles with Brian (although not romantically) and starts talking again with her father, and it looks like, with this story as her project, that she will pass English. D.J., it appears, will be allowed to be a somewhat masculine (although definitely straight) female character, and Amber (whose story would also be an interesting one to hear) may be moving toward a more open expression of her sexuality.

Two. Beyond Deliver Us from Evie

The most recent of the lesbian young adult novels discussed in this chapter is Charlton-Trujillo's *Fat Angie*. It illustrates the variety of ways in which a young woman might be ostracized at school: because of her weight, her mental health issues, and her attraction to women. Before the novel starts, there are these three sentences on an otherwise blank page: "There was a girl. Her name was Angie. She was fat" (n.p.). Angie is defined simply by her weight and by her gender. As the novel opens, Angie is being bullied at school, in part for being fat and in part for breaking down and attempting to commit suicide at school after she hears her soldier sister is missing in Iraq. In what is now becoming a pattern in lesbian YA fiction, Angie meets a new girl in gym, the aptly named KC Romance, "the girl that sound tracks played for whenever she stepped into the room" (10). When she finally gets up the nerve to call her, Angie's life is "changed" (48). When Angie sees KC the next day, "butterflies-in-belly fluttered. It was as if the crowd of chattering, texting kids parted like the Red Sea for the sexy Ms. Romance" (63). As has been noted earlier, an important feature of recent YA LGBTQ fiction is this representation of same-sex attraction in the florid language previously reserved for heterosexual romance.

When KC assumes that Angie is "gay-girl gay," she is surprised. "But there had been no pamphlets. There had been no rainbow-in-the-sky epiphany. There had been nothing. Had there?" (99). There had been "no dancing Care Bears blasting belly rainbows in Fat Angie's dreams either" (99). Still, Angie says she does prefer Lady Gaga and KISS singer Gene Simmons (she doesn't know which she likes better) to Barbies. "The Barbies were too perfect. Fat Angie did not like too perfect. That much she was certain of" (100). Still, when she thinks about it, she realizes that "to be seen—to be touched—Angie could not remember such a time since her sister had disappeared" (122). Angie realizes "she had never been Fat Angie to KC. She had just been her. A smile erupted with no hesitation, and she knew what she had to do" (144). What Angie realizes is that love is love, no matter what form the object of affection takes. She also realizes that love isn't about being perfect (or thin) but about being seen for who one really is.

The two girls finally kiss, midway through the novel, and her brother sees them and outs them to their parents and the school. Angie recognizes the seriousness of this situation: "People might forget crazy. They might even forgive fat. But *dyke*. Throw that into the teen mix of conservative Dryfalls, Ohio, and there would be no escape" (169). Dryfalls "isn't exactly rainbow friendly," her friend Jake tells her (177). Fearing repercussions, she tells KC she "made a mistake" about them being together (178). Even though she tries to undo her action shortly afterward, KC tells Angie that she's had her fill of girls who "crawl through my window at night. Feed me some rich spiel with super-size lies on the side" (199). Soon after, Angie admits to KC that she's "gay-girl gay" although she didn't know until she met KC (202). This uncertainty—and recognition of the double burden Angie faces as a fat girl and a lesbian—provides a healthy complexity to this teen romance.

In a way that is reminiscent of D.J.'s trying out for football, Angie makes the basketball team, and her coach gives Angie her sister's jersey number (190). Angie does well, her sister's body is finally found, and they have a funeral, and Angie seems stronger for having confronted her fears and her grief. KC, on the other hand, goes back, briefly, to cutting as a way of dealing with her depression and anxiety, although this seems less to do with KC's lesbianism and more with her general unhappiness. This scene is reminiscent of the suicide attempt in *Letters in the Attic*, and, as in that novel, it serves more to create drama in the plot than it does to reinforce the tragic-lesbian stereotype.

The novel ends with Angie taking KC's hand, saying that they don't know what will happen next: "The two girls neared the end of the cul-de-sac-, turned the corner, and …" (263). Again, there is both optimism and uncertainty. The closing lines of the novel echo (and then significantly alter) the first: "There was a girl. Her name was Angie. She was happy" (264). Angie, like D.J. in *Dairy Queen*, can be different from other girls—in her size, in her interest in sports (and in other girls)—and she can still be happy.

The novels in this chapter span nearly 20 years of contemporary lesbian YA fiction, and they show the ways the girls in these works explore their sexuality, often refusing to identify explicitly (or sometimes exclusively) as lesbian. They also treat same-sex attraction as, for the most part, similar emotionally to opposite-sex attraction. It is true that there is some ancillary homophobia lingering in the margins of their stories, and their parents aren't entirely thrilled when their daughters come out (or are outed), but, for the most part, parents are accepting (if initially confused or concerned), and the girls' friends are supportive, even if they occasionally resent not being informed about their relationships. In addition, a wider lesbian community—of people, of books, and of online information—is being made available to these girls. Perhaps most importantly, the girls in this chapter are funny, smart, quirky, feminine, masculine, confident, troubled, mouthy, shy, talented and ordinary. In short, they are simply girls—flirting, dealing with high school drama, negotiating friendships, and falling in love.

THREE

"But that's young gay love for you"
Contemporary Gay Young Adult Fiction

> It's one thing to permit talk about homosexuality; it is quite another matter to let the homosexual talk—Kirk Fuoss, "Portrait of the Adolescent as a Young Gay," 165

> There are worse things in the world than a boy who likes to kiss other boys—Benjamin Sáenz, *Aristotle and Dante Discover the Secrets of the Universe*, 307

According to Thomas Crisp, young adult novels (at least through 2008) about gay teenagers can't win for losing. Most adolescent novels with gay male characters, Crisp says, "still often rely on heteronormative or heterosexual assumptions" (335). In addition, many gay adolescent novels, he argues, "use homophobia as the foil against which characters with non-normative sexual identities struggle in order to find happiness as a monogamous couple" (335–36). To make matters worse, "the portrayal of gay characters with either stereotypically 'feminine' or 'masculine' traits limit the extent to which such books constitute a departure from heteronormative traditions." If books go outside of these realistic tropes, on the other hand, they "imagine away homophobia by showing gay characters building relationships in an environment relatively free of discrimination" (336). Finally, Crisp claims, authors of such novels end up "reinstat[ing] heteronormativity" and "strengthen[ing] homophobia" (339), and he concludes that "there has not yet been any book that really inscribes queerness" (344). Clearly, the landscape of gay young adult fiction is littered with characters who are either gay stereotypes in heteronormative settings or living in a fantasy world.

Roberta Trites agrees, although she uses a more Foucauldian frame: "Books about gay male teenagers," she says, "superficially seem to promise the reader freedom from past constraints, freedom from continued repression, freedom from narrow-minded discourse—but simultaneously, such books often undermine that alleged liberation" (143). Homosexuality in gay young adult literature, she despairs, "seems at once enunciated and repressed" (143). Both gay and straight readers are not provided with "transformative experiences" (144), and, even worse, the reluctance to depict intimate relationships explicitly in these novels "divorces it from pleasure, thus disempowering gay sexuality" (149). Both Crisp and Trites see gay YA fiction playing on stereotypes, showing gayness as a barrier to happiness, representing happiness for gay teens only in utopic homophobia-free worlds, and, for the most part, failing to acknowledge sexuality for gay teens.

Granted, Trites is writing in 1998, and she only includes novels written before 1990, when the literary landscape was decidedly different from today, but Crisp's essay was published in 2009 and includes early 21st century novels by Alex Sanchez and David Levithan. I hope to show instead that recent novels are doing more than reinscribing heteronormativity and therefore delegitimizing gay sexuality/romance. My choices—Paul Robert Walker's *The Method* (1990), Cynthia Voigt's *David and Jonathan* (1992), Alex Sanchez's (2001–2005) and Brent Hartinger's (2003–2013) series, Benjamin Alire Sáenz's *Aristotle and Dante Discover the Secrets of the Universe* (2012), and Bill Konigsburg's *Openly Straight* (2013)—demonstrate a clear progression toward diminishing the effects of homophobia on the characters, expressing gay sexuality and romance, and exploring the various identities and communities possible for young gay males.

The novels discussed in this chapter have also gone beyond Kirk Fuoss' criticism in "Portrait of the Adolescent as a Young Gay," in which he outlined the problems of gay young adult books from 1969 to 1986. Early gay adolescent novels like John Donovan's, Fuoss says, "grant physical expression of homosexual love all the presence of an ellipsis" (164). Gay sexuality is completely elided, he rightly points out, but, unfortunately, "there appears to be no prohibition against depicting homophobic violence" (164). He also notes "sustained resistance to the articulation, by a gay narrator, of his own story. In addition, homosexuality "presumably belongs only in the characters' past, not in their futures" (167). Bottom line, the gay characters in novels written before 1990 operate "as a sort of ghost in the machine, a gay poltergeist whose role is central to the text but whose actions are more often than not marginalized and ghettoized, occurring offstage and out of sight" (170). Amusing as the idea of a "gay poltergeist" might be, contemporary writers of young adult fiction featuring gay characters have clearly taken Fuoss' words to heart, offering young gay men who tell their own stories, gay sexuality that is overt (if not always explicit), and same-sex attraction that is a visible and permanent part of their lives. The early novels discussed in this chapter still show need for improvement in these areas, but by the second decade of the 21st century, it is possible to see progress in the areas of visibility, identity, and, finally, claiming one's own story.

The first novel discussed here received decidedly mixed reviews. *Publishers Weekly* called Paul Robert Walker's main character Albie in *The Method* "likable" but "unfortunately surrounded by a cartoonish supporting cast." These characters, the review continues, "are little more than sexual stereotypes," whose "sexual preferences seem designed to titillate rather than illuminate." Nevertheless, in spite of its "dubious voyeuristic appeal, this novel hints at interesting, complex issues, but none are developed enough to capture the attention of serious readers." *Kirkus Reviews*, on the other hand, said that while it is difficult to feel sympathy for Albie's typical adolescent "blend of insensitivity and awkwardness," he is nevertheless realistically drawn and able to learn from his mistakes. Finally, the review says, the novel is "a pungent, unsentimental picture of an immature but talented boy at a pivotal time." I think that novel is stereotypical *and* interesting, voyeuristic *and* unsentimental. However, I also believe it represents the beginning of a new wave in gay young adult fiction, one that attempts (not always successfully) to integrate gay characters into life in high school. While two of the gay characters—a young man and an adult—might be seen as sexual predators, they are also charismatic and inspiring figures, and the other gay character offers a useful corrective to their somewhat unsavory behavior.

As the novel begins, Albie, 15 and likely straight, has been accepted an elite acting group called The Company, which consists of a six-week summer acting session. As his mother tells him, hopefully and prophetically, "if your old mother can find a boyfriend, anything is possible" (30). Albie finds out over the summer that just about anything *is* possible. The dramatic tension arises in the form of Cliff, who is far more talented, handsome, and confident than the rest of the students. As the narrator says, "There was something about Cliff that made Albie feel everything

Three. "But that's young gay love for you"

was going to be all right" (80–81), although Cliff becomes both Albie's professional and romantic rival.

Cliff seems willing to seduce anyone who might advance him personally or professionally, including their instructor Mr. Pierce, who is, according to Cliff, is "an old fag" (85). At one point in the novel, a friend takes Albie to a Gay Pride Parade (167–68), and they see Mr. Pierce and Cliff there (170). This parade (admittedly a cliché) is also a coming out point for Albie's friend and the pretext for a discussion about whether people who are gay can be identified visually. Albie says his friend can't be gay because he's "built like a brick, and he's got hair on his chest like you wouldn't believe." Mitch says, amusingly, that "being hairy is not queer insurance," and then shortly after tells him, "I'm gay. I'm queer. I'm a faggot. I'm a homosexual. This is not a joke. This is my life" (175). When Albie asks if Mr. Pierce and Cliff are gay, Mitch says he doesn't "have a built-in queer detector" (184). Albie tells him that they are still friends (177), and the novel moves back to acting class—and (for the most part) straight teenage romance. However, this scene provides an example of coming out of the closet, which, while dramatic, is both lighthearted and doesn't create a conflict between gay and straight male friends.

Back in class, Mr. Pierce tells Albie, significantly, that "Hamlet must decide between being and not being. He would like to choose not being—that is, he would like 'not to be.' It would certainly be easier. However, he is so afraid of not being that he chooses the harder path. He chooses to be" (201). This seems emblematic for the closeted life that Mr. Pierce is living and also for the closets of identities that all young people find themselves in. Albie, for example, can't become the actor he wants to be because he refuses, at least at the beginning, to accept who he is (which is never the romantic lead). On the other hand, in this dramatic context, a closet is also a place where all sorts of costumes exist, a safe space where young people can try on various identities until they find what best fits them. The closet thus implies both hiding and experimenting.

After a number of romantic misadventures—with Cliff and without him—the novel comes to a close. Granted, Albie's attraction to Cliff is not resolved, or is resolved by a definitive return to heterosexuality, but Mitch remains gay (and Albie's friend), and Mr. Pierce's unethical (and illegal) behavior with students seems to have no lasting repercussions for any of them. Unlike with many earlier novels about the LGBTQ young adult experience, there are no tragic accidents, no tearful coming out scenes, and very little ambient homophobia. Of course, the novel is set in an acting class, which is in itself a gay cliché, but at least within The Company, it is possible to figure out who one wants "to be" with only a minimum of drama.

Cynthia Voigt's *David and Jonathon* is a good bit darker than *The Method* and in many ways suffers from the stereotyping and tragic representations of homosexuality that Crisp, Trites, and Fuoss lament. Henry (15) and Jonathan's (16) friendship is disrupted when Jonathan's mysterious cousin David, who was a child during the Holocaust and who eventually commits suicide, comes to live with Jonathan's family. *Publishers Weekly* says the two protagonists are "gratingly precocious," which certainly is true, but *Kirkus Reviews* rightly calls the novel "intelligent, thoughtful, and challenging." Lobban and Clyde correctly note that "Henry's sexuality is a small part of a complex, disturbing story" (192). These reviewers have acknowledged both the strengths and weaknesses of this novel, which is not one of Voigt's strongest (although one of her most troubling) works.

When Henry first meets David, he notices that Henry's "eyes darkened by hope, the face alight with it." Henry's body also "matched the intensity of David's eyes; the long flat muscles of chest and belly, running down into his groin, tightened in anticipation" (80). Henry dreams about David, whose "long-fingered hands touched Henry's ribs, and brushed down them-and Henry stood helpless as his body fused all of its separate parts together, and he ejaculated" (82–83). Henry thinks that David made him have the dream, which he thinks is "creepy" (107). Clearly, in this relatively early novel, same-sex attraction is, for the young protagonist, a cause for concern, uncertainty, and even resentment.

These feelings for David cause Henry to question who he is, to think at one point that "you couldn't count on yourself to know the truth" (122). When David tells Henry he'd rather have sex with Jonathan than with Jonathan's sister (whom, strangely, he plans to marry), Henry feels "sick" (178). He worries about his own sexual identity, thinking that his feelings for David might be "already in there" (179). Although he remains disturbed, David is slowly accepting that he might not know himself as well as he thought, a productive state of mind for adolescent characters—one that leads to growth and change.

Three. "But that's young gay love for you"

After David, who may or may not actually be a relative, commits suicide, Jonathan's sister reveals she is pregnant with David's child and has an abortion (which renders her sterile), and their mother becomes an alcoholic (240). If that's not enough, there's also the possibility that David has had an affair with Henry's father. David has been a clearly destructive presence, to himself as well as to others, and this destructiveness is in part linked to his "dangerous" sexuality. Sterility, suicide, alcoholism, infidelity, and mental illness all seem to stem from homosexuality.

However, this is not the end of the story. The novel is framed by a later event in an Army hospital, where Jonathan is a patient, and Henry is the surgeon. When the novel returns to the frame at the end, which has the two men grown up and soldiers, Jonathan asks Henry if he loves men, "not *agape, eros*. Love men *eros*" (237), and Henry denies it. At the very end, however, Henry tells Jonathan that he will try to live his life (one presumes authentically) (248). Although one gay character is doomed and destructive, the other (although closeted and apparently alone) has decided to live his life on his own terms, and this rather gloomy novel ends, surprisingly, with laughter.

In spite of this somewhat hopeful ending, *David and Jonathan* represents a step backward in gay YA fiction. The gay character is disruptive and self-destructive and causes psychological turmoil in one of the main characters, who eventually chooses to live alone rather than acknowledge his sexuality. However, it does show a lasting friendship between a gay and straight man and a tentative acceptance of "eros" attachment between men. It is also important to recognize that David's problems have as much to do with his traumatic experiences during the Holocaust as they do with his sexuality. His desire to seduce both Henry and Jonathan's sister (and perhaps their father) may arise more from his PTSD than from his sexuality. With that in mind, the novel still places homosexuality as the crisis in the lives of several of its characters and thus more resembles earlier GLBTQ young adult fiction.

Brett Hartinger's *Geography Club* inaugurates a welcome new voice in gay young adult fiction. As *Publishers Weekly* says, the novel "does a fine job of presenting many of the complex realities of gay teen life, and also what it takes to be a 'thoroughly decent' person." Writing *in The Horn Book*, Claire Gross says that "coming out is about community as much as romance. The best books capture the exhilaration and relief of finding a place in the world where you can be all of yourself." *Kirkus Reviews* says that while "Hartinger has to jiggle the plot to make it work … overall the book is provocative, insightful, and, in the end, comforting." The same holds true for the other books in Hartinger's playful and charming series. Gay and lesbian characters do still struggle with coming out and with romantic entanglements, but their homosexuality isn't nearly as dramatic as the events in their high school (and summer camp).

The first novel begins, as will become familiar throughout the four-book series, with a melodramatic statement, which will prove to be somewhat less extreme in reality. Russel Middlebrooks, a sophomore in high school, is "deep behind enemy lines, in the very heart of the opposing camp" (1). Actually, he is in the boys' locker room where he feels threatened (because he's gay), but his "cover was holding—for another day at least" (5). That cover won't hold for long, though, as Russel and his friends are planning to start a Gay-Straight-Bisexual-Alliance Club in their high school. They decide to call it The Geography Club because "no high school students in their right minds would ever join that" (63).

When a rumor begins going around that he is gay, Russel comes out to one of his best friends, Gunnar, who has been cluelessly setting Russel up on heterosexual dates throughout the book so that he could score himself, now claims that he has known for five years that Russel was gay (in part because of his love of animated Disney musicals) (211). In the meantime, Russel is having a relationship on the down low with Kevin Land, a fellow baseball team member. Russel wants to make their relationship public, but Kevin wants to see him in secret. Russel reluctantly breaks up with Kevin, thinking, "I'd like to say I didn't look back, but I did. I think I always will" (223). The coming out scene is handled, much like the one in The Method, with no disruption between the gay and straight friend, but the Kevin affair shows that keeping sexuality secret is still one the primary plot drivers, at least in this first novel.

The novel ends with the kids starting an officially-sanctioned Gay-Straight-Bisexual Alliance Club and thinking about how they'll be ostracized for it. None of them care, though, because "even the ugliest place in the world can be wonderful if you're there with good friends" (225). Tison Pugh says the fact that "the novel concludes with even an ironic endorsement of homophobia illustrates the ways in which homosexuality is denigrated within its pages, despite being written from a pro-gay perspective" (163). This seems ungenerous to me. The accepting nature

Three. "But that's young gay love for you"

of Russel's friends and their determination to be honest about their sexuality trumps their acknowledgment that, for a variety of reasons, that high school can be "the ugliest place in the world."

The Order of the Poison Oak (Book 2) begins, again melodramatically, with Russel saying, "I was surrounded by fires, angry blazes raging all around me" (1). This will have more literality later in the novel, but at the start the "fires" are caused by Russel starting the Gay-Straight-Bisexual Alliance and the whole school knowing he is gay. The bulk of this novel, though, centers on friends Russel, Min, and Gunnar working as counselors at a summer camp during a session for kids with serious burn injuries. Love triangles ensure, as is often the case at summer camp: both Min and Russel have a crush on Web, who appears to be bisexual and sexually promiscuous, Gunnar meets Em and starts a relationship with her, and Russel eventually falls for Otto, a counselor who is also a burn survivor.

On a group hike, Russel discovers that while some of the male counselors have turned the hike into a race and the female counselors have made it a nature walk, Russel is simply doing was doing "everything he could just to keep his kids moving in a forward direction" (48). This clearly becomes a metaphor for the various ways one can confront life. It can be a race, a nature walk, or simply a struggle to keep moving forward. Of course, it is also possible to see this as a metaphor for sexuality—one can jump into coming out, meander slowly through forest that is high school, or just try to stay "moving in a forward direction," regardless of how others respond.

Russel decides that he wants things to be different for his campers, telling the difficult youngsters that they are "Rainbow Crows ... with hidden beauty" (81). He continues this line of persuasion by creating The Order of the Poison Oak for people with "special powers." "You guys know what it's like to be teased and misjudged," but he tells them they have the power that if their "skin gets damaged in any way, it grows back thicker and stronger than before, so it can't be hurt again" (113). Obviously, Hartinger wants kids to think about the ways in which children who are bullied have the opportunity to build hidden strengths. These strengths are tested when there's a fire in the woods, and some of Russel's campers are in danger, although, since he knows them "inside and out, body and soul," he knows where to find them. The friends rescue the kids, who are in a patch of poison oak. Russel and his most challenging camper, Ian, "were completely unaffected by the poison of the plant" (162), but Em and Gunnar take two weeks to heal. The message is reinforced: the more struggle one has the more resilient he becomes—to bullying, to homophobia, or to poison oak. At the end of the novel, Russel feels "like there's absolutely nothing that can affect me. Not knives, not bullets, maybe not even Kryptonite" (172). Even though he acknowledges that this feeling may wear off when school starts, he thinks it may linger "maybe a little" (172). The second installment of the series has moved further than the first, with the main characters gaining more confidence in their own identities and in their abilities to lead others toward a healthier conception of themselves.

A two-part book, *Double Feature: Attack of the Soul-Sucking Brain Zombies and Bride of the Soul-Sucking Brain Zombies* (Book 3), is told first from Russel's point of view, and secondly from Min's. The novel opens at the beginning of the school year after the summer camp in the previous book, when the kids decide to be extras in a zombie movie. Twisted love plots ensue, once again. Russel is having a long-distance relationship with Otto, and, to complicate matters, Kevin comes out and comes back into Russel's life.

The most dramatic part of the novel, and the one most relevant to this study, comes when Russel's parents find out he is gay. Russel is shattered by their negative response: "My parents were good, decent people," he says. "They gave money to charity, and they voted. They didn't litter. They didn't make fun of the homeless, or laugh at insult humor, or tolerate racial stereotypes. And they loved me—I had never doubted that. Which is why I was so surprised by the way they reacted to my being gay" (18). His father tells him, interestingly: "You're confused…. Lots of kids go through a phase like this. I know I did" (20). This is never followed up on, but the suggestion is clearly that Russel's father might have had some same-sex attraction in his younger days but rejected it in favor of more "mature" heterosexuality. His mother says that homosexuality is "disgusting" (21) and "a sin" (40). His parents want him to talk to someone, which Russel interprets to mean "to talk to me, but not listen to a single word I said in response" (40). The bottom line for Russel is "being rejected by your own parents just for being yourself is really, really tough" (22). This sounds very much like the parental responses seen in earlier novels, although there is no indication here that Russel's parents will throw him out of the house, and Russel seems able to con-

Three. "But that's young gay love for you"

tinue his romance with Otto, regardless of their disapproval. In fact, much of Russel's personal life is conducted out of his parents' line of vision, and, as readers have seen in the first two novels, they don't find out he is gay until several years after he has come out to his friends.

As an antidote to his parents' homophobic responses, Russel clarifies what being gay has meant for him. "Being gay was never that big a deal for me," he says. "Maybe it was because I always felt so unbelievably different from other kids in so many other ways anyway—this was just one more thing" (20). He reiterates that he isn't "'questioning my sexuality.' For me being gay was just finally finding the word to describe the way I'd always felt" (21). This sounds very much like the responses of characters in David Levithan's novels, for example, and is very typical for the rhetoric surrounding gay and lesbian identity in novels since the beginning of the 21st century. (M.E. Kerr's *Deliver Us from Evie* offers an early version of such an approach.)

In the midst of Russel's tumultuous coming out to his parents, he is forbidden to have Otto, who has up until this time been represented as a platonic friend, stay at their house for Thanksgiving. Russel tries to explain that Otto is a great guy: "My mom stared at me with this bewildered look. Like she didn't recognize me—like I was someone who had just wandered in off the street, someone she'd never even seen before" (64). Otto comes anyway and stays at Gunnar's. When they meet at the airport, they kiss. "I knew people were staring at us, two teenage boys kissing," Russel acknowledges, but he is not embarrassed; he is "busting with pride" (93). They go for a walk later, but they step apart every time a car passes. "It's one thing to be stared at in airports; it's something else entirely to have been bottle thrown in your direction from passing pickup trucks," Russel comments. "But that's young gay love for you" (93). Both the milder and more extreme versions of homophobia are on display here—stares at the airport and bottles thrown (or at least anticipated being thrown) from cars. Still, "young gay love" is not just possible in public in this novel—it is joyous.

Min's story is somewhat less dramatic, which befits her status as a secondary character in the series. It concerns her coming to terms with a girlfriend who wants to stay in the closet. Min has a crush on one of the girls in the movie, Leah, who is clear about her sexuality but doesn't want to come out at school or at home. Min has to learn to accept different ways of being gay but also to make some ground rules so she won't be marginalized or disrespected by Leah's friends. The end of both Min's and Russel's versions of the story is tentative but optimistic, as is true for most YA fiction, whether the characters are gay, lesbian, trans, or straight.

In *The Elephant of Surprise* (Book Four) Russel is 17 and a junior in high school. He breaks up with Otto, although they remain online friends throughout the novel. Russel meets Wade, a "freegan" (who lives off of dumpster diving), and develops a crush on him. They find out the freegans are part of a radical environmental group planning to blow up a water tower to flood a golf course, which they believe to be environmentally insensitive. Wade isn't involved but has to flee anyway, lest he be implicated. Although he used his sexual appeal to recruit Russel to his cause, Wade turns out to be straight. Still, he is not repulsed by Russel's desires. Wade says that being same-sex attracted is "a little *like* being a freegan. Wanting something, but not being quite sure what it is. Not being able to put it into words. And then finally experiencing it and realizing what it was you were missing all along" (155). Here, Wade acknowledges that Russel is living his most authentic life.

At this point, Kevin returns to the story and turns out to be a nicer guy than Russel thought in *Geography Club*. When Kevin finally kisses Russel at the end, it was "like that gazebo in *The Sound of Music* after all, except with hot guy-on-guy action" (216). The novel ends in the misty, cold morning after the boys have stayed up all night, and Russel says the future is "wild and unpredictable," which doesn't scare him, and, on the contrary, he can't "wait for it to begin" (219). With this ending, the Russel Middlebrooks series has moved from coming out, through brief romances, to extended relationships, to reconnection with lost loves. By the end of the series, Russel is far less concerned with his homosexuality and more with having an honest romantic life. The boy in the enemy territory has passed through flames, zombies, and wild elephants of surprise to arrive at the cool dawn morning and the expectation of a brighter future.

Another series continues the trajectory started by Hartinger. According to Blackburn and Buckley, Alex Sanchez's *Rainbow Boys* series provides balance as it disrupts stereotypical notions of gay men by focusing on three very different male protagonists (206). The reviews, overall, were positive, and the novel has been awarded a number of literary prizes. As Thomas Crisp puts it: "To say that the books are beloved

Three. "But that's young gay love for you"

almost seems an understatement: readers across a range of sexual identities and ages and from a variety of professional backgrounds (i.e., students, critics, scholars) have affirmed them as both realistic in their portrayals and positive in their content" ("The Trouble" 238). Not surprisingly, though, given the predominant attitude of literary critics to LGBTQ young adult fiction, Crisp is also unhappy with these books. "'[R]ealism' is produced in the trilogy," he says, "through Sanchez's reliance on homophobia as a mechanism for establishing believable ways in which the characters interact with one another and within the world in which they live" ("From Romance" 336). In addition, "although the protagonists of the *Rainbow Boys* series identify as homosexual, they embody characteristics that reinforce normative conceptions of gender, and, by extension, sexuality" ("The Trouble" 238). According to Crisp, the series creates realism through homophobia and reifies heterosexuality.

This is not all, however. "[T]he series appears to call for the gay population to become resilient to the injustices enacted upon them by homophobic heterosexuals," Crisp continues, "as the world is constructed as a frightening and dangerous place where homosexuals find solace only when isolated from the heterosexual population" ("The Trouble" 239). The bottom line about the positive reception the novels received, Crisp says, is that "readers refer to the novels as 'honest' and 'true' because these are stories with some heart, but they rely upon familiar tropes that have become recognizable as a result of their repeated portrayal across literature and media. This feels 'realistic' because these are motifs we've seen again and again" ("The Trouble" 259). I agree that the books are realistic, but I disagree that it is created by trading on stereotypes and acceptance of homophobia. The engaging gay characters in this series spend more time mocking homophobia than they do being diminished by it, and their exuberant same-sex attractions resist heteronormativity.

In the first book in the trilogy, *Rainbow Boys*, readers are introduced to the three main characters, who will individually narrate the story in alternating chapters. The most dramatic of the three is Nelson, who is openly gay with a "million earrings, his snapping fingers, his weird haircuts," according to Jason, another of the main characters (2). His mother is completely supportive, and his father is mostly out of the picture. Nelson's absentee father asks why he can't be "normal" (221), and Nelson decides that while his dad might never change, he can (222). After nursing a crush on Kyle through most of novel (which is unrequited), Nelson has a one-night stand, without protection, and worries he might be HIV positive (it turns out later that he isn't, although this isn't resolved in the first novel). Eventually, Nelson meets Jeremy, who is HIV positive, and they kiss on a first date.

The jock, Jason, has a girlfriend at the beginning of the novel and concludes, since he has had sex with her, he couldn't be gay: "Homos couldn't do that. Ergo, he couldn't be a homo" (3). Still, he worries about why he continues "to have those dreams of naked men—dreams so intense they woke him in a sweat and left him terrified his dad might find out?" (3). He thinks he might be bisexual, but "[h]is mind spun with questions" (8). Jason wants to talk to someone, but he doesn't feel safe sharing the secret with the adults in his life, and his jock friends make "fag jokes" (33). Eventually, Jason comes out to his girlfriend, Debra, and she worries that someone abused him (123) and breaks up with him. Jason then tells his alcoholic father, who becomes violent, and his somewhat more supportive mother asks if he wants to see a psychiatrist (200). Jason's character will be the most familiar to readers of earlier LGBTQ fiction—the adolescent who is initially uncertain about his sexual identity and who struggles to find sympathetic adults in his world. However, he is only one of three very different young gay male characters in this series.

The third boy, Kyle, is out to his friends but not to his parents, and he has a crush on Jason, who might, or might not, have feelings for him. Since Kyle was little, he'd known he was different, though he couldn't explain exactly how. When other boys began to talk about girls, he never "felt interested" (12). When he meets Nelson, however, he knows that he's "no longer alone" (13). Kyle finally tells his mother that he is gay, and his mother becomes "despondent" because she believes that he'll never have kids (75). She says she just wants him to be happy, and his father says it's a choice whether or not to be gay (103). Kyle, at least in the first novel, also represents a kind of gay character seen in earlier works, one who knows who he is but struggles with his parents. The fact that he is open with his friends, though, distinguishes him from earlier LGBTQ characters and aligns him more clearly with protagonists like Russel Middlebrooks.

After being outed at school, Kyle experiences gay bashing for the

Three. "But that's young gay love for you"

first time, and he understands Nelson's position (130). He tells his parents, and they stand up for him, which Kyle recognizes as "a shift" (171). Although his father is still saying that he doesn't want him to "do something that you'll regret later," he asks about PFLAG (205). As a way of healing the rift between them, Kyle asks his dad if he wants to go to Jason's basketball game, and his jock father breaks into "a huge smile. You would have thought the prodigal son had come home" (207). After finally sleeping with Jason, Kyle forgets his cap (which he has worn all his life) and decides that it is time to stop wearing it, signifying, most likely, that he is ready to become an adult (214). At the end of the novel, the boys get their GSA officially approved by the school administration, and the novel ends with the first meeting, and Jason stepping inside (233). This moment of previously-closeted Jason proudly asserting his sexual identity is a significant moment in LGBTQ young adult fiction.

Picking up where *Rainbow Boys* ended, *Rainbow High* opens with a Gay-Straight Alliance (GSA) meeting and all three boys out of the closet—in some form or another—for their senior year. Nelson finally finds out he's HIV negative, and he is still with Jeremy, who is HIV positive. His mother is worried that he might become infected, and their good relationship founders. Jason's conflict concerns when—and how much—to come out publically. His principal tells him he should think carefully about coming out to his team members before the state playoffs (96). Jason has told his coach, however, and there's a possibility he might lose his college scholarship (which he eventually does).

One of Jason's teachers (a lesbian) tells him: "So few things in life truly matter. Chief among them are being true to yourself, and being honest with others" (69). After this good (but possibly impractical) advice, Jason comes out to the team, and his coach supports him. Crisp acknowledges that "Coach Cameron will eventually serve as one of the few positive portrayals of a heterosexual character in the entire series. It is clear he cares deeply for Jason and he does his best to advocate and provide support" ("The Trouble" n. 247). The team teases him, but Jason knows "their kidding was a cover-up for the awkwardness. And yet he was grateful. He laughed along, aiming his face into the shower spray, hoping no one would notice the tears of relief streaming down his face" (132). He gives a TV interview and begins receiving mail "applauding his courage for coming out" (189). During the finals, he takes the crucial shot and wins the state championship, and then he kisses Kyle (193) in front of the TV cameras and stadium full of fans. It didn't make the news, though. "Shootings and gore they'll show," Nelson says, "but teenage boys kissing? That would scare people too much" (195). Nelson's (and the media's) response notwithstanding, the kiss is a significant milestone in YA fiction, even if it can't (yet) be shown on television.

Like Jason, Kyle has his sports woes. At a swim team meet, the boys say they won't room with Kyle, and his coach does nothing (177). Kyle gets mad, walks away from the team, is threatened with expulsion from the meet, and his newly-enlightened dad works things out with the coach. "He isn't such a bad guy," Kyle thinks. "If only he'd learn to stop getting so worked up every time I want to do something that doesn't match his expectations" (183). At this point in the series, Kyle's dad has moved from acceptance to activism on behalf of his son. Toward the end of the novel, the boys go to the prom, an iconic ending for much young adult fiction but with a twist. The morning after, Nelson, Jason, and Kyle are in the front seat of the car, watching the first golden rays of sun splash onto the road ahead, and Nelson is smiling about nothing "and everything" (247). Like the ending of the Russel Middlebrooks series, the future looks bright for these rainbow boys.

In *Rainbow Road*, Jason has been asked to speak at the opening of a LGBTQ high school in California. Nelson is jealous: "'How unfair is that?" he asks. "I've been out since kindergarten. Where the heck's my expenses-paid trip?" (6). This is a good question. Then, as now, prominent public figures are more interesting when they come out than "ordinary" LGBTQ people. To make matters worse, Nelson's mother says that she should invite Jason to speak at her PFLAG group. "Nelson cringed. How come she'd never asked her own son to speak to the group?" (18). This resentment of Jason's privileged status as gay sports hero rankles Nelson throughout the novel, and it highlights some of the tensions within the gay community.

The boys decide to take a road trip to get to California, and, early on, Nelson steers them to the Radical Faerie sanctuary. Nelson loves it, listening "eagerly" to the men describing a worldwide collection of such communities, "imagining a place where no one hassled you for being crazily queer, a place where you could be totally yourself" (70). Nelson says, "It's like *The Wizard of Oz* when you suddenly go from black-and-white to Technicolor. I haven't felt this excited since Madonna kissed Britney" (73). Jason and Kyle are nonplussed. When Jason calls it "weird,"

Three. "But that's young gay love for you"

Nelson says, "It's the rest of the world that's weird. Why shouldn't you be able to dress how you want, act how you want, and love who you want? If you're so straight-acting, then why don't you have the guts to just let yourself go and be who you are" (81). Although the boys' reactions to it are mixed, this is one of the first examples in gay YA fiction of an extended gay community.

Jason, who was not at all impressed with Faerie land, takes time out in Nashville to play basketball and reassert his jock identity: "Within seconds he'd hit his first shot and his teammates were clasping his hand. It felt great to be around normal guys again, who played by clear, established rules; guys who looked and acted like guys were supposed to look and act, in contrast to those wacky Faeries" (86). He thinks it was a relief "to take a break from 24/7 gayness" (86), although he's troubled by Nelson's criticism. Although Crisp says "masculine" is routinely privileged in the series ("The Trouble" 246), this criticism applies only to Jason. In addition, Jason's concern about not always being identified by his sexuality is one that is going to appear with more frequently in recent LGBTQ young adult fiction. As same-sex attraction becomes more visible in the high school setting, the more characters are going to demand that they be defined by more than their sexualities.

On their way to New Orleans (it is, admittedly, a convoluted route), they meet BJ, who is a trans girl. Jason thinks the "whole thing creeped him out. What made the guy want to be a girl in the first place?" (109). Even Nelson, who dressed up in his mom's "blue chiffon dress" when he was little, "knew he was a boy. And he had no wish to alter that. It was the *illusion* of being female (and freaking out his dad) that had thrilled Nelson" (111). For Nelson, cross dressing is more about illusion and annoying his father. BJ travels with them to New Orleans, and when she leaves, she gives them a hug. To Kyle "it no longer seemed the least bit odd that she was really biological male. She was their friend; that was all that mattered" (120). This is one the first examples of a trans kid in YA fiction who is not engrossed in hiding (or finding) his or her identity.

Along the way, they meet an older gay couple and a homophobic Christian family with a young gay son, whom Nelson encourages to be himself (162). They lose money, destroy a cell phone, Nelson gets briefly hospitalized for food poisoning, and they are chased on a mountain road by some homophobes, whom they outrun. This road trip has exposed the boys to all kinds of reactions to their gayness, but it has also shown them that they are tough, resilient, and adaptable.

Finally in California, Jason acknowledges that Nelson should be the one to give the speech, but Nelson, although pleased, says Jason was the one they invited (222). Jason calls Nelson his best friend in the speech and says that he met "some amazing people ... living free and being themselves" in Tennessee. "[W]hen we stop being alone, we get what I had on the court," Jason says, "a team to play with, to work with, to encourage each other, and to be there for one another, stronger than any single one of us could ever be" (225). As he is signing autographs after the speech, Jason imagines "a future world in which boys and girls like him would no longer be afraid of—and miss out on—getting to know such kids" (226). At this moment, Jason is finding a way to reconcile his gay and his jock identities.

At the end of the novel, Jason and Nelson are reconciled, with Nelson mastering "a fairly decent layup, and Jason offer[ing] up finger snaps at every play" (239). Nelson decides to stay with Manny, a boy he met at the school who likes sports and works in an auto repair shop. Crisp says that Nelson "remains virtually static throughout most of the entire series: he never learns from his experiences or thinks before he acts" ("The Trouble" 252). I disagree—Nelson has made a dramatic change in his life, one that will move him toward his first real relationship and away from the security of his supportive mother. Also, the series ends with Kyle looking at Jason and thinking every time Jason smiles at him that he "couldn't help seeing a lifetime ahead" (243), which suggests growth and development on the part of the other two main characters.

In spite of his objections, Crisp does think these novels can be effectively taught to young people, with a teacher or other adult figure helping adolescents to "begin to identify how these pieces of contemporary realistic romance fiction depict homosexual and heterosexual people ... in ways that rely upon and reinforce heteronormative and stereotypical constructions of gender and sexuality" ("The Trouble" 259). This seems an ungenerous way to approach these playful and relevant novels. Crisp argues that it might be better to "begin looking for depictions that reflect for gay adolescent readers the possibilities of who they can become" ("The Trouble" 259), but it seems a shame to abandon the Rainbow Boys series because it doesn't conform to a particularly orthodox representation of gay sexuality. Perhaps the better solution might be to teach these works in conjunction with other, more recent novels.

Sprout, by Dale Peck, for example, might be more easily taught to young people, with less of the scaffolding Crisp deems necessary for *Rainbow Boys* and the other books in that trilogy. At the beginning of this delightful novel, main character Daniel Bradford (who calls himself "Sprout") and his father move from Long Island to Kansas after his mother dies of cancer. His father is an alcoholic, and Sprout dyes his hair green to match his assumed name. In addition, Sprout has a secret, which everyone knows, but "no one talks about it, at least not out in the open. This makes it a very modern secret" (3). Much of this engaging book revolves around the apparent need for keeping secrets, the repercussions of revealing them, and the need, eventually, to dispense with them.

His first attempt at revelation is a mixed bag. Sprout's father throws a dictionary into the computer after he finds Sprout looking up gay sites on the internet (70–71), and he says, "I should have seen it coming. Absent mother, poor role model for a father. I apologize, son. I should have found another maternal figure for you" (71). After that, he seems to accept, grudgingly, the inevitable. "Hey. You're a fag. I'm a drunk. Nobody's perfect," although he relents and says, "That was mean. You're gay. I'm an alcoholic. Now toss me a beer" (72). This casual cruelty combined with gruff acceptance might be more the result of Sprout's father's alcoholism and depression after the loss of his wife than any genuine homophobia, however.

Adding another wrinkle to the question of coming out, Sprout's English teacher, Mrs. Miller, starts coaching him for a writing/scholarship contest and When Sprout announces that he's going tell people at school that he's gay, Mrs. Miller says she doesn't want him to get "sidetracked" from the essay contest. "Kids who come out in school have a hard time," she tells him. "They get singled out. Their whole life becomes about being gay. By keeping your private life to yourself you can focus on your future" (74). This is, as I've said earlier, fairly typical for recent LGBTQ fiction. Young people are aware of their same-sex attractions, but they don't want to be defined solely by them. So, when his friend Ruthie wants him to come out at school, Sprout says he doesn't want to be "the gay guy. The token homosexual. The school fag. I don't want to have to try out for every stupid school musical, wear pink triangle pins, and start a letter-writing campaign to bring my boyfriend to the prom. I just want to be *me*" (115). He tells the reader, "When I started writing about myself, I waited as long as I could before I told you I was gay, because once you reveal that, it seems like it's all anyone can think about" (179). Like dyeing his hair green, Sprout wants to be a quirky iconoclast, not simply the gay boy. Mrs. Miller also tells him he can't turn in an essay about being gay because, if he does (in Kansas), "the judges aren't going to see your inventiveness, your humor, your compassion. They're just going to see your sexuality. And they're not going to like it" (187). This reaction, she argues, could hurt his chances for the scholarship funded by the contest.

At this point, Sprout finds out he will have Social Security money to pay for college and won't need the money from the essay contest, and, simultaneously, Mrs. Miller reconsiders her advice about keeping silent, worrying that "all the mixed messages I was sending you about when it is or isn't okay to say you're gay somehow made you think your sexuality was something you should hide to protect yourself. The truth is, that's how it gets power over you. Not when you're open about it, but when you have to spend all your energy keeping it secret" (273). This theme of the dangers of keeping secrets is going to reappear in other novels discussed later in this study. Eventually, Sprout writes the essay, which begins: "And so I picked up my pencil and started writing furiously. But this time I wasn't writing to run away from something, I was running after something, and I wasn't going to stop till I caught it" (277). At this point, Sprout seems confident about sharing who he is with the world, even though he still hesitates about having his sexuality be his primary defining characteristic.

Benjamin Alire Sáenz's *Aristotle and Dante Discover the Secrets of the Universe* may well represent one of the books that reflect "the possibilities of who they can become," which Crisp wants to see. Aristotle (Ari) is 15 when the novel opens, his father is a Vietnam vet with emotional issues, and his brother is in prison (and the family never mentions him). "The problem with my life was that it was someone else's idea" (8), Ari says, referring to the silences in the family and his mother's insistence that he live her version of his life. In addition, Ari doesn't get "the whole guy thing" (16), and he has "a feeling there was something wrong with me. I guess I was a mystery even to myself" (16). This is far as the novel gets with Ari's sexuality until much later in the book, but

Three. "But that's young gay love for you"

it does suggest that boys, especially, often feel that they don't conform to limited masculine models.

Ari meets Dante at the pool, and he teaches Ari how to swim, which is an important step in Ari's independence and self-determination. His growing relationship with Dante also allows him the freedom to explore his emotions, which he's been keeping pretty carefully hidden. Looking through the telescope one night with Dante, he thinks, "[I]t was all so beautiful and overwhelming and—I don't know—it made me aware that there was something inside of me that mattered" (42). After Ari saves Dante from getting hit by a car and ends up with two broken legs, Dante tells Ari he loves him (150), but Ari believes he is straight. Clearly, though, Ari is conflicted about his relationship with Dante and his sexuality (171).

When Dante goes to Chicago with his parents because his father has a visiting professorship. He writes Ari that he is experimenting with kissing girls, although he'd rather be kissing boys. Ari thinks, "I didn't know exactly what to think about that, but Dante was going to be Dante and if I was going to be his friend, I would just have to learn to be okay with it" (202). When he comes back, the boys make rules, including "No trying to kiss Ari" and "No running away from Dante" (248). This respectful stalemate appears to be the basis for a future relationship between the two boys. It is not dissimilar to the one between Min and her closeted girlfriend in *Zombies*, one in which a romantic partner or friend's sexuality is kept at bay but is nevertheless treated with respect.

Ari attends the funeral of his Aunt Ophelia, and finds out she has had a long-term female lover, and he realizes that it doesn't bother him (286). His dog, Legs, stays with Dante while they are at the funeral. Ari imagines Dante (who loves to kiss) kissing his dog, comforting him during a thunderstorm. Thinking that he doesn't like kissing himself, Ari speculates that "maybe kissing was part of the human condition. Maybe I wasn't human" (298). Still, Ari comes to realize that Dante has "saved my life and not the other way around. I wanted to tell them that he was the first human being aside from by mother who had ever made me want to talk about thing that scared me" (308). At this point, though, it isn't completely clear, at least to Ari, what it is that "scared" him.

The novel seems headed toward an uncertain ending, especially about a main character's sexuality, which was fairly typical for gay young adult novels of an earlier time. Ari wonders: "What would happen to me after I graduated? College? More learning. Maybe I would move to another city, to another place. Maybe summers would be different in another place" (336). He maintains his separation from others, asserting that, he is "unknowable" (337). At the end of the novel, however, Ari realizes that he is love with Dante:

> This was what was wrong with me. All this time I had been trying to figure out the secrets of the universe, the secrets of my own body, of my own heart. All of the answers had always been so close and yet I had always fought them without even knowing it. From the minute I'd met Dante, I had fallen in love with him. I just didn't let myself know it, think it, feel it [358-59].

In part, the "secrets of the universe" include Ari's love for Dante and also his need to connect to others—both inside and outside of his family. The novel concludes with these words: "Imagine that. Aristotle Mendoza, a free man. I wasn't afraid anymore" (359). The popularity of this recent young adult novel (which now has a sequel) clearly comes from the touching innocence and growing acceptance of the narrator of his desire to love and be loved.

Along with *Aristotle and Dante*, *Openly Straight* by Bill Konigsberg might also be one of the books that meet Crisp's criteria for better gay young adult fiction. The last novel discussed in this chapter, and perhaps one of the most interesting, has main character Rafe, who has grown up in the liberal city of Boulder, CO, coming out to his family when he's in 8th grade, and then to his friends and soccer teammates in high school during freshman year: "And no one's head exploded," Rafe says. "And nobody got beat up, or threatened, or insulted. Not much, anyway. It all went pretty great" (3). Still, he's tired of being seen only as gay: "The image I saw was so two-dimensional," he says, "that I couldn't recognize myself in it" (3). He decides to go to Natick, a private boy's boarding school and not tell them there that he is gay, so he could have "a chance to live a label-free life" (4). He doesn't tell his parents of his choice to go back into the closet, in part because he doesn't want to face their disapproval but also because he wants to carve out an identity without their influence.

In a way that differs significantly from earlier LGBTQ young adult fiction, Rafe's sense of himself as gay is presented early in the novel as a fact, rather than a dramatic realization: "So it wasn't like I was sitting up there and I had this epiphany: *Wow! I'm gay!*" he tells readers. "I had known that for a long time. I guess if there was an epiphany, it was like,

Three. "But that's young gay love for you"

I've got a feeling and no one else knows about it. Maybe I should tell Mom and Dad. So that was it. No major breakdown, no thoughts about whether I'd be homeless. More like, I could *enjoy* chocolate ice cream, but I prefer strawberry" (78). Sexuality becomes a preference no different than one for a particular flavor of ice cream. His mother, who is extremely supportive, responds with books, and Nick is less than enthusiastic: "*Thanks for making this exciting new thing a chore, Mom. Awesome*" (79). He also wonders why being gay has to be part of every dinner conversation: "It was sort of like Mom was the gay one now. Me, I was basically the same kid I'd been the year before. Still a virgin. Still not dating" (92). Technically, all Rafe has at this point is same-sex attraction; he hasn't done anything about it yet. This, of course, is frequently true for LGBTQ teens and thus is a plot point with which they would identify.

When he gets to Natick, Rafe's writing teacher asks them to keep journals to "tell me who you are." "*Great*, I thought. How the hell was I going to do that?" (42). This is in part because he is keeping his sexuality secret but also because he isn't sure exactly who he is or, more importantly, how he wants to appear to others. Eventually, he tells his parents about his plan, and they aren't happy. In his defense, he tells them "I'm so tired of being the gay kid. I don't want this anymore. I just want to be, like, a normal kid" (133), and he informs them that they need to go along with his choice (134). After watching him play football, his mother says, "I hadn't understood that desire in you, the desire to do those sorts of boy things. I don't know how I missed that" (179). He also has to "reverse come out" to his best friend from home, Claire Olivia (182), and she is angry as well.

During all this drama, he has a closeted relationship with Ben, who doesn't know Rafe is gay and thinks he might be bisexual himself. When he finally comes out to Ben, he is furious at Rafe for being dishonest with him. Rafe comes to realize that "there's no such thing as openly straight" (212), and he comes out to his friend Albie, who has shared that he, too, is gay (280). "[B]eing able to pass for something you're not is a kind of curse," Rafe thinks. "Especially if you try it" (282). He qualifies this: "I don't think being gay is a curse. Definitely not. But we all know that being open about it comes with a lot of things that make life harder. Even if you have great parents and a school where you're treated well, it adds stuff to your life. The worst to me is how everybody looks at you differently. I got so tired of being looked at" (295). However, he acknowledges, "as soon as I tried to remove the label, a lie formed. In the end, that lie created a barrier way worse than the original one" (298). This has become a common message in more recent LGBTQ young adult fiction: the keeping of secrets is seen as more damaging than same-sex attraction.

As a result of these insights, Rafe comes out fully and joins the Gay-Straight Alliance (another common trope in recent fiction) at his new school. At a meeting, a classmate puts things into perspective for him: "Straight people don't have to think, every time they talk, about whether they are coming out. We do. That might be hard, but that's also why we have to come out" (308). Rafe also learns that his secret has hurt others, and he apologizes to Ben: "I had been out of tune with how important I was to him, and how much lying to him would injure him" (313). This lesson about empathy is an important one for all young adults: the world, no matter how it might seem, does not revolve around you.

Empathy and understanding is not enough, though; this novel goes further. Back in Boulder with Claire Olivia after Christmas, Rafe ends the novel with this image, inspired by a street scene: "We were dancers and drummers and standers and jugglers, and there was nothing anyone needed to accept or tolerate. We celebrated" (320). This is the key difference between these later gay young adult novels and those of the past: there is no longer a call simply for acceptance or tolerance; young gay men are asking for a celebration, even when they aren't entirely sure what they are celebrating.

Secrets of the universe, being openly straight, rainbow roads (and high and boys), young gay love with fires, poison oak, and zombies, *agape eros*, and acting companies make up at least a part of gay young adult fiction of the late 20th and early 21st century. Homophobia still exists, although the violence against gay young men appears less in these novels, especially over time. There is some confusion over identities (and how, where, and when to share those identities) and there is, at least in the early novels, some self-loathing as well. By the later novels, though, gay kids are worried more about whether they want to be thought of as only gay, whether their identities are solely determined by their sexual attractions, and they more fully consider the connections between sexuality and relationships (and love). There is also more gay community as the novels move through time, and GSA clubs start making an appearance.

Three. "But that's young gay love for you"

Parents still worry about whether their gay children will be happy—and have children—but, for the most part, they have already accepted their children (sometimes with a vengeance!) and seek to educate themselves and about sexuality. Not all parents are perfect, but this would be the case if their children were straight as well. The novels are primarily narrated by the gay characters now (not the straight sibling or friend), and a variety of same-sex attracted characters are presented: queens and jocks, nerdy shy kids, and mouthy overly sophisticated ones. Gays and lesbians are also starting to appear in the same novels, and there is a budding gay community being created, with older gay characters acting as role models and supporters and the younger boys seeking out groups of similar and sympathetic teens.

Things are not utopic, of course. The communities of gay and lesbian older people could be represented in more detail, including gay and lesbian parents, contrasts could be made between gay life in cities and small towns, and novels could explore bisexuality and transsexuality more fully. It might also be interesting to have gay young adult novels have gay characters in them in which sexuality was not a primary focus, just as these novels have moved away (somewhat) from focusing exclusively on the coming-out narrative. It's true that gay characters in these novels (with one exception) don't commit suicide or have fatal car crashes, they don't come down with AIDS as a matter of course, and they are not routinely (or continuously) bullied for their sexualities, but homosexuality is still the main subject, as opposed to the romantic relationships, conflicts with parents, and search for identity of most straight YA novels. However, the final chapter of this study, which focuses on gay/lesbian utopias and dystopias might offer a productive direction for such new fiction.

Four

"Gender is a choice, not a life sentence"
Young Adult Narratives of Trans Identities[1]

> Gender is many things, but one that it is surely not is a *hobby*. Being female is not something you do because it's clever or postmodern, or because you're a deluded, deranged narcissist. In the end, what it is, more than anything else, is a *fact*. It is the dilemma of the transsexual, though, that it is a fact that cannot possibly be understood without imagination—Jennifer Finney Boylan, *She's Not There*, 22

> Everybody can be everything—Cameron, "Variables," 97

A bill introduced in the Wisconsin legislature in October 2015 attempted to force public school students to use school bathrooms based on their sex assigned at birth, not their gender identity. Commenting about this legislation, Emily Mills, columnist for the *Milwaukee Journal-Sentinel*, said in an October 2015 editorial that "the more we let go of our fear of things we don't immediately understand, a fear that holds us all down, the more we're going to be able to forward and help support the world that our kids already know exists and is so much brighter" (C2). Such legislation, which failed in Wisconsin but has recently been debated throughout the country (and enacted in some places), speaks to the anxieties that continue to surround trans children in the public sphere and suggests that there remains a need protect the youngest and most vulnerable from reactionary social policy and legislation. Also, while it highlights the fear and misinformation in some parts of the straight community toward trans people of all ages, it also can provide an opportunity for learning and empathy. This might be facilitated through a clearer understanding of the historical and theoretical background of transsexuality, personal stories of trans people, and works of fiction that address the states of mind and social pressures experienced by those who transgress (or transmute) traditional gender binaries. As Mills suggests, many young people already know that a "brighter" and more tolerant world can exist, if only we weren't so caught up with legislating bathroom use.

This issue matters for more than just a few isolated individuals, as some have claimed. Stephanie Brill and Rachel Pepper write in *The Transgender Child* (2008): "No one knows how common transgender children are. Some specialists say that one in 500 children is significantly gender-variant or transgender. This may be a reasonable statistic, though the rate may actually be higher" (2). Trans writer Jennifer Finney Boylan reports that recent research suggests that "the condition is more common than cleft palate and multiple sclerosis" (249). Rather than punishing or stigmatizing people who are trans, a far better move would be toward understanding the complex and still-shifting emotional and social issues surrounding trans identities.

A good place to start might be with a working definition of trans behaviors and identities, a historical account of trans activism, and a discussion of its reception in the public sphere. In her thorough and engaging 2008 history of transgender activism in the United States, Susan Stryker defines transgenderism as "the movement across a socially imposed boundary away from an unchosen starting place" (1). This stresses both the repressive nature of gender boundaries and the involuntary aspect of gender identity. However, she also tellingly remarks, "because most people have great difficulty recognizing the humanity of another person if they cannot recognize that person's gender, the gender-changing person can evoke in others a primordial fear of monstrosity, or loss of humanness" (6). Thus, confusion can lead to alienation and eventually to demonization of the trans individual.

This "monstrosity" has been dealt with in a number of ways, from the kinds of legislative restrictions mentioned above (keeping the "monsters" safely contained in their "proper" bathrooms, colleges, sports teams, neighborhoods, careers) to medical interventions of various sorts. Medicine, Stryker points out, has always been a double-edged sword— its representatives' "willingness to intervene has gone hand in hand with their power to define and judge. Far too often, access to medical services for transgender people has depended on constructing transgender phenomena as symptoms of a mental illness or physical malady, partly because 'sickness' is the condition that typically legitimizes medical intervention" (35–37). In other words, unless you are "sick," you don't need medical intervention, so being trans becomes a treatable illness, but an illness nevertheless. In addition, surgical and hormonal interventions, especially in the late 1960s and 70s, "became entangled with a socially conservative attempt to maintain traditional gender, in which changing sex was grudgingly permitted for the few of those seeking to do so, to the extent that the practice did not trouble the genre binary for many" (94). Certain people were allowed to transition to their "proper" and stereotypically-defined gender, leaving the rest of the population safe from gender confusion.

This was also a period of an increasing separation between the transgender and gay and feminist communities, Stryker points out. However, by the 1980s, people began thinking about "all the imaginable genres of gender difference there could be, if only the medically dominated discourse of transsexuality were shattered. In doing so trans people could simultaneously circumvent older feminist ideas that regarded transsexuals as duplicitous, dupes of the patriarch, or mentally ill. All genders—all genres of personhood—would be on the same plane" (129). In addition, vulnerable trans populations like Latinos and African Americans began to receive federal funding as a way to prevent the spread of AIDS into wider communities (132). The current era seems somewhat brighter the past. "The remarkable expansion of the transgender movement in the mid–1990s," Stryker says, "would not have been possible without the Internet's even more remarkable and rapid transformations of the means of mass communication" (146). However, she says, "even though gay and lesbian people who conform to gender norms seem poised for mainstream acceptance ... discrimination against gender-norm transgression remains legal" (152), as the debates in Wisconsin and more recently in North Carolina show.

In 1992, Marjorie Garber writes in *Vested Interests: Cross-Dressing and Cultural Anxiety* that "one of the most important aspects of cross-dressing is the way in which it offers a challenge to easy notions of binarity, putting into question the categories of 'female' and 'male,' whether they are considered essential or constructed, biological or cultural" (10). Choosing to conflate transvestism with transgender under the aegis of cross-dressing, she says it "*is a space of possibility structuring and con-*

Four. "Gender is a choice, not a life sentence"

founding culture: the disruptive element that intervenes, not just a category crisis of male and female, but the crisis of category itself" (author's emphasis, 17). She adds:

> Paradoxically, it is to transsexuals and transvestites that we need to look if we want to understand what gender categories mean. For transsexuals and transvestites are *more* concerned with maleness and femaleness than persons who are neither transvestitism nor transsexual. They are emphatically not interested in "unisex" or "androgyny" as erotic styles, but rather in gender-marked and gender-coded identity structures [110].

In Garber's formulation, the cross-dresser has much to teach people about gender identity and representation.

Activist Kate Bornstein is less concerned with particular gender identities and more about rigid gender binaries that lock people into a particular identity. She says in her 1994 book *Gender Outlaw* that "in living along the borders of the gender frontier, I've come to see the gender system created by this culture as a particularly malevolent and divisive construct, made all the more dangerous by the seeming inability of the culture to *question* gender, its own creation" (12). Informed by the feminist movement's view of gender as a cultural construct, Bornstein wants to push toward an even more flexible definition. In her 2012 book *A Queer and Pleasant Danger*, she says that she realized at four and half that she wasn't a boy, but even until adulthood she "never had the courage to correct them. Instead, I lied to everyone telling them I was a boy. Day and night, I lied. That's a lot of pressure on a little kid." What she did instead was learn "how to act" (13). For Bornstein, gender is more performance than fixed identity, but that performance remains locked within certain designated parameters.

Suzanne Kessler, in her 1998 landmark study of the history of surgical responses to intersexed children, shows how medicine (and the science behind it) is shaped by cultural perspectives about gender and sex. As she puts it, the common belief among endocrinologists and pediatric surgeons was (and, for the most part, remains) that "gender and children are malleable; psychology and medicine are the tools used to transform them. This theory is so strongly endorsed that it has taken on the character of gospel" (15), even though the biological anomalies of intersex infants and children suggest that gender duality "is not mandated by biology" (31). A child's gender can be changed in early life, the argument goes, but a child must nevertheless be assigned a particular gender. "[I]f culture demands gender," she says, "physicians will produce it, and of course, when physicians produce it, the fact that gender is 'demanded' will be hidden from everyone" (75). Medicine turns gender identity into a choice between two options, rather than allowing people to choose *not* to choose.

She concludes that "intersexuals in the political vanguard, like transsexuals in the past, have turned to gender theorists not because we have tremendous influence on the medical profession but for an articulation of the grounds of gender's authority" (120). The result of this questioning might also mean that "[d]efining sexual orientation according to attraction to people with the same or different genitals, as is done now, will no longer make sense" (124). Finally, she says, "by subverting genital primacy, gender will be removed from the biological body and placed in the social-interactional one. Even if there are still two genders, male and female, how you 'do' male or female, including how you 'do' genitals, would be open to interpretation" (132). Sexual identity, sexual attraction, and gender presentation might well become a range of possibilities, a series of deliberate actions, rather than an imposed set of very limited options.

These historical and social-scientific ways to both do and manage gender obviously have much in common with current literary theoretical positions on gender, as well as to narrative representations, both fictional and non-fictional, of sexual and gender identity. In his 1998 book *Second Skins*, Jay Prosser makes this connection, arguing that "to name oneself transsexual is to own precisely to being gender displaced, to being a subject in transition, moving beyond or in between sexual difference" (2). "[T]ranssexuality is always narrative work," he continues, "a transformation of the body that requires the remodeling of life into a particular narrative shape" (4). For writers and readers, he argues, "transsexual narratives place us in a stronger position to understand how dynamic and complex are the relations of authorship and authorization between clinicians and transsexuals and to reexamine the whole problematic of the subject's construction in postmodern theory" (9). Theory, narrative, gender, and identity are therefore linked in the transgender story.

In *Queer Time*, Judith Halberstam continues this discussion of the relationship between transgenderism and postmodernism. She argues that transgenderism, "with its promise of gender liberation and its patina of transgression, its promise of flexibility and its reality of a committed

Four. "Gender is a choice, not a life sentence"

rigidity, could be the successful outcome of years of gender activism; or, just as easily, it could be the sign of the reincorporation of a radical subculture back into the flexible economy of postmodern culture" (21). Halberstam makes the excellent point that "[e]ccentric, double, duplicitous, deceptive, odd, self-hating: all of these judgments swirl around the passing woman, the cross-dresser, the nonoperative transsexual, the self-defined transgender person, as if other lives—gender-normative lives—were not odd, not duplicitous, not doubled and contradictory at every turn" (57–58). Thus the transgender individual raises questions about the instability and fluidity of all gender representation.

Of course, much of what feminist and queer theorists have come to understand about the performative nature of gender comes from Judith Butler's work, starting with *Gender Trouble* in the 1980s. She continues that work in *Undoing Gender* (2004), where she explores transgender identity:

> The very criterion by which we judge a person to be a gendered being, a criterion that posits coherent gender as a presupposition of humanness, is not only one which, justly or unjustly, governs the recognizability of the human, but one that informs the ways we do or do not recognize ourselves at the level of feeling, desire, and the body, at the moments before the mirror, in the moments before the window, in the times that one turns to psychologists, to psychiatrists, to medical and legal professionals to negotiate what may well feel like the unrecognizability of one's gender and, hence, the unrecognizability of one's personhood [58].

To be uncertain about gender can mean, in our society, to be uncertain about one's humanity. For trans people, this can mean assuming a fixed gender identity in order to be allowed access to the not only drugs and surgeries they desire but also to the realm of the sane. "In San Francisco," Butler says, "FTM candidates actually practice the narrative of gender essentialism that they are required to perform before they go in to see the doctors, and there are now coaches to help them, dramaturges of transsexuality who will help you make the case for no fee" (71). Butler argues, not surprisingly, that these culturally-inflected narratives, not innate biological or psychological gender dysphoria, fix the gender of an individual. People play the part of a particular gender so that they can convince medical professionals to transform them physically into their given role. As do many other theorists, Butler wonders whether a new and more flexible definition of gender and sexuality might make this practice unnecessary.

In her 2010 article, Shanna Carlson argues that the transsexual could be "the unconsciously bisexual subject for whom sexual difference is only ever an incomplete, unsatisfactory solution to the failure of the sexual relation. In this way, transgenderism would figure as a solutionless solution to the impasses of sexual difference, a sort of unconscious scene of undecideability, but an undecideability fundamentally shared by all human subjects, no matter their seeming 'gender'" (65). All of us, in Carlson's formulation, might be bisexual, as she uses the term, unable (or unwilling) to decide on a gender identity. However, there might be "another way of reading transgenderism" that would be "as an expression of the logic of sexual difference" (65). Sexual difference would thus be embodied in a single person. Such doubled sexuality, however, can only be seen on the margins of the young adult fiction discussed in this chapter, although it might be possible to view adolescence as perfectly representing a time of gender uncertainty, of development and change.

In *Enigmas of Identity* (2011), Peter Brooks says that who we are and what others call us "seems to have become a problem with entry into the modern age in a way that it wasn't before" (4). Narrative art, especially, "becomes largely devoted to the understanding of personal identity in a world where that identity seems ever more important while at the same time ever more threatened by the anonymity of the modern, by the sheer numbers of others among whom one lives" (5). Unfortunately, though, individuals' sense of identity "seems to resist the state's classificatory impulse—which throws individuals into categories" (27). This is undeniably true with sexuality identity, especially with the insistence (begun at the end of the nineteenth century) on more discrete categories of homo- and heterosexuality (27). Same-sex attraction, Brooks argues, "turns everything around, gives new valence to all social encounters, new identities that revise those we thought we knew" (32). What much modern literature teaches us, however, "is that we live multiple identities, those assumed for the world and those that we harbor in our heads," although The State has much invested in categorizing, normalizing, and policing those identities (91). Thus, narratives of transsexuality might therefore be seen as the most transgressive *and* the most modern of narratives, ones that put into question not just sexual attraction but sexuality itself.

In a 2014 article, Kate Drabinski agrees with Brooks that narratives of sexuality, and in particular trans stories, are fundamentally political

Four. "Gender is a choice, not a life sentence"

in the ways they impact social life (305). Narratives of transsexuality in the 1950s, she argues, created a story of "transnormativity" that "invoked gender normative tropes largely to make sense of lived experiences that prior to the circulation of such stories remained mostly unintelligible." Although they reified gender norms (Male-to-Female, or MTF transsexuals, for example, adopted extremely feminine visual identities), they also offered, Drabiniski argues, "a radical critique of the normative assumption that gendered realities match only certain bodies" (309). Contemporary narratives, on the other hand, "resist the terms of gendered identity altogether, arguing that the language available cannot fully express their experiences of themselves as gendered people" (322). Finally, she says, these narratives "understand gender as no longer anchored in a core internal identity, but rather understand self-making as located in the narrative process itself." Gender is "produced by storytelling," rather than being "the ground of those narratives" (322). In Drabinski's formulation, one tells oneself into a gender, a situation that will render the fictional and non-fictional narratives discussed in this chapter even more important.

Contemporary transgender autobiographies reveal, in more practical terms, much about the tensions and multiplicities of gender discussed by these theorists. For example, in their collection of trans narratives, David Levithan and Billy Merrell include a narrative by Eugenides Fico that argues, "All gender is an act. There's just a very big difference in people's minds about when that act is 'right' and when that act is a 'lie'" (15). Fico doesn't want a sex-change because sex isn't the problem: "The problem is that people are too intent to categorize me as a person who enjoys shopping and makeup and boys, simply because I look a certain way" (19). "My gender is an act," Fico continues, "but acting is open to interpretation" (19). Clearly, Fico sees sexual identity as a deliberate act, but an act that can be interpreted by others in unintended ways. Another writer in the collection recounts a sense of loss of a male identity that is embodied, visceral: "I feel the boy I was slowly ebbing away, more quickly than you would think. I find myself a little sad for his loss. He is dying, after all, so I may live. If he was ever alive in any real sense is something that will be left for me to think about for what I suppose will be the rest of my life" (170). As these two examples show, sexuality can be either a fluid representation or a battle to the death, a both/and versus either/or dynamic.

English professor and novelist Jennifer Finney Boylan's autobiography *She's Not There* (2003) tells the story of her MTF transition and highlights some of the contradictions in the previous narratives. In the preface to the 10th anniversary edition of the book, Finney Boylan stresses the need for stories like hers for younger trans kids. She says that as a teenager she searched for stories that resembled her experience: "Without much in the way of dependable narrative or contemporary myth, there were ways in which I felt, back then, as if I did not exist. Talk about phantoms! Surely, if there were no books about lives like my own, I was fated to live a life in which I could only be invisible" (xii). Recent memoirs and textbooks about transgender people, however, "have helped change trans issues from something extraordinary to something more commonplace, from a single, simple narrative to a series of messier ones" (xii). This messiness might actually be good for teens who are trying to fit their own conflicted attitudes about gender and sexuality into the world.

Throughout the book, Finney Boylan offers a variety of metaphors for thinking about the transgender experience, which are often repeated in the fictional narratives. The conversation about being transgender, she says, "frequently resembles nothing so much as a conversation about *aliens*" (21). As a child she understood that she should keep quiet about her situation, intuiting that "the thing I knew to be true was something others would find both impossible and hilarious" (21). She also posits that "best way to understand gender shift is to sing a song of diaspora" (113); the transgender individual has, like immigrants from Ireland during The Famine, left a familiar homeland for another world and identity, leaving him or her with a sense of loss and displacement—and, perhaps, nostalgia. Using another metaphor, she says that "the line between male and female turns out to be rather fine. Although we imagine our genders as firm and fixed, in fact they are as malleable as a sand castle" (137).

As she transitioned, Finney Boylan noticed that sometimes people saw her as male, other times as female. In an email to her friend, novelist Richard Russo, who was having difficulties understanding her transition, Finney Boylan says, "I really did 'choose' to be Jim every single day, but that once I put my sword down I haven't chosen Jenny at all; I simply wake up and here I am" (180). The default state for Finney Boylan is female; the confrontational/challenging self was male. The bottom line (and primary frustration) for Finney Boyle is that "no matter how much

Four. "Gender is a choice, not a life sentence"

light one attempts to throw on this condition, it remains a mystery. Worse, it is a mystery that everyone has an *opinion* about" (248). For trans teens as well, the world has confident opinions about what to them often seems confusing and even disturbing.

While adult narratives of the trans experience can provide comforting assurances to teens that others have gone through this process before them, stories from adolescents can be even more helpful. With this in mind, writer and photographer Susan Kuklin sought to document the lives of transgender teens, arranging to visit with several at the Health Outreach to Teens through the Callen-Lourde Community Health Center in New York City. Jessy, a FTM transgender young adult, says, "I've always loved my body, and now I love it even more because it fits how I feel" (3). In response to the pronoun question (what gender-inflected or gender-neutral pronouns the transgender person prefers), Jessie says, "I don't really care about pronouns anymore. A pronoun doesn't define who I am. I have a male role in society. I'm proud to be transgender. It's an enriching experience and a big part of my life. But yet I can't get rid of the fact that I was born a biological female. I've had the privilege of being born into a female body and living in a masculine body. I like the fact that I've changed my sex" (24). Jessie sees her sexuality as a role, but a role that doesn't change her original identity as a female. Both girl Jessie and boy Jessie live inside her, although her outside now matches her current emotional state.

Christina, a MTF trans girl, has more conventional ideas about the markers of her gender identity. Born a boy, she didn't' want to ride bikes, or play football or Frisbee, presumably what boys want to do. Instead, she's "been drawn to shopping all my life" (39), which, in her mind, defines her as a girl. Christina hopes to "finish college and get a job and have a husband. I just want to be a housewife. I want to cook and I want to clean. I want to take care of the kids" (42). Not surprisingly, given her definition of girlhood, her vision of an adult life is stereotypically feminine. She also adopts a clichéd version of female sexuality. Taking female hormones and diminishing the testosterone in her life makes her happier, although it eliminates much of her sex drive. "The constant need for sex is annoying—it really is," she says (56). Christina and Jessie thus represent two ways of enacting gender—embracing a kind of dual identity versus accepting wholeheartedly gender norms, even at the expense of sexual experience.

Cameron, on the other hand, takes a different path, choosing to dress more androgynously, sometimes as a "girl" and sometimes as a "boy." "I don't have body issues," Cameron says. "My body is a pretty nice one. It works" (112). Some of the differences between transgender teens may have something to do with the relative acceptance and economic class of the young person's family and community. Those kids whose parents are educated professionals—and who have come to terms with their gender identity (or lack of it)—seem to be willing to embrace less traditional gender identities. Kids from more traditional families, like Christina, may want to transition from one sex to another, but they reinforce conventional gender roles.

Becoming Nicole, by Amy Ellis Nutt (2015), is the most recent of the books and the most extended treatment of the childhood and young-adult trans experience. The biography tells the story of Wyatt Maine's MTF transformation to Nicole. Nutt intersperses her narrative of Nicole's transformation and her parents' response to it with other stories of transgender life. For example, Nutt discusses David/Brenda Reimer (who was surgically changed into a girl because his penis was burned off in an surgical accident and who eventually committed suicide) and concludes that his suicide was caused by his "remaining tortured" after his parents made him live as a girl (even though he transitioned back to being male as an adult) (34%, location 1466). This case, she says, "did much to turn the focus on the nature versus nurture debate, at least as regards gender, back to the brain" (35%, location 1472). Although she admits that this situation "did nothing to explain how there could be a disconnect between sexual anatomy and gender identity" and indeed may have made the problem more difficult to solve (35%, location 1474).

Nutt then talks about recent research into the gender "spectrum," but she insists that "for those whose sexual anatomy is truly discordant with their mental identity, there is no such thing as psychosexual neutrality," and she supports this with the results of a study of 32 transgender children, whose response to a series of questions indicated that they as clearly identified with their chosen gender as did cisgender children (35%, location 1491). About this research, she somewhat surprisingly concludes: "It is that incongruity between body and mind that is the source of a tortuous physical alienation…. When it comes to that physical self, for a transgender person every waking moment, every conscious breath, is a denial of who they truly are…. There is only one way out of

Four. "Gender is a choice, not a life sentence"

the alienation, and that's to make the body congruent with the mind" (35%, Location 1498). It seems, however, that there might be a number of ways "out of the alienation" other than surgically altering the body to conform to the mind.

Later in the book, Nutt even acknowledges "gender identity itself is not a fixed target. Rather, it is only one ingredient of a person's sense of self, and for some the sense of being male or female is simply not as central as it may be for others." Nevertheless, she says, "the binary view of male/female and the pathologizing of anything that doesn't conform to these expectations is stubbornly entrenched" (75%, Location 2446). She concludes that "if there is no one test for gender, if it rests somewhere in that illimitable space between nature and nurture, then gender truly is less about biology and more about what we tell ourselves—and others—about who we are" (59%, Location 2517). This calls into question her earlier statement that the body should be altered to conform to the mind, given that gender identity might not be as fixed in some children as others and that gender might be more of a story we tell ourselves. The novels discussed later in this chapter will address a variety of responses to the issue of transsexual surgery and further elucidate these conflicts.

Another issue that comes up frequently in transgender narratives is the situation of the other siblings in a family with a transgender child. Jonas, Nicole's twin brother, found it had to be "the other child, the other twin, the one without the unusual story." Jonas often felt "like a bit player in the theater of his own life" (75%, location 3201). Wayne and Kelly, Nutt says, "had asked a lot of their only son, and sometimes they forgot the sacrifices he'd had to make being Nicole's brother" (76%, location 3246). This issue about siblings can also be seen in *Luna*, and it appears in gay and lesbian novels as well, where the most troubled gay or lesbian teen gets the most attention in the family or among friends.

As she concludes Nicole's story, Nutt says, "We are, all of us, always crossing borders. Everything seems to happen all at once when we're young, but as we get older we see that we are always moving away from one thing and toward another, never still, never without motion. We live in liminal time, each moment sliding into the next, the future into the present, the present into the past. We believe all things are possible, and that there are always more stories to be written" (90%, location 3829). This applies well to the transgender child, who is almost always the one on the move, "crossing borders" of gender identity and transgressing societal norms, sometimes with a personal and often with a public price to be paid.

Although they follow in the path of autobiographical narratives of trans experiences, the novels discussed here, stories of trans young adults written in the decade between 2004 and 2014, represent a new direction in LGBTQ fiction. They take every possible position on the spectrum of responses to transsexuality: transphobic hostility and violence, refusal on the part of parents and friends to accept the transition, medicalizing of the issues (often hormones and less frequently surgery, as the protagonists have not yet reached the age of consent), and also embracing a multifaceted gender identity. In most cases, the romantic partners of the trans kids eventually distance themselves from the protagonists, and the novels frequently end, as do may YA works, with the main characters embarking on a new and independent lives.

In *Into the Closet* (2008), Victoria Flanagan says that children's literature frequently offers "a nonsexualized and temporary construction of cross-dressing which focuses on the cross-dresser's potential to destabilize normative gender categories through the simulation of a differently gendered subjectivity" (xv). The most common type of cross-dressing is from female to male (xv), Flanagan says, and the male-to-female cross-dressers "are much less successful at interrogating gender stereotypes." She continues: "Instead of questioning the concept of gender in order to make a crucial statement about its application to individuals, male-to-female cross-dressing narratives are rarely able to construct cross-dressing as anything other than a short-lived, comic gesture which is used to reinforce the priority of patriarchal masculinity" (xvii). However, the novels discussed here, which mostly concern MTF trans adolescents, do raise questions about the stability of gender.

These novels also avoid what Jody Norton calls the effect of traditional literature's reinforcement of binary gender norms on children. Norton argues, "the hegemony of the binary model of sex/gender [which] effaces the indefinite range of variant genderings, enforces that effacement with taboo: Gender 'deviance,' if it is visible at all, is sick, disgusting, and immoral" (300). Norton calls for "an unabashed romanticism of imagination" that includes "a range of child subjectivities so grand, and at the same time so individually distinct, as to constitute what I have called a sublime realism. For it is my contention that the child does not

Four. "Gender is a choice, not a life sentence"

only long, in some transient way, for the transformation of the real into the imaginary, but that, in fact, the most profound desire of the child is precisely to transform the romantic (the fantastic, the fantasmatic) into the real" (309). Certainly the novels discussed here do show the ways in which the desires of the child can become a reality and, sometimes, make what might seem fantastic—that a boy can become a girl or vice versa—into the real.

One of Nicole's favorite novels, *Luna*, by Julie Anne Peters (2004), is told from the perspective of Regan, the younger sister of MTF trans young adult Liam/Luna. Regan knows that Liam has always wanted to be a girl, even though when Liam goes to school he dresses in "boy role" (6). "No one will ever know the person I am inside," Liam tells Regan. "The true me. The girl, the woman. All they see is this ... this nothing" (20). Although she loves her sibling, Regan's annoyance with Luna begins early. "Ever since I started school," Regan says, "I felt like I had this older sister to live up to. She was smarter, nicer, prettier—or would have been if she could dress the part. Liam's footsteps were way too big for me to follow in. I kept tripping on his high heels" (30). Regan has all the troubles associated with being the second born, combined with the fact that she has to keep her brother's hidden identity a secret from the world.

Throughout the novel, Liam's gender self-expression creates troubles for Regan. At Regan's slumber party, Liam reveals himself as Luna, which causes strained relations with Regan's friends. Still, Regan notices the ways in which Liam—and everyone—is constrained by gender binaries. While babysitting, Regan thinks that gender is created in part by the way children are socialized: "There were lines you didn't cross, in clothing, behavior, attitude" (50). She also realizes that "the gender scales didn't extend equidistant in both directions. For example, if you were a girl you could be off-the-scale feminine and that's be fine, but if you acted or felt just a little too masculine, you were a dyke" (51). Liam's body "didn't reflect his inner image. His body betrayed him" (51). At this point, the little boy she's babysitting comes out holding a G.I. Joe and wearing high heels: "So much for gender expectations," Regan thinks (51). In spite of her growing awareness and Liam telling her that "there are shades of gray to people's gender" (69), when Regan realizes that he wants to have a sex-change operation, a "wave of nausea" passes over her (71). She loves her brother *as* her brother and doesn't want to see him change his physical form. On the other hand, she also recognizes that her brother's secret and his struggle is "sucking the life right out of [him]" (117). Still, she knows that Luna emerging from her brother is like "a butterfly emerging from a chrysalis." Unfortunately, though, Luna "is forced to rein in her wings and reinsert herself back into the cocoon every day. Every single day, she has to become this shell of a person" (126). At some level, Regan knows that Luna can't stay inside the shell forever.

This new-found sympathy is tested, though, when Liam babysits for Regan's charges, and he dresses up as Luna. When the parents come home and find Luna dressed in the wife's clothes, they fire Regan. She lashes out at her sister: "It's the only thing I had that was mine.... It was the only place I had to go to get away from *you*." Liam doesn't understand. (171) Regan feels as if *she*'s in the closet: "Just once I wanted to be able to hold a conversation with a person without having to watch every word I said," Regan thinks. "Or worry about saying too much, divulging the truth, giving her away. I wanted to be free of this secret, this lie, this brother who wasn't a boy" (172). She feels like she's "trapped," "suffocating" with Liam's secret (180).

As a result of this realization that she must be honest about her identity, Luna comes out to her parents, and her father says she's "sick," and threatens, "If you walk out that door, don't bother coming back" (223). As the rest of the novels discussed in this chapter will show, this is a fairly typical response, sometimes from the father and, less frequently, from the mother. However, both fathers and mothers usually come around, in part because in YA novels (unlike in life) the goal of writers is often to present a hopeful conclusion for teen readers. In *Luna*, Regan finds out that their mother knew about Liam's desire to be a girl and told him to keep it a secret (241) to avoid destroying their father. Regan, who initially judges her mother harshly and even thinks she may have engineered Luna's suicide attempt, eventually comes to reassess her mother and her choices and realizes that she may have been doing the best she could under the circumstances.

At the end of the novel, Luna decides she has to leave and go to Seattle to stay with another trans woman until she can have the surgery. In a reversal of what Regan thought at the beginning novel, Luna tells her sister, "Don't you know, you're the girl I always wanted to be" (246). Regan thinks, "She freed us both." At the end, Regan runs to the door of the airport, saying goodbye to Liam and hello to Luna—and herself

(248). This relatively early trans young adult novel doesn't show a way for Liam/Luna to remain true to herself and stay with her family, and it does present surgery as the only possible route for happiness, but Regan, at least, is able to empathize and love her sister, while at the same time being free of the burdens of her secret.

Victoria Flanagan says that *Luna* was among a small number of novels at the time that used "transgendered identity simultaneously to expose the artifice of socially constructed gender categories and to teach the reader/viewer of the importance of values such as tolerance and compassion" (7). The novel also provided readers, Flanagan says, "with a representation of cross-dressing that embraces the complexity of transgendered subjectivity" (214). Still, one has to admit that the novel, while somewhat hopeful at the end, is nevertheless filled with heartbreak and loss, both for the transgender character, her sister, and their family.

A more exuberant novel, James St. James' *Freak Show* (2007), is not about a trans kid but a boy who presents himself to the world in gender-challenging ways. Living in Florida with his inattentive father (after his mentally-ill mother sends him away), Billy Bloom, 17, is starting at a new school as the novel opens. Dressing for the important first day, he thinks, "Although my sexuality is still largely theoretical at this point, I hope that I don't actually LOOK gay—you know, all pursed and twittery with big, bulgy, 'gay' eyes. It's a new school after all. I need to test the waters first before I break out the tiaras and leg warmers" (11). However, his dramatic and unconventional clothing (he *does* "look gay," at least to the other students) and feminine manner causes him to be harassed and bullied at school.

To make matters more complicated, Billy falls in love with Flip Kelly, a high school football star, but at first Flip does not reciprocate. However, when Billy unwisely comes to school dressed as a Swamp Queen, he is brutally beaten and ends up in the hospital, where Flip, who is a genuinely nice guy (if a bit dim), comes to see him. They have a straightforward talk about sex, and Flip asks Billy how far he's "gotten" with a guy. Billy tells him he's a "teenage spinster." "Really," he says, "I am so totally homo-challenged, I might as well be straight.... I'm going to hermetically seal my ass now and save future archeologists the problem" (142). Like many YA novels, the sexuality of the main characters, gay or straight, is, for all intents and purposes "theoretical," as Billy puts it. Still, Flip doesn't seem threatened by Billy's attraction to boys (and to him), and they continue to be friends.

After Billy recovers and comes back to school, the kids are nice to him, in part because there's been a crackdown on bullying and hate speech. However, Billy says that homophobia is "always there. A bit of gay terror. Bubbling under the surface. Threatening to pop up and expose you. I mean, you can't un-gay yourself whenever it's inconvenient for you. Despite what Republicans seem to think" (159). Still, as a sign of how much things have changed upon his return, when Billy gets a hard on when looking at the captain of the football team during swimming class, the matter is dropped because students are afraid of the repercussions after the hazing incident.

Eventually, Billy kisses Flip, but as they look through the windows of Billy's waterfront bedroom, a tour boat full of people sees them rolling around on the bed, and Flip is furious and worried about his reputation as a football star. Billy is devastated, but he decides to go back to school: "Sure, I could keep running, and never look back," he says. "But then I would never know how it all turned out, if I had what it takes to survive in that world, or possibly even triumph" (195). With the help of a classmate, Mary Jane, he hatches a plan "to earn their respect and their acceptance, or die trying, and along the way, drag them into the twenty-first century" (202).

Billy intends to run for homecoming queen, and, not surprisingly, he begins to get the attention of the media. He and Mary Jane try to think about how to promote him, and come up with "preen queen," "transvisionary," "gender obscurist," "gender obliviator," "glitteroid," and, finally they decide on "Superfreak" (218). These terms suggest the possibilities of gender in the 21st-century. In his speech, Billy tells the student body, "GENDER IS A CHOICE, NOT A LIFE SENTENCE. I'm going to change the world, one dress at a time!" (217). While sexual attraction may not be a choice (regardless of what the republicans say), gender, or the ways in which one might represent genre, can very well be. He tells the media that "Homophobia IS SO LAST CENTURY! ... Heal the world, and vote for the sissy!" (223). Billy (and St. James) have established the "sissy" as a viable posture, even in high school.

As a result of the publicity, Billy begins to hear from other teens that he is their role model, and from "drag queens and transgender types, who told me about similar ordeals they went through in high school, and the horrific torture THEY endured. (And that's always reassuring.)" (234). What this ironic commentary suggests is that Billy's brave new world comes at the price of "ordeals" and "torture," and a bright future isn't possible for everyone.

In his final speech to his classmates before the homecoming game, Billy tells them that all teenagers are "freaks":

> Alone in our rooms at night, we are all weirdoes and outcasts and losers. That is what being a teenager is all about! Whether you admit it or not, you are all worried that the others won't accept you, that if they knew the real you, they would recoil in horror. Each of us carries with us a secret shame that we think is somehow unique. [247]

He admonishes his classmates to "accept the Universal Freak Show in us all" (248).

Billy doesn't win the contest for queen, but he says that, actually, "it was about winning them over. Showing I was WORTHY of being their queen" (281). After the homecoming dance, Billy is attacked by a closeted classmate but decides that he won't be a martyr or a victim (290–91). At the end of the novel, Billy reconciles with his father, plans to start a GSA club at school, and is kissed by Flip. The last lines of the novel are "And there were fireworks and rainbows and a hail of 'hip, hip, hooray's' as church bells rang and the whole world cheered and danced in the streets. Yes, there was peace on earth when love saved the day and Flip and I lived FABULOUSLY ever after. Well, of course!" (298). Readers enjoy the delightfully happy ending, but they also know that Billy, from the beginning of the novel to its end, is not always the best judge of any given situation. Billy loves his rose colored (and sequined and cats' eye) glasses far too much to have a realistic idea of how his life will turn out. Still, this ending doesn't deviate that much (with the exception of the fireworks and rainbows) from the ambiguous but usually optimistic endings of most young adult novels.

Ellen Wittlinger's novel *Parrotfish* (2007) is a more typical problem novel than *Freak Boy*. It opens with Angela, a female-to-male (FTM) trans kid wondering why gender is so important. "Not all of us fit so neatly into the category we get saddled with on Day One when the doctor glances down and makes a quick assessment of the available equipment. What's the big rush, anyway?" (3–4). This is a question that continues to challenge trans and intersex advocates. This ambiguity is reinforced when Angela reminds her parents that she now wants to be called Grady.

"It's a name that could belong to either gender," she tells her sister. "Also, I like the gray part of it—you know, not black, not white. Somewhere in the middle" (6). This celebration of the "grayness" of gender will become a common motif in later trans novels for young adults.

When Angela/Grady started high school (after being home-schooled) Grady said he was a lesbian because it prevented "giving everyone hope that someday I'd turn into a regular hairdo-and-high-heels female." Still, he knew he was "crawling toward the truth on my hands and knees" (9) that coming out as a lesbian "was just a pit stop on the queer and confused highway" (18). He soon discovers that he "can only lie about who you are for so long without going crazy," so he cuts his hair, binds his breasts, and starts wearing boys' clothes (19). His father accepts the change because he's "addicted to happy endings" (23), and Grady notices that in general the "male members of [his] family seemed to be taking this better than the females," possibly because he is rejecting their gender (33). Grady worries that he won't ever be able to normal again with his mother and that she would "always have that sad look on her face" when she sees him (36).

Grady's friend Sebastian says he's like the stoplight parrotfish, which changes its gender when needed (43). "Nature creates many variations," Sebastian says (71). The principal, on the other hand, doesn't want to see "the school gets turned upside down for nothing" (55). His gym teacher lets Grady use her private bathroom, so he could "urinate—or hide out—without fear" (75). He starts feeling fearful in spite of that, not meeting people's eyes or raising his hand in class, and jumping at every noise (76). Later his gym teacher defends Grady to the principal and tells him it's up to the schools to educate children about trans issues (189).

Grady thinks that maybe if everyone wasn't so rigid about gender that he could have been "a crew-socks-wearing person who played on the boys' soccer team and it would have been okay" (106). When the football players dress as girls for a pep rally, Grady thinks that maybe "they needed a break from performing that whole machismo act day after day" (124). To further clarify, Sebastian draws the metaphor of a football field, with the most feminine woman on one end and the most masculine man on the other. He says that "there would be a lot of people in the middle of the field" (128). Grady wonders what that means for him and for his classmates: "What made a person male or female, anyway? The way they looked? The way they acted? The way they thought? Their hormones? Their genitals? What if some of those attributes pointed in one direction and some in the other?" (131). These sorts of questions will be raised in many of the trans YA novels discussed here.

Clearly, identity is a fraught matter in the story. Grady worries that he's going to have to think about every little thing he does. "Why couldn't people just leave me alone?" Grady wonders. "Who was I hurting, anyway? Why did I have to defend my right to be the person I was?" (181). Grady tells some nosey girls that he is "a person who's capable of loving other people. That's all that matters" (196). Grady concludes, unlike the gender-changing fish that change "only when it's necessary for survival," that living as a male is "necessary for my mental survival, if not actually all that great for my day-to-day physical life" (209). Like many of the trans kids in both the autobiographies and the novels, Grady comes to recognize that he has learned a great deal from being female and male. "I was a boy who had once been a girl. I was some of each. Which was beginning to feel okay" (227). He also discovers that cis-gendered teens also have troubles with gender identity. Her football-player friend Russ, for example, says that he doesn't always feel like a "man," and he wishes "we didn't have to be one thing or the other" (228).

As the novel comes to a close, Grady realizes that although the past month has been difficult, he is "beginning to like not knowing what would happen next. Now that I knew there were people who'd help me roll with the punches, it was kind of exciting" (264). Grady recalls the football field metaphor at the end: "We spend a long time trying to figure out how to act like ourselves, and then, if we're lucky, we finally figure out that being ourselves has nothing to do with acting. If you don't believe it, just look at me, the kid in the middle of the football field, smiling" (287). This is an interesting conclusion, given that it implies that identity is *not* an act. Still, Grady is in the middle of the field; he could run in either direction, it appears, and be happy either way.

Like *Luna*, Almost *Perfect*, by Brian Katcher (2009), is one of Nicole's favorite books, but unlike Luna, the main character is not related to the trans kid but is romantically interested in her. Logan Witherspoon, 18, has been cheated on by his girlfriend when he meets a new student, Sage Hendricks, who is MTF trans, although no one knows this but her family. He is attracted to her, but her parents are very protective and won't let her date, and she sends him mixed signals. After a long conversation one evening, Logan notices that Sage looks like she's "fearful of some impending disaster" (83). A little while after that, Logan kisses her, and when she tells him she's a boy, he feels that he has "fallen for [her feminine appearance] completely" and worries that he might be a "fag" (100). If other students find out, he thinks that even their flirting in biology "would be enough to paint me pink for the next twenty years" (103).

During this difficult time, a boy calls Logan a "faggot," and he explodes, punching him. He also begins to reflect on his anger toward Sage and is "scared" by it (122). Still, he remains attracted to her. When Sage shows up at his house, Logan doesn't "want to have to question my own sexuality every time she smiles at me," but he doesn't ask her to leave (161). Growing up in the small town of Boyer, Missouri, Logan has never met "a homosexual, a Muslim, a Jew, a Communist, or a New Yorker." People like Sage were "just perverts who appeared on talk shows. And now I was friends with one" (163). He decides that Sage isn't as much of a "pervert" as his best male friend though, and he chooses to stay with her (172).

Logan and Sage have sex (very discreetly portrayed), the first time for both of them, on a college tour trip to the university his sister attends. Logan thinks after the trip that he'd "been Sage's boyfriend for months now. I'd only just realized it" (260). His sister finds out when Sage stays with her in the dorm that Sage is biologically male, and she tells Logan, assuming that he doesn't know. Logan breaks up with Sage because he can't live with his sister thinking he's gay (269). "Why couldn't she just be a real girl?" he wonders. "Our lives would be great. She was so close to the real thing. But close didn't count" (285). Sage gets beaten up by a frat boy she met at the university, dated, and revealed her gender to, and Logan wonders why it is "such a big deal" that she's trans (292). Still, he realizes that he himself had had "a thousand opportunities to be selfless and understanding, but I'd always been small-minded and cruel" to Sage (298).

As the result of the rape and the stress of being trans, Sage is admitted to a psychiatric hospital. She tells Logan that she's realized that she's "never going to be a woman. Even if I have the surgery, I'll be faking it. I'll always be a boy to my family, and I'll live the next sixty years wondering if my secret will get out. I just can't take it anymore. I tried and failed, so I'm quitting. I wish we could stay friends, but after what we did together, we couldn't face each other man to man" (331). Later she decides

Four. "Gender is a choice, not a life sentence"

not to go back to being a boy, but she doesn't know what she's going to do in the future.

Eventually, Logan and Sage realize that they won't ever become a couple. Logan thinks:

> Sage drove me crazy but I didn't regret knowing her. She made me too happy. She once told me I made her feel beautiful, special, like she belonged. I'd never told her she did the same thing for me. I'd never forget her.... Any future relationship I had wouldn't be nearly as complicated as the one I'd had with Sage. And probably not as fun [355].

At the end of the novel, Logan is a college freshman, and he meets a girl in the dining hall. He's interested, but he thinks, "There was no point in worrying about the next girl in my life right now. All I knew was that she would have a hard time measuring up to Sage" (357). Although the trans character in this novel is abused and traumatized, she is treated with affection and respect by the protagonist, and Logan's final statement implies that Sage is as much of a "girl" as anyone—and more fun.

Unlike the earlier novels, which focus on primarily on relationships, *I am J*, by Cris Beam (2011) raises a wider variety of trans issues—from chest binders, to hormone injections, rejection/resistance from parents, the relationship between gender identity and sexuality, homelessness, the need for schools and places to live for trans kids, and conflicts between the gay and lesbian and trans communities. In this novel, J (a FTM trans kid) runs away from home, claiming that he's "nobody's little girl" (125), but, as is the case for many trans young adults, his leaving home creates far more problems than it solves.

One of J's major reasons for leaving home is that he wants to start taking testosterone, which his parents won't allow. However, he finds out that the clinic he visits won't give him shots right away, in part because he's underage. He gets a room at a cheap hotel and meets Marcia, who is likely trans, and she tells him, "Oh, honey, we're *all* transgender" (137), implying that everyone has some kind of issue with gender or sexuality, or at least that everyone (especially those who are young) is in transition from one identity to another.

When Marcia tells him about a house for gay and lesbian kids, J is reluctant to go there, thinking that he will have nothing in common with them. "Your homophobia's *real* tired," Marcia comments. "We all gotta get along" (139), suggesting that long-standing animosities between the gay and lesbian and trans communities might be ending, or at least raising that possibility. In spite of Marcia's admonishment, J goes to the LGBTQ shelter and school, but he is convinced he isn't "anything like these people" (148), although he soon discovers that he has things in common with MTF trans teens. When J meets Chanelle, a MTF trans girl at school, she tells him, "I hate it that the transwomen and transmen are so separate all the time. That's why I talked to you. You seemed different" (199). This is a new element in trans young adult fiction, one that suggests a wider trans community and some of the connections and problems in that community.

While he is living on his own, J feels "that his very body was divided in parts," with one part belonging to his new life in the shelter, another with a new love interest (who doesn't know he's trans), and the third with his parents and his past (149–50). A reconciliation is attempted with his family, but his mother tells him that he's selfish and should concentrate on getting into college, not on his sexuality (162). "You can learn to love the life you're handed," she says (166). J moves in with Melissa, in part because of his mother's resistance and his father's refusal accept his being trans, and he asks his mother for a letter allowing him to get testosterone shots (he's not quite 18).

J goes back to the clinic where he earlier asked about getting testosterone shots, and he looks at all the trans men in the room. J wonders about what makes a person male or female. "If there wasn't a word for male and female, would everyone just be a person? Would that be easier?" (203). Still, J thinks, vaguely, that he needs to be a man, even though he realizes that he "learned to hate [his] body because of other people" (204). Around this time, J also decides to be honest about his being trans. J gets his first testosterone shot with Melissa, Chanelle, and Zak, a young man leading a transgender support group. "It was like a family, a holiday, a graduation, a birthday, a plane taking off, a circuit overload," J thinks (299). Melissa represents the link to his past, Chanelle to an acceptance of his changing body, and Zak, to political activism and community. Again, this is breaking new ground for trans young adult fiction, while at the same time raising complex issues about gender identity and physical transformation.

Toward the end of the novel, J confronts his father at his parents' anniversary party (to which he was not invited), and his father tells him that he is "disgusting," "sick," and "needs help" (316). This, of course, is not an uncommon response from parents in trans YA fiction. He turns his back on them both—on his mother for choosing his father over him and his father for not accepting him as his son. As is usually the case with almost all YA fiction, things improve before the novel ends. In the last pages, J is still living with Melissa and visiting his parents on the weekends. They are on "good behavior" when he sees them, and he feels "newly supported" by his dad. At this point, J thinks that he is "like a camera before things went digital; the film in its roll could imprint any picture at all. People could project images into his line of sight all they wanted, but he was the one who pushed the shutter" (325). He is accepted into a college photography program, and when he tells Melissa, "his new, deep voice didn't crack" (326). J has learned how to "push the shutter" on his life; he, like most of the trans kids in these novels, is moving forward in a positive direction.

Winner of the ALA Stonewall Book Award, Kirsten Cronn-Mills' *Beautiful Music for Ugly Children* (2012) tells the story of FTM trans kid Elizabeth/Gabe, who lives in small-town Maxfield, Minnesota. The small town is a common location in GLBTQ YA novels, creating conflict by stressing the isolation of the young person and providing and contrast with the city, which is usually a site of information and community. "My birth name is Elizabeth, but I'm a guy," Gabe tells readers on the first page of the novel. "My parents think I've gone crazy, and the rest of the world is happy to agree with them, but I know I'm right. I've been a boy my whole life" (8). Gabe loves music and has an older friend, John, who is a DJ, and who functions as his surrogate grandfather. Although no one's ever beaten him up and his parents love him, Gabe says he's been holding his identity inside and is about ready let it out. "I'm like a 45," he says. "Liz is my A side, the song everybody knows, and Gabe is my B side—not played as often but just as good" (12). It seems that Gabe is poised to play that other side for the world.

Gabe's friend Paige knows he's trans, but he hasn't told John. Paige tells him that John will "get used to it, just like everyone else has" (18). If Gabe doesn't tell John, Paige says, "you'll still be in limbo. Haven't you been in between for long enough?" Although Gabe has promised himself that he'd "get on the Gabe road for good after high school," he sometimes wants "a detour, to some place like Antarctica where people wear so many layers of clothes that nobody cares who you are" (18). Gabe finally tells John, and John says, "You are you. That's all there is to it" (39). John gets him a DJ job at the radio station, and he goes on as Gabe. John's acceptance and support is crucial for Gabe; he is getting validation from an adult role model, along with concrete help toward furthering his career.

He is not getting this from his parents. Gabe's father tells him, angrily, "You may think you know who you are and what you want, but you're also young and maybe a little foolish," and he admonishes Gabe to get a job (65). Gabe's mom tells him it's hard to make the transition to thinking of him as a boy. "You have this sweet little baby, and then, all of a sudden, she tells you it's a mistake. We created a mistake" (156). Again, these are not uncommon responses from parents in trans novels; a crucial difference here is that Gabe has adult support elsewhere.

One of the reasons Gabe hasn't applied for jobs is because his ID says he's a girl, an issue many trans activists cite this a primary stumbling block for trans people. However, he eventually finds a job at a record store, where the manager doesn't care that he's trans, and he also gets a series of groupies for his radio show, including one girl named Mara who has a crush on him (but doesn't know he's trans). Frightened about his date with Mara, Gabe wants to "quit" being trans and have his mother tell him everything will be all right (143), but he goes ahead with the deception. After their date, Mara finds out he's a boy, is furious, and outs him online. Word gets out, and some transphobic guys threaten him online and in person.

Gabe meets his fans for a party, and Gabe thanks Mara for outing him. "You shoved me off the cliff. Turns out I can fly," he tells her, realizing that although this statement is "dorky," it is how he feels (226). The boys making the threats show up at the party; John gets hit with a baseball bat and ends up in the hospital. John survives, and he sells his valuable Elvis guitar and gives Gabe some of the money for college or perhaps sexual reassignment surgery. Gabe's still holding out for a possible relationship with Paige. The novel ends with Gabe headed to community college and John and Gabe arguing about band names (232). Sounding very much like Logan in *Almost Perfect*, and almost all of the trans teens in the novels discussed earlier, Gabe is uncertain about what's going to happen in his life. "That's what bites about the future," he thinks; "there's no way to predict it. You just have to show up and see what happens" (203). Gabe, newly out to everyone, has decided to "show up" as himself.

The importance of being honest about one's identity is also a theme

Four. "Gender is a choice, not a life sentence"

of Rachel Gold's *Being Emily* (2012). The novel features MTF trans kid, Chris, who as the book starts is dating a girl, Claire, who thinks Chris is a boy. Chris wants to tell her, but she remembers that it didn't go well when she tried to tell other friends. However, "the truth welled up in me so thickly I knew I couldn't hold it back much longer" (2). Chris feels that she's "dressing up as a boy" and that she is living amidst a "pile of deception" (4). When he tells Claire, she remembers how much he loved *Ozma of Oz a*nd how, like the title character, she "searched everywhere in my life for the magic to turn me back into my rightful self" (19).

An interesting feature of this book is that it is told through both Claire and Chris's perspectives, which allows readers to be both inside and outside of the trans experience. In her version of the story, Claire feels angry at first when he tells her but then "sad for herself" (22). It makes her "feel sick" to think about guys turning into girls. "There were men and there were women and you couldn't just go from one to the other" (25), she thinks. It all seems "unnatural" to her (25), and she wonders why someone would need "all that medical intervention" to change. "Who needed to take a perfectly good working body and turn it into something else?" (25), she asks. However, she also thinks that "the world was made for joy" and trans people should be included in that joy (27). Claire says that Chris has "a girl brain in a boy's body," which makes her "a lesbian trapped in a straight girl's body" (54), but she grows more accepting of the situation the more she considers it.

Dressing as a girl represents both the best and the worst for Chris. She hates being "a freak," but she also goes from "being a charcoal outline of a person to being a flesh and blood human being" (29) when wearing women's clothes. Chris meets Natalie, a MTF trans girl, in a transgender chat room, and she tells them "my whole life isn't about my gender identity, you know," when Claire asks if they should call her trans (64). Natalie says that when she started dressing as a girl, her mother noticed the positive change; she was fully of "confidence and optimism." She tells her mother that she's "always been like that, I'd just spend so much energy fighting against that other thing that I had nothing left over" (70). Natalie gives Chris some of her hormone pills (108). Still, one half of Chris is happy to have a girlfriend and a support group and hormones, but the other half "was a paper-mâché shell that looked like a guy on the outside and was hollow within" (110).

Natalie's mom helps Chris transition to Emily at a slumber party at their house. Chris thinks "that heaven was probably populated with people like this" (134), and afterward, Claire says that there is "a lot more mystery in the world than she'd thought" and that she is "gender euphoric" (140). When Claire watches Emily and Natalie, she notices that "being beautiful wasn't a burden, it was a self-expression they were willing to fight for. Their feminine beauty was the battle standard for claiming their own identity. She had never realized that femininity could be a radical act" (151). For Claire, "the more she spoke up for Emily, the more Claire felt those parts in herself come forward: the vulnerable, soft, creative elements of her own being" (186). This is an important moment in trans YA fiction; the cisgender teen is more fully coming to understand herself and her gender identity through her experiences with the trans young person.

Toward the end of the novel, Emily comes out to her parents, and they are initially upset, but they eventually accept her new identity. Both a useless and a helpful psychiatrist are involved in the process, and Chris' father actually takes him to the doctor to get the hormones. Claire and Emily continue to date, but they go off to separate colleges, and they eventually break up. By the last pages, Emily has had facial surgery and is saving up for more and has decided that she'll "take my ordinary moments and enjoy every one of them" (210). This optimistic tone is familiar from the novels discussed earlier, although through its narrative structure, this text has gone further in exploring the implications of and reactions to trans kids.

Kristin Elizabeth Clark's *Freakboy* (2013) differs from the other novels in that it tells the story from three different perspectives and is written in verse. The novel, which is the story of Brendan, a MTF trans teen; his girlfriend, Vanessa; and Angel, a trans young woman who works at a LGBTQ center, begins with this preface:

> A pronoun is a ghost
> of who you really are
> short
> sharp harsh
> whispering its presence,
> taunting our soul.
> In you
> Of you
> But not
> All you [3].

Four. "Gender is a choice, not a life sentence"

This suggests the importance of pronouns for trans people but it also reminds readers that it only reflects a part of one's identity, a "ghost" of who one is.

Brendan's attempt to define herself and her situation looks like this:

> Transgender.
> Transwoman.
> Transformed into a freak.
> Transported to hell.

Here, Brendan stresses both the transformational aspect of being trans but also the sense of being trapped in a life of difference and pain. Perhaps naively, Brendan and Vanessa both hope that "love heals everything" after they have sex (113), which, of course, it doesn't.

The two trans characters speculate about the slippery relationship between bodies and identities. Angel thinks that "my junk doesn't dictate who I am" (188) and doesn't believe that surgery is "that important/to how I see myself" (188). In keeping with this idea, Brendan wonders "Can't I just be/a girl with a dick?" (266). Although Brendan thinks that she's "in the wrong skin," she can't "make it right" because she doesn't like "long fingernails,/high heels, or skirts / either." Both Angel and Brendan are coming to accept that physical transformation might not be necessary, and certainly that adopting an earlier model of trans-womanhood—an ultra-feminine one—will not be the answer. Sadly, though, Brendan thinks:

> I'm Freakboy and
> there will never
> be a place for me [379].

Brendan and Vanessa eventually break up, and Brendan asks to see a psychologist who is accepting of her being trans. The novel ends this way, in Brendan's voice and on an optimistic note:

> I'm in just the right
> Body, I'll leave it
> as it is. My fu-
> ture is murky
> and some days are
> more femme than the
> others but today, on this day,
> and in this moment, I can
> live with that [427].

Brendan appears to have decided that he doesn't need to change her body to be a woman and accepted that she may be "more femme" on some days than others. She may still feel freakish from time to time, but it looks as if she can "live with that," which is important give the exceedingly high suicide rate for trans teens.

Gracefully Grayson, by Ami Polonski (2014), features the youngest of the protagonists discussed in this chapter. Main character Grayson, a MTF trans kid whose parents were killed in a car accident when he was four, has moved to Chicago to live with his aunt and uncle. When the novel starts, Grayson is in the sixth grade. In keeping with the protagonist's age, much of the imagery in the novel is taken from fairy tales. For example, as Grayson looks in the mirror she sees herself this way:

> I spin in a slow circle and my wide pants legs puff out like sails. I watch myself. They're still pants, and my chest tightens. I spin again, not like a dainty princess, but like a tornado. I'm making myself nauseous and dizzy, but I don't care. And finally, with the wave of a magic wand, with glitter flowing in its trail, in a blur of gold and rush of hot blood and wind, my clothes transform, the way they have for so many years, into a dress [13].

This is a violent but effective transformation from boy into girl, less "dainty" than wild. It is also somewhat painful, causing nausea and fever. At this point his cousin calls him to dinner, and, as the spell is broken, she "follow[s] my evil stepbrother to the dining room, wearing a golden gown that only I can see" (14). At this point, Grayson realizes that her pretend princess world is no longer working as well as it used to (26).

Grayson and her friend Amelia (who does not know she's trans) go shopping at a thrift store (where Grayson secretly gets his feminine clothes), and they find a mechanical bird in a cage, which they manage to break: "The bird is lying on the floor of the cage, one of its wings still twitching, as the music continues to ping" (41). Clearly, the author is equating Grayson with the broken bird, no longer able to even pretend to fly free. Grayson thinks back to fifth grade, when pretending was enough (50), and wishes she was a playwright so she could change her ending (63). This gets him thinking about acting, and an idea "takes shape and floats into my mouth, and it waits there" (72–73). As a result of this insight, Grayson tries out for the school play, *The Myth of Persephone*, and she gets the part of Persephone. Her English teacher cautions

Four. "Gender is a choice, not a life sentence"

her to think about how people might react to her playing this role (75), but when she reads the lines for the part, she feels like Persephone, and she starts to smile (82).

During another trip to the thrift store, Amelia catches her trying on a skirt, and she's disturbed and worries that others will think Grayson is "crazy" (95). Grayson worries about being labeled as "the boy who tried on a skirt—a beautiful, beautiful skirt" and that "nobody will ignore me again" (96). This, ultimately, may be what Grayson wants: that she won't be ignored and that she'll finally be seen for who she is.

Of course, Grayson gets the role of Persephone, but her aunt and uncle don't want her to take the role. Grayson, however, "can't turn my thoughts away form a vision of myself on stage, in the spotlight, in a beautiful, flowing gown," but her aunt tells the drama teacher that she's "creating a monster" (123). The principal is concerned, the PTA gets involved, and the drama teacher decides to leave at the end of the school year to avoid further conflict. Even though her teacher is leaving because of him and her aunt thinks he's a "monster," when Grayson is playing her part she sees herself the way she's "supposed to be—my inside self matched up with my outside self. And now, everyone else will finally see it, too" (214). The play goes well, and after it is over, she is reconciled with her aunt and uncle, and the uncle invites her to go with him to see a professional play (237).

Although she's been wearing girl's t-shirts underneath his boy's clothes to school, at the end of the novel, Grayson puts the pink shirt on top: "I think of all the years that I spent wearing boys' clothes and pretending that I looked like I do right now, and I think about how I wished and pretended that everyone else could see me the way I'm supposed to be, the way I really am" (243). She heads back to the classroom. "I'm scared, but I do it anyway—I open the door and walk inside" (243). This optimistic ending echoes the ones in earlier novels, and, although this trans kid has yet to fully transition or experience sex (or really even desire), the author presents a hopeful picture of her future. Grayson is moving into her new life, and her new identity, with grace (and the right clothes).

The most recent and probably the most comic novels discussed here is Jeffrey Self's *Drag Teen* (2015). Subtitled *A Tale of Angst and Wigs*, the novel recounts the adventures of JT Barrett, who wants to get out of Clearwater, Florida, and the life his parents have planned for him as a mechanic in the family gas station, so he decides enter a drag contest in New York City for a college scholarship.

JT is gay, and he tells readers on the first page of the novel that it isn't "one of those stories about a heartwarming journey toward accepting my cursed homosexual identity. No. First of all, being gay is far from a curse. It's more like an extra order of fries at Wendy's because the lady in the window isn't paying attention when she fills your bag. It's awesome" (1). Still, this wouldn't be an adolescent novel if JT didn't have some self-esteem issues (he worries about his body), but being gay is "one of the only things I actually like about myself" (1). He also worries about being popular, and being gay doesn't help, although not in the way that readers might think: "being a gay kid in this decade of equality and anti-bullying and all that stuff that gay celebrates liked to talk about on TV had so many advantages, but one of the biggest disadvantages was that I couldn't blame why I felt like an outsider on being gay any more. Gay was in, but that didn't mean that all gay people were" (4). One of JT's challenges is to accept himself enough to believe that he is entitled to his handsome boyfriend Seth, who is "in" (21). To be perfectly clear, JT tells readers that he is "insecure about almost everything, but at least I had the freedom to be proud of being a gay person, even if I wasn't wild about the person part" (42).

JT, Seth, and their friend Heather take road trip to New York City and of course have lots of adventures on the way. All sorts of hijinks and sabotages occur during the contest: JT doesn't win, but the Dolly Parton–like famous country singer he meets on the road trip to New York City (who lent him her costumes and wigs) offers to pay for his college. His parents also show up at the pageant and accept his plans for the future, which don't include Clearwater, Florida. At the after party, Seth and JT see themselves "surrounded by dancing couples of all genders, sexualities, appearances, races, tribes" (260) and know that "that no matter how we feel, someday, this wonderful world of wonderfully weird and beautiful people, all of it, it's ours" (261). Reminiscent of *Boy Meets Boy*, *Openly Straight*, and the entire world of the Weetzie Bat novels, the ending of *Drag Teen* creates a queer community for TJ and Seth that is beyond open and accepting—it is joyful.

Drag Teen, Gracefully Grayson, Freakboy, Being Emily, I am J, Beautiful Music for Ugly Children, Almost Perfect, Parrotfish, Freak Show, and *Luna* chronicle the experiences of trans kids from 11 to 18, in big cities and small towns. Some of the kids are supported by their parents and others are rejected, some have fully transitioned (although not surgically), and others are just starting to wear the clothing of their chosen genders. Many are questioning the bifurcated nature of gender and wondering if they can remain girls with male genitals or if they can be boys who like to wear sequins and makeup. They are falling in love—and usually falling out again. They are on their way to college, or, in Grayson's case, 7th grade. They have found teachers who are supportive and suffered under those who are not. Some have been harassed (and even brutalized) by transphobic people, and all have learned that in order to grow up, they are going to have to empathize with those who love them but are troubled by their identities and to sympathize with (if not condone) the behaviors of those who fear them. Certainly these are the books that will inspire (and have inspired) trans kids like Emily and Cameron, and they point the way toward future stories that tell of trans kids who are simply part of the general rough and tumble of middle and high school and not the center of attention (good and/or bad) at all. They may also help inaugurate a world standing wherever one wants on the "gender football field" (to borrow the metaphor from *Parrotfish*) is just fine.

Five

"Difference matters"
LGBTQ Families in Young Adult Fiction

> The stories of today's adult children of gays and lesbians are compelling, but, fortunately, the more negative circumstances of their young lives—the closet their parents conceived them in and subsequently emerged from—are gradually passing away. By the time my son and his generation of kids raised by gays and lesbians—kids whose parents were never closeted—are old enough to share their stories, having queer parents won't be as remarkable as it is today, and with luck, their stories won't be as painful or harrowing—Dan Savage, "Preface," xii

> My family is as good as anyone else's. Why can't people just leave us alone?—Cristina Salat, *Living in Secret*, 141

In her foreword to a book about children growing up with gay, lesbian, and transgender parents, Col. Margarethe Cammermeyer (the highest-ranking service member to be discharged for being lesbian or gay)[1] said:

> As the lives and stories of nontraditional families are portrayed on television, and in movies and books, all our lives will become easier. We will learn to use different words to ask questions about families. One day we will be able to enjoy the uniqueness of our families without fear of rejection. It is important to remember that accepting and embracing same-sex couples and their families does not diminish the institute of heterosexual marriage or those families. Rather, it illustrates the diversity our common humanity, which is to be valued and treasured [xvi].

Col. Cammermeyer makes the important point that all lives will improve when the lives of LGBTQ families improve, as they are starting to do today. When this book was published in 2000, during the era of Don't Ask, Don't Tell and the Defense of Marriage Act (DOMA), that future had not yet been realized. In that same volume, Sophia Gould writes of the loss she felt when her mother's partner left the family: "We know what these words mean. *Mother. Daughter.* And we have ways of understanding the separation of one from the other. To that loss, we would automatically ascribe unbearable devastation; we would expect far-reading psychological consequences. Imagine if that loss had to be a secret, essentially unspeakable or haltingly revealed to a few trusted intimates" (Gould 12). The loss of a parental figure can be traumatic for children, even if the couple is heterosexual (and therefore more able to be open), but when a same-sex couple feels the need to keep the relationship a secret (as they often did until very recently), the loss is even more devastating because it can't be shared. Unfortunately, in spite of the Supreme Court's 2013 declaration that DOMA was unconstitutional (thereby paving the way for legal same-sex marriage across the United States), we are still not fully accepting of our "common humanity" when it comes to same-sex parenting.

As this book has stressed throughout, cultural products, in particular literary ones, can have a profound effect on changing hearts and minds (while the court system, one hopes, does the rest). Young adult novels, in particular, can reach the new generation and lead them toward the empathy and respect for diversity of which Cammermeyer speaks so longingly. As early as 1989, critic Virginia Wolf spoke about the dearth of novels about gay and lesbian parents and the need, at that time, for more novels celebrating (or at least exploring) same-sex parenting. Children of gay and lesbian parents, she says, "need to know that being different from the majority does not make them bad or worthless, but rather special and valuable in their own way." She also stresses that children of same-sex couples aren't the only ones who need to read books about LGBTQ families. "[B]ecause books provide readers with the experience of gay families and thereby extend their understanding," Wolf argues, "they can be one way to combat homophobia. It is, therefore, doubly an injustice that there are only a few, largely inaccessible books. They can't begin to do the job of education needed, and, indeed, they do not" (52). At the point that Wolf was writing her article, for example, there was "not one book about children of gay parents who chose to have children after they had become a couple" (57). Fortunately, this situation has changed since 1989, but there is still a need for more (and more diverse) books about same-sex parents and their children.

The non-fiction world has perhaps better explored the experiences of same-sex parents and their children. Although these books would be less likely to appeal to young readers, they do offer models of the kinds of experiences young adult writers could fold into their fiction. Jesse Green, for example, writes movingly about his experience as the partner of a gay man who adopted two children in his book *The Velveteen Father* (1999). He also places the increasing (albeit slow) acceptance of same-sex parents in a historical context. The opening of doors to gay and lesbians adopting children, he points out, sadly, was prompted by "no bright force ... but a dark one: desperation" (14) caused by the rise in crack use and AIDS in the early 1980s, which led to an overloaded child protective services system. In spite of this desperate need for adoptive parents, gay men still struggled against the homophobic perception that they might be pedophiles (34). In addition, the AIDS epidemic's focus on death left little energy in the gay community for "those few men who sought any opportunity to talk—moonily, sunnily—about birth" (35). As if that wasn't challenging enough to any prospective gay parents, many in the community accused those who wanted to adopt of living a false heteronormative dream (51). The straight world saw gay men seeking to adopt as predators; the gay world saw them as unrealistic dreamers.

Nevertheless, Green asserts that love for his partner's children "made me real" (99):

> Adulthood becomes a tricky concept for those who don't procreate, or who wait longer and longer to do so. For gay men especially—but more and more heterosexual women, too—the question of what forms a mature identity has been left, since the first days of the sexual revolution, unanswered. And often unasked [104].

Gay men (and anyone, for that matter, who doesn't have children when young) face the unanswered and often unasked question of whether or not they are truly adult. Having (or adopting) children legitimizes the parents as grown-ups—and thus could be seen as an essentially selfish act.

When their baby arrives, however, most of Green and his partner's concerns fade. Green finds that the baby has "an affectional village [of caretakers, and 'uncles,' friends and family] that may have seemed chaotic from the outside but was a blessing from within" (137). When taking their son out, Green notices to his delight (but also somewhat to his chagrin) that "fatherhood trumps gayness," and that he and his partner begin to experience "kindly attention" that was nearly unknown for

Five. "Difference matters"

gay men. "[I]t was as if a secret parallel world of heterosexual privilege and bonhomie was suddenly opened" to him (155), he comments.

This acceptance comes at a price, however. Although they were "no longer gay to straight people, we were no longer gay to most gay people, either" (159), Green says. He notices that he and his partner (and their baby) are not particularly welcome at the gay (and usually child-free) social events that they had attended in the past. Parenthood also reveals new insights about sexuality—this time their child's sexuality. When their son develops a crush on a female character on Sesame Street, Green says that he and his partner were proud of his apparent heterosexuality "because it proves that he is not embarrassed to exactly who he is, even in a home that does not model the specific kind of passion he feels. Which is more than can be said for the millions of kids, both gay and straight, who grow up in homes that model no passion at all" (205). As gay men who have had to fight for the right to love whomever they choose, both Green and his partner can model *both* passion and tolerance.

The final lesson of this book is that gay parents are really no more "abnormal" than the rest of American society. At the time the book was written, fewer than half of American families consisted of straight, same-race biological parents, which means "more of us are alternative than not" (222), and the number of "traditional" families has surely decreased since then. Finally, Green issues a call to gay men:

> [T]o the extent gay men have abandoned younger people, whether because of the pain of their own youths or the intimidation of bigots, I hope they have the nerve to return. Not in the way they returned to the gym—with a vengeance—but the way they returned from their long years of internal exile to the crowded field of the civic realm. What did all those demonstrations demonstrate if not connectedness? [233].

Just as gay men return to childhood—and to children—so do the writers of fiction for children and young adults need to embrace LGBTQ parents and demonstrate the "connectedness" that Green both feels and encourages in others.

More sarcastic and profane than *The Velveteen Father* (but as heartfelt), Dan Savage's *The Kid*, also published in 1999, tells the story of Savage and his boyfriend's open adoption of a son. Like Green, Savage never assumed when he came out in 1980 that he would be a parent: "After all, gay men didn't have families—we were a threat to families" (22).

Although at first Savage feels different from the straight couples trying to adopt because of infertility, he notices that their shame about their inability to produce biological children mimicked the shame many gay men feel about their sexuality: "[N]o one can spend a lifetime in the closet. Now we all had some common ground" (26). Mirroring Green's insight, Savage admits that the reason he wanted a child, is "about self-fulfillment. Kids are a self-actualization project for the parents involved.... Something for grownups to do, a pastime, a hobby" (34). Neither he nor his partner Terry wanted "to be anybody's forgotten old gay uncles. Kids wouldn't keep us young, but they would keep us relevant, something other hobbies wouldn't do" (35). As well as keeping them "relevant," being parents could be seen as a political act (36). Finally, choosing to become adoptive parents, Savage argues, might make them more thoughtful and grateful than many biological parents:

> Since gay men and lesbians don't have children by accident—it's hard to get drunk one night and do an adoption, or slip and fall into the stirrups at an artificial insemination clinic—all our kids are wanted kids, planned for and anticipated. All parenting experts agree that a wanted child is usually a loved child, and a loved child is a well-looked-after child [59].

Although they were more likely to be good parents than many heterosexual couples, disapproval came from a variety of places. In ways similar to what Green describes, Savage says that a gay academic friend accused him of "adopting a 'heteronormative' lifestyle, and a gay Communist accused me of selling out" (64). On the other hand, what the conservative right fears, Savage says, is not that gay dads will be bad parents or turn their children gay (or sexually abuse them) but that they'll be *good* parents. Echoing Cammermeyer, Savage notes that "once straights have seen boring gay parents at a PTA meeting bitching about class size and school uniforms ... we're not going to seem so scary anymore, even if (like a lot of straights) we do have old bondage equipment in our basements" (183). Gay parents start looking like boring (and sometimes flawed) straight parents. Thus, both Green and Savage's books chronicle the struggles—and the joys—of becoming parents as gay men, but they also insist on the common ground between parents of all races, sexualities, nationalities, and religions. Novelists writing about their experiences with LGBTQ parenting, it is hoped, would do the same.

Although Savage and Green's books speak to the struggles and joys of gay parenting, not much has been written expressly for young people about LGBTQ people becoming parents. Although the novels discussed in this chapter (from 1988 to today) tell stories about gay and lesbian families, there are still no books about LGBTQ couples *starting* families, although the scenarios developed in earlier chapters do imply that the adolescents beginning relationships will, eventually, have families of their own. It is possible, too, that the lives of LGBTQ parents are less interesting to adolescents (after all, an adolescent protagonist is a hallmark of YA fiction), but most LGBTQ young adult books about same-sex families either have the gay or lesbian character be a second-level relative (like an uncle), show the sexuality of the parent as a conflict to the family, reveal the sexuality of the parents after the child is an adolescent, or expose the adolescent to an already-existing family with same-sex parents. The story of trans parents has yet to be written.

A delightful early book featuring gay family members, *The Arizona Kid* by Ron Koertge (1988), focuses on a boy's relationship with his gay uncle. The novel, according to Lobban and Clyde, has "believable characters, [a] fast pace, hysterically funny situations, and lighthearted treatment of serious themes." Readers have enjoyed, they say, "Billy's self-deprecatory humor, open-mindedness about differences, and desire to be a supportive romantic partner" for his girlfriend. Billy's gay uncle Wes, they continue, "is a warm person who talks openly with his nephew about feelings, relationships, problems, and safe sex" (40). Although the gay uncle might be seen as a literary cliché, Koertge treats his character (and his relationship with his nephew) with respect and subtlety.

As the novel opens, main character Billy Kennedy, 16, goes to Tucson to spend the summer with his uncle Wes. He finds work at a racetrack and falls in love with an exercise girl, Cara Mae, clearly establishing his heterosexuality (and thereby, one assumes, his appeal to straight readers). His uncle is very good looking, and Billy says it "really blew me away," that while he could have any woman he wanted, his uncle isn't interested (6). He finds it "unbelievable" that his uncle likes men and says that the idea of men kissing "made my stomach feel funny" (17). This incredulity about "normal" seeming people who are nevertheless homosexual is a fairly typical response for characters in young adult fiction, as is the discomfort that Billy feels. Still, he's Billy enjoys Wes's company, although he realizes that he is "going somewhere new to live with somebody who was really different from me" (17). He also thinks his classmates back home wouldn't understand and isn't sure how to talk about his uncle being gay at first, especially since his father has told him to "be cool about it" (19). Having a straight parent support a homosexual adult and encourage his child to do the same is relatively unusual, especially in such an early novel.

In spite of his father's tolerance, Billy isn't sure how people back home would respond to Wes. His uncle is a minor celebrity in Tucson for his gay rights activism, while in Billy's hometown, "most people thought gay men should go away and hide, and here my uncle got his picture in the paper" (59). Cara Mae asks him what it's like living with a gay man, and Billy tells her it's "like living with anybody else, I guess," and he notes that after a few weeks it no longer feels "funny" (152). The plot centers on Billy's life at the race track and a bet the kids make about a horse (which they win) and the romance between Billy and Cara Mae (and Billy's purchase of a cowboy hat and boots). In one dramatic moment, his uncle loses a friend to AIDS and gets drunk, but for most of the novel he tends to his business, has parties with both gay and straight people, volunteers at an AIDS hotline, and lives a fairly conventional life. At the same time the novel stresses the pervasiveness of homophobia (especially in small towns), it insists on the normality of Billy's life with his uncle.

As Billy gets ready to head home, his uncle tells him that he'll "pat you so heartily ... that we'll look like two he-men and not one straight teenager and one forty-year-old sissy" (282). Billy replies that he doesn't care about that, showing that Billy has moved on from feeling "funny" at even the thought of same-sex attraction to being comfortable hugging his "sissy" gay uncle. However, this scene acknowledges the need to acquiesce to the culture's generalized homophobia that forces them to pretend to be "two he-men." After (literally and metaphorically) embracing his uncle, Billy takes the train home and thinks that he's "really on my way" (283). Sounding much like almost every other young adult protagonist, Billy is confident that his future is beginning, and he realizes that his experiences in the novel taught him much about the complexities of life.

Published a year after *The Arizona Kid*, *Jack* (1989), by A. M. Holmes, has been lauded by the critics. According to Lobban and Clyde, the novel is "a rich, leisurely book, in which sexuality, as it is in life, is only one part. It is also funny and touching and life-affirming" (71). Day says that the book "has been praised for its humor, panache, and charm,"

Five. "Difference matters"

and she notes that other critics have called the protagonist "a doggedly funny, endearing, and attractive human being." She also comments that Jack's father is "a multidimensional person who is trying to do his best to be a good parent" (36). Although this novel treats the parent's sexuality as the primary crisis for the protagonist, it does show the main character learning to accept both his father's new life and his parents' divorce.

Jack is 15 when the novel opens, looking backward on his relatively short life. His father moved out when he was 11 without an explanation, and Jack feels a profound void:

> When you're a kid and you've got a father who reminds you of Superman, who seems like he can do anything, a father who's the kind of guy that climbs up onto the roof to rescue your dweeb GI Joe when it gets stuck up there during some idiotic experiment, and then one day he's gone, totally disappeared into a million green plastic garbage bags, no explanations offered, nothing anyone says later makes a bit of difference [9].

In part because he doesn't understand the reasons behind his father's departure, Jack is convinced that nothing can make things better—and they are about to get much worse. Trying to prepare the ground for his coming out, Jack's father tells him that you can love all kinds of people: "It's not something you can control, although you can try," he says. "It just happens.... Love doesn't have limits" (16). When shortly after he tells him he's gay, while they are out in a rowboat, Jack feels "sick" when he hears: "I looked out at the water. Dragonflies were hovering over the scum I wanted to get up, to run, but thanks to my dad, we were in the middle of a goddamned lake. I thought I was going to throw up" (20). Afterward, he sits in his room, "trying to figure out how my father could be queer. I mean, historically, queers are not fathers" (21). In a way, Jack is right—"queers are not fathers" in the media or in Jack's personal experience, but readers know that nothing physiological prevents a gay man from fathering a child with a women. In the 1990s, though, as Green and Savage's books remind us, very few gay men were parenting children in openly same-sex relationships.

His father's revelation leads Jack to what should now appear to readers of this study a rather predictable worry about whether or not he might be gay. He thinks he'd kill himself if he was "queer," and he wishes that "a bolt of lightning or something would crash through the window and stab me in the chest, just so I wouldn't have to deal with this anymore" (30). No child likes to think about his or her parents' sexuality, and, in Jack's case, his father's being gay causes him to question his own identity as well as feel as if he'd rather be struck dead than having to deal with a gay father.

Not surprisingly, it takes Jack awhile to adjust, but when some kids write the word "faggot" on his school locker, he gets a glimmer of empathy for his father's situation: "I thought about my dad. I wonder if people did or said horrible things to him on account of being gay. I mean, whoever wrote *faggot* on my locker had gone out of their way to rub my wrong side, but what if it was true? What if I was a faggot, then how would I feel?" (66). This is a key moment in LGBTQ fiction for young adults: when the straight protagonist begins to understand viscerally the ramifications of homophobia. The straight teen thus models empathetic responses for other straight readers.

School teaches Jack other lessons as well. When Jack tells his homophobic friend Max that his and his soon-to-be girlfriend Maggie's fathers are gay, Jack insists that "you can't *make* a person queer. They either are or they aren't" (71), showing that he has internalized at least part of his father's message about homosexuality. When Jack's basketball coach calls the boys on the team "faggots," in a misguided attempt to motivate them, Jack thinks that the coach is a "joke," who could easily be beaten by his very athletic father in basketball, and he wonders "what incredible idiot stands in a junior-high gym and tells twenty guys that if they don't kill, they're faggots. And you wonder why some people grow up and become mass murderers and stuff" (91). Here Jack appears to understand that homosexuality and athletic prowess are not mutually exclusive and that the relentless homophobia and misogyny of many high school coaches is at best deluded and, at worst, potentially dangerous.

As they are wont to do in novels, various plot elements ensue. Jack severely sprains his ankle playing basketball, he begins driver training, and he and Maggie start to date. On a trip of a family farm, Jack's friend Max's parents fight (his father hits his mother) and split up, and Jack sees how a marriage can fall apart in more dangerous ways than his parents' did. Jack's father comes to pick him when he returns from the farm, and as he and his father reconcile, and his father's sexuality begins to matter less than his dad's reliability in a crisis (74). The now-extended family (including his father and his boyfriend, Bob, his mother and her boyfriend, Max, and Maggie) has a party for Jack's 16th birthday. Afterward, he thinks:

Five. "Difference matters"

> [W]hatever he or any of them were or weren't didn't really have anything to do with me. We were all separate. I'd only wished I'd known it a couple of years ago. I'm Jack, that's all. I'm Jack, just Jack out there by myself. And I know it sounds stupid and obvious and all that, but I didn't really understand it until just then, and even then I wasn't sure I understood it completely [215].

This is a significant realization (even it is as yet imperfectly understood): the lives of parents and the lives of their children are separate. Jack can become whoever he wants to be; having divorced parents, even having gay parents, makes very little difference in his future.

At the end of the novel, Jack knows he's attached to all the people in his life, but "more than anything I was plain Jack, no strings attached' (218). Playing basketball at the end of the novel, he thinks 'I was Fast Jack, and I knew I would be okay, permanently. Right there on the basketball court, I knew I would make it'" (220). It is significant that several aspects of Jack's life are intertwined here: his love of basketball, his love of his parents, and his growing confidence in his own identity. Even 25 years after it was written, *Jack* has an important message for young people—gay and straight—about their own imperfect (but hopefully loving) families: a family stands by you in good times and in bad and "love has no limits."

Unlike *Jack* and *The Arizona Kid*, *Living in Secret* (1993) by Christina Salat features a female protagonist and a lesbian mother. Main character Amelia, Lobban and Clyde say, "is a strong hero, and the novel eschews sentimentality for emotional honesty. The characters are real and engaging, and the plot intriguing" (154). This relatively early novel about lesbian parents, unfortunately, sees the lesbianism as a direct threat to the family, although it accurately reflects the legal and societal realities of its time. LGBTQ parents in the 1990s were often denied custodial rights and considered to be unfit parents.

Consequently, *Living in Secret* is in many ways a thriller—with secrets, suspense, and surprising conclusions. At the beginning of the novel, Amelia (also known as Amy and later as Julie) has run away with her mother and her mother's girlfriend to San Francisco. She is almost 12 when the novel starts, which, along with Melanin Sun (who will be discussed later), makes her one of the younger characters in this chapter. They have to keep her identity a secret, so she can't go to school, but she makes a few friends, although she becomes increasingly distressed about having to keep secrets. She also blames her mother for her newly restrictive lifestyle, which includes some amount of economic distress. For example, Amelia is jealous of her friend Elizabeth because of her "TV-show family," which she thinks she would have if her parents had stayed together (65).

She also begins to become aware of a LGBTQ community that is larger and more accepting than she had previously imagined. At one point in the novel, Amelia and her mothers go to a New Year's Eve party that is "full of people dancing. I notice men are dancing with men, and women are dancing with women [and men and women dancing together].... Nobody seems to mind anyone else. I am amazed. I didn't know gay people and straight people ever hung out together" (94). As with Jack, readers are encouraged to be "amazed" with Amelia and see that gay men and lesbians are not much different from other people at a New Year's Eve party.

Still, all is far from perfect. Like Jack, Amelia worries that she might also be a lesbian. Her mother tells her that she can be whoever she wants to be (96), and Janey tells her mother that she is giving Amelia the freedom to be herself (98). Also like Jack, Amelia makes an equation (as do other characters in later novels) between racism and homophobia (her friend Elizabeth is black): "It's kind of the same as being gay, I think.... It's not fair that people hate each other for being different. Nobody's exactly the same as anyone else" (105–06). However, Elizabeth's father says that he doesn't think homosexuals should fight for equality, reflecting the conflict at the time between LGBTQ communities and people of color: "I wish those people would stop taking steam from the real battle for equality.... This world needs *racial* equality. If homosexuals want to sleep together, fine, let them sleep together. They don't deserve special privileges for that" (120). This, of course, was (and, to a certain extent, still is) a common sentiment from the African American community, which wants to confine the struggle for civil rights to matters of race.

In addition, Elizabeth and Amelia get into a fight while playing Life (where players pretend to attend school, get jobs, choose mates, have children), because Amelia chooses to put a pink peg (indicating the imaginary spouse's gender) in her car, implying that she is marrying a girl (126). As a result, Amelia worries that it might be "weird" for girls to marry girls (128). Another girl, Kasha, who has two dads (and a mother and stepdad), helps Amelia realize that she doesn't need to be embarrassed by her unconventional family (133), but shortly after that, Amelia tells her mother that she's tired of being different (138). This scenario reflects the situation in *Jack*, which also featured a homophobic friend and another whose parents were gay. In such novels, the protagonist has the opportunity to educate the homophobes and to model the acceptance seen in the lives of the more tolerant friends. The alchemy is that once readers can begin to identify with kids in novels who have LGBTQ parents, they can transfer that empathy toward LGBTQ people in their own lives.

This novel, however, is realistic about the obstacles Amelia and her new family face in the outside world. On a trip to Chinatown, for example, some tourists comment negatively on Amelia's mother and Janey holding hands. Amelia is first embarrassed, then angry: "I'm tired of everyone pushing us around making us run away and be scared just because they think we're not a regular family. There are all kinds of families ... not just one kind that is the right kind to have!" (141). Some good comes out of this difficult situation, though, when Amelia finally tells Elizabeth about her mother and Janey. "There's no point in having best friends if you can't tell them the truth about something that's a big part of your life" (148), she thinks. In spite of their conflict over Life and her father's political objections to LGBTQ rights, Elizabeth accepts the news calmly. Shortly afterward, Amelia has a dream in which her mother and Janey get married, with her father's approval (154). This, of course, would have been recognized as only a dream in 1993, even in San Francisco.

At this relatively peaceful point, though, her father shows up and drags her back to Connecticut, telling her that she going to have a "real family now." Amelia becomes angry and insists that she already has a "real" family (165). Her father tells her not to let her friends know about her mother because they might tease her, but Amelia disagrees: "Real friends don't make fun of each other. I'm not ashamed of my mother. So, she's different, so what? At least she's not fake like you, I think. And neither am I" (173). This, of course, sounds very much like typical teenage mouthiness and the kind of manipulation that children of divorced parents often indulge in, but the stakes are high here, as Amelia is in danger of never seeing her mother and Janey again.

In spite of being returned to her father's more conventional life, the ending is hopeful, as is typical for young adult novels. Her mother and Janey write to her, and they suggest that they will take the custody ruling to court, if Amelia wants it. "Now I know things can change, because they do change all the time," Amelia thinks. She imagines going to court and living back with her mother and Janey, where they will save all the letters of support they receive and "burn the rest of the letters and our fake ID's, in a welcome marshmallow roast for me" (183). Amelia imagines a future where lesbians will be allowed to parent children and where Janey and her mother might get married. This book is probably the most dated of the novels about LGBTQ families and one whose plot might (thankfully) seem rather dramatic and strange today, but it certainly reflected an unfortunate reality at that time.

From the Notebooks of Melanin Sun (1995) by Jacqueline Woodson feels more contemporary than *Living in Secret*, although the sexuality of the parent (also the mother) still represents the primary crisis in the novel. Nevertheless, this work combines both sexual and racial conflicts in a way that still seems fresh today. Lobban and Clyde call it "lyrical" and praise the way the novelist reconciles these conflicts of race, class, and sexuality (210). Day says that Woodson has written a novel "that encourages readers to push beyond walls of hatred, secrets, and lies to find the common bonds that connect us all" (59). Although some readers might find this rather evaluation rather sanguine, Woodson does offer hints at what might allow readers to cross those prickly and seemingly insurmountable boundaries.

Protagonist Melanin Sun, whose name is a celebration of his dark skin color, is "almost fourteen" when the novel opens (2). He lives with his mother, and they have no contact with his father. Because of his family situation, the dark color of his skin (his mother is lighter), and because he is "on the quiet side" (2), Melanin feels that he's "on the outside of things," and he opines that "difference matters" (3). In spite of their external differences (or perhaps because of them) Melanin and his mother share a pair of pierced earrings (she wears hers in her nose). He knows this might seem "strange" to others, but his mother says that all that matters is "what feels right to us" (13). From the beginning of the novel, readers are encouraged to respect difference.

Even before he knows that his mother is attracted to women, Melanin is quite concerned about his own sexuality. He worries that collecting stamps, which he enjoys, might be "faggy," but he says he doesn't care. He also believes that there are "two kinds" of "faggy," one, like

Five. "Difference matters"

Melanin, "that really isn't super macho and has notebooks to write stuff down in," and the other, which is the "really messed up kind. That kind actually wanted to be with other guys the way I get to feeling when Angie comes around. That kind made me want to puke every time I thought about it—which wasn't a lot" (19). Fears of being perceived as gay (even though he clearly has sexual feelings for a girl) hem Melanin in and cause him to feel guilty about his love of stamp collecting and writing. Carefully policing his sexuality comes at a high cost—one that it will prove impossible to sustain over time.

Soon after this, Mom's new "friend" Kristin comes to dinner. She is the first white person to come into their world, and Melanin is not happy. He thinks there is "[n]o use for them in this neighborhood. This was *our* place—people of color together in harmony away from all of *their* hatred and racism. I didn't dislike white people, I just didn't think of them" (30). Like many people, Melanin feels safer in a space filled with others like him, and he resents Kristin's incursion into it. "White, before Kristin, didn't matter at all," he says (75). By making Kristin white and lesbian, Woodson has opened the novel to discussions of both race and sexuality.

Interestingly, after his mother tells him about her relationship with Kristin, there is a reference to *Jack*, which Melanin has read. Melanin remembers that when Jack's father told him he was gay, he was "stuck with this big chunk of info and no way back to shore" (54). Melanin, too, feels like "bobbing and gasping, then going under" (55). He worries, as did Jack and Amelia, that his mother's sexuality would somehow transfer to him: "If she was a dyke, then what did that make me?" Also like Jack, Melanin is trapped (not in a boat but in a car) when his mother tells him, and wants to scream that he's not a "faggot," jump out of the car, and get "hit by the biggest thing coming" (57). He hates his mother and simultaneously wants to hold her while she's crying (58), and he begs her not to "be a dyke" (59). He avoids his mother for weeks and worries "maybe Mama hated men. Maybe she hated me" (62). Melanin also worries about how his friends will respond. He fears that Angie "would run screaming if she knew. Screaming, screaming, back to her big, big family. Back to her normal life" (93). Of course, his friends do find out, and he fights with one, but another friend says "what goes on with your mother doesn't have to do with anybody else, right?" (109). Similar threads run through the three novels discussed so far: friends who are judgmental and who are supportive, fears about sexual "contamination" from the gay or lesbian parent, and difficulties accepting the parent's sexuality.

As in the other two novels with gay and lesbian parents, Melanin and his mother reconcile, and Kristin joins their life. Mel and Kristin start talking, and "something melted" inside of him, "some small closed-up space for Kirstin started opening, growing, filling itself in. Like an eclipse—the way the moon rushes out to cover up the sun" (125). Melanin and his mother are "[g]roping for some sort of light on the other side of all of this. Something that would guide us somewhere, help us find our way back to each other," but he is confident that they will find it (126).

The ending of the novel is reminiscent of the other works discussed so far in this chapter (and in the rest of the book). Melanin thinks, "I didn't know what would happy tomorrow or the next day or the next.... I didn't know if it would every stop mattering what people thought. But I was sure of mama, sure of my notebooks. And for the quickest moment, walking backwards against the sun, I was sure of me. Maybe that's all that matters" (126). Like Jack is sure of his basketball skill, Billy knows that he can fend for himself (and find a girlfriend), and Amelia has faith she'll be able to spend time with her mother and Janey again, Melanin knows his mother will always be there for him, that he is a writer, and that he can also depend on himself.

Unlike the young adult novels about LGBTQ families written in the 1990s, works from the 2000s treat gay and lesbian parents less *the* problem and more of one problem among many (and often not the most important one). The coming out of the parents has usually already happened, and, for the most part, the young protagonists take the situation in stride. However, the parents' sexuality still causes the protagonists to question their own identities and to worry about how they will be perceived by their peers (especially their straight love interests). They also try to appeal more directly to a wider audience of gay and straight, male and female readers.

Jon Ripslinger's *How I Fell in Love and Learned to Shoot Free Throws* (2003), although it features a young woman with two mothers, is clearly designed for the heterosexual male reader. From its straight male protagonist, Danny, to the tattooed bicep on the cover to the sports-oriented title, to the author's insistence (on the back cover) on his marriage to a

Five. "Difference matters"

woman and six children, the book is intended for that often-elusive reluctant reader. The novel even opens with the main character eyeing the blonde "Stone Angel" as she plays basketball. Angel, who offers to help Danny with his free throws, is hesitant to let him into her life, and the people around him gossip about Angel's mother and her connection to a woman who "looks like a dyke" (57). Eventually, Angel tells him that her mother is in a relationship with a woman and defends her secrecy, saying, "Try being a sixth grader and having your classmates laugh at you at recess because one of them saw your mom and her lover holding hands at the grocery store.... Wait until your best friend gets mad and calls you a faggot and tells your worst secret to everyone else.... My whole life, all I've wanted is just to be thought of as normal" (91). Danny helpfully (and self-interestedly) offers to help her squelch rumors about her sexuality by becoming her boyfriend and displaying enough hetero affection to defeat all the gossip (94). Angel turns down that offer and says they can see each other but only in secret, telling him that "the fewer people I'm close to, the fewer people who know me, the better," even though that is not what her mother and girlfriend want for her (97).

However, Danny comes out of the closet Angel has placed them in fairly quickly by telling his friend and father about both his relationship with Angel and her mother's sexuality. Danny's dad (who already knew about Angel's mother but kept it from Danny) tells him to see someone else, as dating Angel "might put her in contact with a lot of weirdo fags and their lifestyle, which I'd rather not have you be a part of" (109). When that doesn't seem to work, he warns him that when kids find out they can be "ferocious. Worse than sharks. That's why teachers keep their mouths shut about that stuff," but then he relents and asks Danny to bring Angel by the house (113). Believing that Angel is "hiding behind a wall" and trapping him there as well (119), Danny talks to Angel's mother, and they agree that she should tell the truth (131). Eventually, the kids at school find out and determine that Angel must be gay because her mother is (151). Danny supports her and, at the end, they kiss on the basketball court for everyone to see (170). Although this novel speaks clearly for the need to tell the truth, the assertive heterosexuality at the end seems like a less-than-optimal message for readers, although, if the target audience is kept in mind, Danny's acceptance of Angel's family does represent progress.

The Saints of Augustine, by P.E. Ryan (2007) broadens its appeal to both straight and gay male readers. It is the story of Charlie and Sam, male best friends who stopped speaking a year before because Sam, in the throes of an unrequited crush on straight Charlie, almost kissed him (and fled in terror of ruining their relationship). Sam's father has moved out to live with his male lover, and his mother has taken up with a homophobic know-it-all whom Sam can't stand. Charlie is coping with his own problems—a father who is depressed and drinking heavily and an unpaid debt to a violent pot dealer. This novel is especially interesting because it features both a gay male protagonist and gay parents.

At first, Sam couldn't understand why his father wanted to "start a whole new life" with David, although he recognizes that his father is happy and relaxed "for the first time in Sam couldn't remember how long" (23). As he begins to figure out the real reason for his father's departure, Sam worries about how people might react and, even more about why he, too, was interested in boys. "It was like his dad had done something wrong, and now Sam wanted to venture into that same territory, which would only upset everyone, and everything, all over again" (26). He wonders, "How would people react if they knew that not only was Sam Findley's dad a full-fledged homo, but that Sam himself was a homo in the making?" (27). This is a new twist on the connection between teens and their parents' sexuality. Sam isn't worried that his father will "turn" him gay, but that his being gay will somehow cause even more trouble and disruption in his family.

This is not the only turmoil in Sam's life, however. When his father leaves with David for London and the trip is extended several more months, Sam feels that his father's being gay is what is keeping them apart, although he acknowledges that his father hasn't stopped being his father—"he was just away" (178). Sam is also lonely because his mother is involved with her boyfriend and seems to disapprove of homosexuality (probably fueled by resentment at her estranged husband). Because of his parents' absence—actual and emotional—Sam is reluctant to share his own secrets.

Unable to stay in the closet, Sam eventually comes out to Charlie, who takes the news surprisingly well and even kisses Sam at one point to relieve the tension between them. He tells Sam that having a gay father could actually be seen as an advantage to a gay kid: "How many gay guys have a gay dad they can talk to—you know, just to … sound things out?

Five. "Difference matters"

It's like finding out you're an alien, and then finding out your dad's an alien, too" (274). The novel ends with Sam and his mother reconciling and Sam admitting his sexuality and interest in Justin. Although the ending of the novel could be seen as happy (or at least encouraging openness about sexuality), non-normative sexuality remains the primary conflict.

Far less serious than *The Saints of Augustine* and other books previously discussed, Amy Brownwen Zemser's *Dear Julia* (2008) is a zany look at French cuisine (à la Julia Child), high school drama, trying to find one's true talent, costuming, burglary, feminism, cooking competitions, and, incidentally, lesbian moms. Main character Elaine has always wanted to be a chef, although she's too shy to admit this to anyone other than her family (which consists of a yoga-practicing, stay-at-home dad, six brothers—one who's trans—and a congresswoman mom who disapproves of women slaving in the kitchen). She finds an unlikely best friend in the outrageous actor-singer-dancer-television producer Lucida Sans (not her real name). Lucida has two moms, who end up being far more supportive of Elaine's dreams than her mother. Although Lucida feels that she needs to explain the "unusual" nature of her family to Elaine before she meets Mrs. Fischberger One and Two, this is quickly resolved with no more comment.

Lucida teaches Elaine that it's fun to dress up in order "to imagine what it would be like to be somebody else" (113), and she encourages her to take changes, to believe in herself, and, finally, to take part in a cooking contest. Lucida also convinces her that Elaine's mother's prejudice against "women's work" in the kitchen is crazy. "I thought having two mothers was nutty. Moms would be thrilled if I was good at anything, practically. Your mother should be proud" (202). Of course, Elaine wins the contest (and has a surprise visit with Julia Child), heads off to college, and her mother reconciles herself to her daughter's future plans. The most interesting thing about this book is that Lucida's two moms are no more eccentric than any other the large cast of characters, and certainly far less odd than their straight daughter. The novel has no drama about keeping secrets or feeling betrayed or embarrassed by parents' sexuality—and no insistence on the writer's part of her own straight "credentials." The plot centers on a girl trying to find a way to succeed at her chosen vocation and teaching her family (especially her mother) to trust her daughter's instincts—both in the kitchen and about her future.

Stealing Parker, by Miranda Kenneally (2012), is not nearly as lighthearted as *Dear Julia*, but unlike several of the other books in this chapter, main character Parker is not interested in keeping her gay parent(s) secret, although she isn't comfortable with the fact. Parker tells readers on the first page of her story that she's given up softball (and all of its paraphernalia) when her mother "announced she's a lesbian and ran off with her friend who was more than a friend" (1). She has also lost 30 pounds, started paying more attention to her looks, and fooling around with as many guys as necessary to prove that she's not a lesbian. Softball, of course, had to go because of its association with strong, aggressive, athletic (and therefore lesbian) women. Parker may acknowledge her gay mother, but she begins the novel weighed down by homophobia—her own and others.'

For example, the fundamentalist Christian church her father insists she attend is, not surprisingly, unsupportive of both her mother's lesbianism and Parker's possible "contamination" as a result of it. Everyone gives Parker's family "funny looks on Sundays during coffee time" (12) and is convinced that Parker might turn out like her mother: "A lesbian. A Sinner" (13). "Apparently," Parker thinks, "'love thy neighbor' changes to 'judge thy neighbor' if your family doesn't follow the church playbook" (14). She's only seen her mother twice since she left and hasn't returned her calls or emails, thinking that if people see her with her mother "it'll wreck my life even more." Parker says her mother "ruined my family" and wonders, "Why did God let this happen to me?" (30). Parker tells her (probably gay) best friend Drew that it doesn't bother her that her mother's gay. "I just wish my family was still together" (52). Throughout the novel, Parker writes letters to God, which she destroys, that try to find explanations for her dilemmas, and for most of the story she is burdened by the homophobia of evangelical Christianity.

In order to reconnect with sports, which she loves and misses, Parker offers to serve as the boys' baseball team's manager, and she starts a disastrous secret relationship with the assistant coach, Brian, while also finding herself attracted to a boy at school, Will. Feeling ashamed for her relationship with Brian and angry at the way he treats her, she thinks "none of this ever would have happened if Mom were here. She would've noticed me sneaking out of the house late at night. She would have spotted the small bruise on my collarbone where Brian kissed me too hard. She would've noticed the condoms in my purse, the ones I brought just in case" (194–95). At this point in the novel, Parker is trying hard to find ways to blame her mother's lesbianism for her own troubles, although it is more likely her mother's absence that is the problem.

Inevitably, she is caught with Brian, and Will feels betrayed and breaks up with her. At this dark point in the novel, Parker finally talks to her mother and apologizes for not calling (and, implicitly for judging her and not caring about her feelings) (208). Her mother tells her that God loves them both (209) and that she has to think about what *she* needs (211). Parker returns to the softball team at the end of the novel, and Will and Parker reconcile. This novel is unique among the works discussed here as it most directly engages church-sanctioned homophobia and raises the issue of straight sexual predators. Although it ends on a resolutely heteronormative note, it also confirms the fitness of lesbian parents and the need for honesty.

Instead of sports, Jessica Verdi's *My Life After Now* (2013) centers around a high school drama club and the usual hetero-relationship angst of many teen novels, along with a production of *Romeo and Juliet*. Main character Lucy has two dads—"the only two gay men in the world who knew nothing about theater"—but who were also "the only parents of anyone I knew who were not only still together, but actually still in love" (10). Lucy is the result of her biological father's college flirtation with heterosexuality; her other father adopted her. Lucy's biological mother (who has an ongoing history of drug abuse) is a mostly indifferent and usually absent parent, who comes to live with Lucy and her dads when she finds herself pregnant again. This novel, like *Dear Julia*, begins with gay parents already out of the closet and successfully parenting their children.

Lucy tells her new friend (and potential boyfriend) Evan that she has two dads, and she admires his equanimity and his "brazenness" for asking her what it was like. People in her "pretty liberal" town were welcoming but rarely asked "direct gay-parent-related questions." Evan, on the other hand, "learned of my unconventional family all of two minute ago and already he was asking questions. It was refreshing" (45). Homophobia is still assumed to be the norm in this novel, but the gay-parent revelation is this time met with curiosity, not judgment.

In another deviation from many earlier gay problem novels for young adults, the gay character doesn't get AIDS, but Lucy does, from a drunken one-night stand (and unprotected sex), even though her father "lived through the New York gay club scene in the nineties" and was upfront about sexuality and protection against STIs (62). Lucy hesitates to tell her fathers because she's afraid they will be mad at her, and when she does tell Evan, he reacts badly, worrying that he may have caught AIDS from kissing her. She eventually does tell her parents and begins going to a support group and gets on medication, although she has a crisis when she cuts herself during a rehearsal of a sword fighting scene, and Evan covers for her, keeping her secret, which is eventually revealed by her drama class nemesis. The novel ends with the production of the play, where she reconciles with Evan and says that she is "absolutely positive" that life isn't that bad (286). Although the safe-sex message is a helpful one, and the two gay dads are accepted as a simple fact of life, one wonders why it was necessary to inflict AIDS on the main character, almost as a return of the repressed punishment for tolerating homosexual parents.

A similar situation unfolds in *Skyscraping* by Cordelia Jensen (2015). Although its format is somewhat unconventional—it is a novel in verse told in the first person by Miranda "Mira" Steward—it uses a fairly traditional problem-novel plot. Set in 1993, and loosely based on Jensen's own experiences, the novel opens with Mira discovering that her father, whom she will soon find out has AIDS, is having a love affair with his male graduate student, James, while still living in an open relationship with Miranda's mother. When Mira discovers them together, she's heartbroken, saying the "the constellation of a family/can shift shape/in seconds" (29). Mira says that the "earth has shifted" (39), that she is "shattered" (41), wonders what she would tell her friends (42). Her father tells her that her parents have "arranged it this way, out of love," but Mira thinks that her family is "lost wandering/in the dark" (46). She wonders, "If your past is a lie, what happens to your future?" (49). As the story moves from fall to winter, Mira thinks that "Icy air coats/our apartment,/the space between me/and my family./Insides matching outsides" (93). Mira believes that she "can't be part of a family/that's built on lies" and that as they try to pull her closer, she's "already/drifted/away" (111). Throughout this, Mira loses her place as yearbook editor, falls out with her college boyfriend, who tells her that AIDS is a "deserved disease" (210), and postpones applying to colleges.

Eventually, as her father begins to fail, her family (which now includes James) comes together. Mira wonders if a family is "something stable,/yet always changing,/because the people inside it are" (232). She also learns "How silence/breeds secrecy, shame./How I hurt myself/being silent./How silence can ruin/lives" (275). In further steps toward reintegration of her life, Mira takes up with a sympathetic classmate, who with her joins the Gay Men's Health Crisis and goes on an AIDS walk. She also tapes conversations with her father for a school project and makes up her mind about college. Her father dies in the summer, and at the end of the book, Mira is driving away to college "blast[ing] into/the summer-gold sky" (342). This novels adds the element of an open marriage and the idea of a village raising a child—and helping a father to die. As a LGBTQ novel for young adults, however, it is less useful, since the gay parent is dying throughout it.

The main female character of Kate Scelsa's *Fans of the Impossible Life* (2015), the final novel to be discussed in this chapter, is also named Miranda, which may say something about the metaphorical potential or contemporary popularity of the name. Told in first (Jeremy), second (Sebby), and third person (Miranda), the book tells the story of two misfit prep school students and a streetwise foster kid who rarely attends his public high school. Brought together by a newly-formed art club and their shared respect for a dedicated English teacher (who has boundary issues with students), they struggle with Sebby's drug use, Miranda's depression, and Jeremy's feelings of alienation because he has two fathers.

After a wide variety of calamities, including Sebby running away, Mira being hospitalized for depression, and the teacher being fired, Jeremy and Mira end up in Provincetown (where his dads own a beach house) for the summer, where they walk hand in hand "through the families and the tourists and the drag queens to the little house where my dads were waiting for us with sandwiches and lemonade" (254). Sebby also appears to be heading their way, remembering a trip that he and Mira took to Provincetown earlier. "Love remembers the places where it touched down. You can follow it back to them," he thinks on the last page of the novel (256). This mention of Provincetown recalls the importance of the town in the wider gay community in Wittlinger's novels, but the novel apparently still regards having gay parents as an affliction equivalent to drug abuse and depression. Nevertheless, the love that anchors the main characters is celebrated in Provincetown and in the gay parent's beach house, which suggests that connection and love might triumph.

Looking at these 11 novels of gay and lesbian parents, patterns begin to emerge: Most of the protagonists are straight (only two are gay males, none are lesbians), the protagonists are divided between young women and young men, and the parents (and one uncle) are equally gay and lesbian. For the most part, the earlier novels imagine dire consequences (except for *The Arizona Kid*) for the main characters if their secrets are revealed, the later novels tend to be more lighthearted and slightly less centered on the parents' sexuality, and, in a few of the novels (*Dear Julia*, *My Life after Now*, and *Fans of an Impossible Life*), the parents' sexuality is merely a fact and not the focus of the plot. This seems like progress, as the gay or lesbian parent becomes less of an obstacle or a catalyst to the adolescent protagonist's development and more part of the background of ordinary life.

Young people—straight, gay, lesbian, trans, or questioning their sexuality—need novels in which LGBTQ parents are represented in a positive light, although the legal and societal conflicts the young people experience (especially in *Living in Secret*) seem less immediate in 2017. Still, the concerns adolescents have about their sexuality remain, and myths about the "contagion" of LGBTQ parents still need to be dispelled. Also, friends and potential love interests might still ostracize teenagers with non-heteronormative parents and might harass and bully them. If nothing else, these novels have the potential to reveal anxieties about LGBTQ parents—both in their young readers and in our culture. As Dan Savage says, the new crop of novels about this subject, one hopes, will be less "painful and harrowing" than the ones that came before.

Six

"What a wonderful world"
Utopias and Dystopias in LGBTQ Young Adult Fiction

[Dystopian writing for young adults] engages with pressing global concerns: liberty and self-determination, environmental destruction and looming catastrophe, questions of identity, and the increasingly fragile boundaries between technology and the self—Balaka Basu, Katherine R. Broad, and Carrie Hintz, "Introduction," 1

It's your future. Choose.—Alex London, *Proxy*, 375

In "Of Other Spaces," Foucault explores utopias, defining them as "counter-sites ... in which the real sites ... that can be found within the culture, are simultaneously represented, contested and inverted." Foucault calls these spaces "heterotopias" and includes in them cemeteries, museums, libraries, vacation villages, brothels, colonies, and boats (24), which makes the heterotopia a place of both freedom and enclosure, other-worldliness and imprisonment. "The ship is the heterotopia *par excellence*," he says. "In civilizations without boats, dreams dry up, espionage takes the place of adventure, and the police take the place of pirates" (27). Clearly, people need escape (or at least the possibility of escape) to prevent them from destroying their societies from within.

LGBTQ young people may especially need such possibilities of escape from the homophobia and heteronormativities of their world. The utopic and dystopic works discussed in this chapter don't take place aboard ship (although one is set on an island), but the characters in them are separated from the "real" world (even if they are only a town away), live in a fantasy version of Los Angeles (with genies and magic), inhabit the empowering world of Nancy Drew and the Hardy Boys, are shipwrecked on an island of beauty queens, or fight evil in the distant and dystopic future. In all of these works, the authors are creating spaces in which the LGBTQ characters can more freely and happily (although not always without conflict or oppression), but, perhaps more importantly, they are creating worlds that invert and challenge the damaging and often dangerous homophobia of our existing culture.

In his foreword to Hintz and Ostry's collection of essays on utopias in children's and young adult fiction, Jack Zipes says that the "utopian tendency of art is what propels us to reshape and reform our personal and social lives" (x), and certainly for LGBTQ youth, much reshaping and reformation is needed. Hintz and Ostry continue this line of thought in their introduction to the same book, saying that utopian literature "encourages young people to view their society with a critical eye, sensitizing or predisposing them to political action." The pedagogical focus of writing for young people "invests utopian satire with particular urgency" (7), the authors argue, calling on readers to critique—and to change—the worlds they inhabit. Utopian fiction is "subversive," they say, in that it "shows the flaws in the adult world—and in the adults that created it" (8). Dystopian fiction is an especially powerful metaphor for adolescence, as adolescents are often "more often under surveillance" (9) in the course of their everyday lives than adults. "The teenager is on the brink of adulthood," they say: "close enough to see its privileges but unable to enjoy them." Utopian and dystopian fiction often gives teens the opportunity to "save the world from destruction," while at the same time "revers[ing] the hierarchy in which real children and young adults are at the bottom." Adolescents, then, are "agents of hope," who "come to embrace their ability to lead" (10). These "agents of hope" might also help create worlds that are welcoming to LGBTQ people.

Rebecca Totaro agrees, arguing in the same collection that "utopian literature supplies a place for practice, not escape—a safe place in which to find and test new information and tools in the battle against common enemies before then trying them out in one's society of origin" (128). Totaro makes connections between the writers of utopian fiction and the writers of realistic young adult novels, who "have always carried this identical burden, educating their readers through the pains of social and physical metamorphosis while entertaining them" (135). Both genres show, she says, that there are "uses for this suffering. Out of it, one may, slowly, with hope and action, emerge into a less painful adulthood" (136).

Six. "What a wonderful world"

For Kay Sambell, authors "must find ways of progressively resisting the pessimistic thesis of the dystopian scenarios they have invoked." This balance between didacticism and individual inquiry, she says, is "so demanding that it is not likely to be achieved lightly nor very often" ("Presenting" 173–74). I would argue that the authors in this chapter do provide both "dark truth" and "hope."

In a later article, Sambell says that dystopian fiction for children's "primary purpose is to puncture old myths and dreams, by proving, in the form of a literary experiment, what human aspirations and ideals are *really* likely to mean for the future of mankind" ("Carnivalizing" 247–48). In children's and young adult dystopian fiction, she says, young characters are "pitted against a powerful adult regime' ("Carnivalizing" 250), and the adults "who ought to look after and protect their children not only let them down, but also, worse, knowingly manipulate and exploit them" ("Carnivalizing" 251). One problem with this, however, is that "[t]he child as an emblem of hope for the future, capable of transforming and transcending adult mores, and the image of the child as helpless victim are often held in acute tension," which can lead "to flawed novels that are imaginatively and ideologically fractured" ("Carnivalizing" 252). Fortunately, the writers I discuss here manage to maintain that precarious balance without sacrificing imagination or ideology.

Lyman Sargent makes the important point that while there are similarities between young adult and adult dystopian novels, there are also key differences. The "safe space" in these novels, Sargent says, "is sometimes quite literally a safe place, a retreat from the problems and dangers of the world outside." However, it is also "a space for testing and experimentation, a place in which to learn and grow, to become aware of who you are." It is also not completely safe and must be protected. The conflict in these novels "helps the young adults define themselves vis à vis each other and the adult world" (233). Thus, young people, unlike adults, must transform themselves as well as their fictional (and real) worlds.

Following Sambell and Sargent, Basu, Broad, and Hintz say that "[w]hile YA books often unflinchingly engage with the problems of adolescents, they are nonetheless tied to the broader tradition of children's literature, which stresses hope. YA dystopias can uphold that tradition of optimism, embrace a more cynical vision or oscillate between the two" (2). Female protagonists in YA dystopias, in particular, "occupy liminal spaces as they seek to understand their places in the world, to claim their identities, and to live their lives on their own terms" These young women also attempt to "recreate the worlds in which they live, making their societies more egalitarian, more progressive, and, ultimately, more free" (3). However, since "very few YA include queer relationships as a central focus," there may be "a reluctance to subvert dominant mores" (8), at least in the area of sexuality. The writers conclude that the "rebellious natures of many adolescent women protagonists, then, must be viewed ... in terms of the generic conventions that these novels frequently blur, reimagine, and, to some degree, reinforce" (11). Several of the novels in this chapter, however, do subvert those "dominant mores."

Sara K. Day agrees with Basu, Broad, and Hintz. Because most YA dystopian novels "illustrate (or perpetuate) questions of control and embodiment through their insistence upon straight romance and desire," she says, "assumptions about heteronormativity also problematizes their message of empowerment through sexual awakening" (89–90). The "parade of straight girls who fall in love with straight boys functions similarly to the implicit insistence on whiteness," Day argues, "inasmuch as other possibilities seem to be ignored or marginalized instead of explored as local options and extensions of contemporary life" (90). Fortunately, the novels in this chapter work to subvert both racial and sexual paradigm, offering alternatives to the "parade of straight girls who fall in love with straight boys."

When asked why there weren't LGBTQ young people in dystopian fiction, science fiction writer Paolo Bacigalupi initially said that the "present day is plenty dystopic enough" for LGBTQ teens. He says that the "real objective in writing a dystopia about being gay would be to rattle a shockingly complacent straight readership into something approaching empathy." Dystopias, he adds, "should force readers to question who they are, what their society is like, and what they take for granted" ("The Invisible Dystopias"). In a posting a few weeks later, Bacigalupi felt the need to follow up, saying that "there's a strange dearth of GLBTQ characters simply living their lives, defying big brother or fighting off the zombie apocalypse, where gender or sexuality is not necessarily the dominant part of the narrative at hand—which is, after all, mostly focused on blowing zombies to pieces" ("Straight-Laced Dystopias"). While no zombies appear in this chapter (blown up or otherwise), the novels discussed here do show LGBTQ characters "simply living their lives"—and preventing a dystopian future.

Six. "What a wonderful world"

To conclude this introductory section, it may be useful to consider at least one of the potential dangers of utopian/dystopian fiction, as well as some of the ways in which LGBTQ utopian fiction might offer possible solutions. In their introduction to *Curioser: On the Queerness of Children*, Steven Bruhm and Natasha Hurley make a provocative equation between utopianism and the representation of children in literature:

> Utopianism follows the child around like a family pet. The child exists as a site of almost limitless potential (its future not yet written and therefore unblemished). But because the utopian fantasy is the property of adults, not necessarily of children, it is accompanied by its doppelganger, nostalgia. Nostalgia is the fantasy of a preferred past (past pleasures, past desires for the future). Caught between these two worlds, one dead, the other powerless to be born, the child becomes the bearer of heteronormativity, appearing to render ideology invisible by cloaking it in simple stories, euphemisms, and platitudes. The child is the product of physical reproduction, but functions just as surely as a figure of cultural reproduction. Thus both the utopianism and the nostalgia invoked by the figure of the child are, in turn, the preferred form of the future [xiii].

This suggests that it may be impossible to offer real social critique in a utopian novel for children or young adults, drenched as they are in nostalgia and heteronormativity. However, the LGBTQ child might well offer a counter-narrative to that reproductive nostalgia and futurity, a child born of opposite-sex reproduction but possibly not representing a future of reproduction, a replication of norms. In the case of the dystopia, even more radical possibilities open.

John Stephens encourages critics to remember that the intention of children's fiction is "to foster in the child reader a positive apperception of some socio-cultural values, which, it is assumed, are shared by author and audience." Writers of children's fiction, he says, "often take upon themselves the task of trying to mold audience attitudes into 'desirable' forms, which can mean either an attempt to perpetuate certain values or to resist socially dominant values which particular writers oppose" (3). "[C]hildren's fiction, Stephens says, "belongs firmly within the domain of cultural practices which exist for the purpose of socializing their target audience" (8). Baccolini argues instead that recent science fiction "has come to represent a form of counternarrative to hegemonic discourse" (519). "[B]y rejecting the traditional subjugation of the individual," he says, "the critical dystopia opens a space of contestation and opposition for those groups—women and other ex-centric subjects whose subject position is not contemplated by hegemonic discourse—for whom subject status has yet to be attained" (520). Women, same-sex attracted and trans people, and/or queer sexualities could well be offered a space—and a voice—in the dystopian universe. Clare Bradford et al. agree with Stephens that "the utopian rhetoric espoused in many cultural texts mimics the liberal democratic rhetoric of assimilation, equality, and freedom, despite legislative, social, and homophobic actions which are hostile to the rhetoric" (133). However, they claim, with Baccollini, that some young adult dystopias, "posit a queer reality which calls into question norms and conventions that restrict the conditions under which people exist, both inside and outside the text" (134). The novels in this chapter suggest that the number of texts that "posit a queer reality" is increasing every year.

The novels discussed below, which feature gay, lesbian, bisexual, and trans adolescents, might well offer a counter to both the nostalgia and the "reproductive futurism" of the child—or they may simply replicate the nostalgia and the heteronormativity of their straight counterparts, depending on who's reading them. They may also help create a "queer reality" that will question existing norms or simply reinforce those norms. However, I believe that what the future may look like for readers of these novels may be very curious—and very queer—indeed.

David Levithan's *Boy Meets Boy* (2003) is not the earliest of the YA utopias/dystopias discussed in this chapter, but it has been quite extensively analyzed and offers a useful critical framework for discussions of these sorts of novels. Although it might be argued that this text is not strictly utopian, it does create a world that does not yet exist in the "real" world. Corrinne Wickens says that the novel is "part love story, part farce, part contemporary realistic fiction. Though the blurring of genres, Levithan in fact crafts a novel to counter normative assumptions around gender and sexuality" (149). The novel, she argues, "undermines heteronormative assumptions by presenting the unthinkable: children as sexual beings, hegemonic masculinity as in fact non-hegemonic and detrimental to success, and homosexuality as normalized and even ordinary" (156). If nothing else, the "unrealistic" and exuberant acceptance of homosexuality and the gender-bending nature of the characters makes the novel utopian.

Amy Patee concurs, arguing that *Boy Meets Boy* "functions effectively as a romance novel, a genre critics have called utopian, and also draws upon and extends conventions of homosexual representation

Six. "What a wonderful world"

found in 'traditional' gay-themed young adult literature and gay pornography to depict a distinctly utopian world of sexual liberation" (156). Interestingly, Patee points out that the novel is "not a separatist one that sanctions only homosexual congress." Borrowing from Foucault, Patee calls it a "heterotopia" (162), where straight and bisexual relationships are treated with equal respect. "Ultimately," Patee says, the novel "reshapes the utopian image associated with the romance while engaging in the political work associated with the GLBTQ novel for teens" (167). This positive assessment accurately reflects the novel's twin desires to show much of teen life as it is actually lived and to suggest how it might be lived in an ideal world—mostly free from homophobia.

Tyson Pugh praises the novel as well, arguing that although the text "posits the end of sexual innocence as the defining feature of childhood, it nonetheless paradoxically retains an air of joyful innocence," which has been freed from "a *Peter-Pan* enforced and eternal juvenilia and thus recast as a boundless exuberance for life and living" (165). *Boy Meets Boy*, he continues, "points to a refreshing new direction for children's literature, one in which gay angst is rendered pointless in a world without sexual closets, and in which neither children nor adults are sacrificed to a fetishized belief in innocence/ignorance as a virtue above all others" (165–66). This may be too idealistic an assessment, however, as at least one of the main characters has to struggle out of the closet created by his religious parents.

Reflecting on this aspect of the novel, Thomas Crisp is somewhat more measured in his enthusiasm. Levithan is actively working against the construction of identity categories, he argues, and the novel is notable in that it gives a feeling of hope uncharacteristic of LGBTQ adolescent literature. However, this feeling "may ultimately be unproductive in that it could forestall any radical restructuring" of society (341). Also, Crisp argues, the book "relies heavily on the ideology of reproductive futurism—faith that the figure of the Child carries with it the possibility of a better tomorrow" (342). In addition, although queerness is not stigmatized (and homophobic characters are usually unlikable), homosexuality "is still constructed as something *different* and therefore in relationship to some "norm," i.e., heterosexuality (343).

Crisp concludes:
> While Levithan does indeed "flip" the binary in *Boy Meets Boy*, in many ways, he simply shows the other side. He repositions the world to bring the inside-

out and the outside-in, but "out" and "in" values persist and ultimately leave the binary intact. Because Levithan is ultimately operating in a binary, difference beyond gay/not gay or extending language beyond the limits of good/bad becomes an impossibility. This is not enough; to truly disrupt heteronormativity, literature would have to be imagined beyond identity categories [343].

Pugh seems to be concurring here with Bruhm and Hurley, arguing that Levithan's utopia simply reinstates, in playful and upside-down form, heteronormative binaries. It may be possible, however, to see this novel as part of a conversation that is continued in the magical realist world of Weetzie Bat and her constructed LGBTQ family, in the bonding of the Pride Pack, in Libba Bray's island of beauty queens, and in the futuristic dystopias of Alex London. But I also think it is possible to challenge Pugh's assertions that the binary of gay/straight is actually challenged in *Boy Meets Boy* from the first page of the novel to its phantasmal ending.

In a recent essay Blackburn, Clark, and Nemeth (2015) articulate this seeming contradiction well. In *Boy Meets Boy*, they say, "several characters in the book adhere closely to an essentialist model of identity development and thus may convey a monolithic ideology with little room for contestation or complication. The idea is we are who we are, even if we don't know it yet" (25). However, when read in the context of our current world, the characters in *Boy Meets Boy* "disrupt the heteronormative expectation of young men identifying as straight, and being desirous of and sexually active with young women" (31). In the way it confounds our expectations of small-town life and romance, the authors argue, "*Boy Meets Boy*'s use of the ironic mode creates a jarring sense of time and space and thus offers multiple and conflicting ideologies around the conceptualization, embodiment, and enaction of homophobia" (40). Thus, while the novel does reinforce a fairly rigid notion of sexual identity, it also works to shake up readers' complacency about gender, small-town life, and romance.

The novel begins with gay main character Paul telling readers about his hometown:

> There really isn't a gay scene or a straight scene in our town. They got all mixed up a while back, which I think is for the best.... Boys who love boys flirt with girls who love girls. And whether your heart is strictly ballroom or bluegrass punk, the dance floor is open to whatever you have to offer [1–2].

In this world, straight guys sneak into the gay bar, gay guys flirt with lesbian girls, ballroom and bluegrass (and punk) meet on the dance

Six. "What a wonderful world"

floor. The novel begins with dance as a metaphor and concludes with an actual dance (albeit in a graveyard), suggesting that learning to separate the "dancer from the dance" might be quite difficult indeed.

The first scene of is in a bookstore, with Paul "mov[ing] through the crowd with ease, sharing nods and smiling hellos. I love this scene, this floating reality. I am a solo flier looking out over the land of Boyfriends and Girlfriends. I am three notes in the middle of a song" (2). This right away suggests a world where one isn't clear to whom the "Boyfriends and Girlfriends" are attached and where Paul's song floats above it all, fluid and transitory. This town of Paul's is a safe haven, but even though there is another world outside his town, where his gay Christian friend Tony lives with his intolerant parents, Paul hopes for "a fair world," where Tony "would shine" (5).

Paul's childhood is untouched by the trauma of a secret and despised sexuality. He says he's always known he was gay, but it was confirmed by his kindergarten teacher, who wrote it on his report card (4). When his best friend Joni kisses him when he was in second grade, he tells her he's gay, and she responds "no problem" and goes on with their game (11). Paul's life isn't completely without homophobia, however. He tells the story of how he was "tackled by two high school wrestlers after a late-night showing of *Priscilla, Queen of the Desert* at our local theater." Happily, he "had gone to the movies with a bunch of my friends from the fencing team, so they just pulled out their foils and disarmed the lugheads." Later, Paul finds out that one of the wrestlers has since become a drag queen. "I like to think I had something to do with that," Paul remarks, archly (13).

This world—where fencing teams defeat bigoted wrestlers (who eventually turn out to be drag queens) continues into Paul's high school. One of the first things readers encounter there is Infinite Darlene, "a six-foot-four football player scuttling through the halls in high heels, a red shock wig, and more-than-passable make-up" (15). Infinite Darlene is not treated as an object of ridicule or even burlesque. Looking closely at her, Paul says he can "see through all her layers. Beneath the makeup and the lipstick and the chicken pox scar on her lower lip, beneath the girl and the boy to the person within, who is concerned and confused and sincere" (106). Darlene and Paul, like many young people of any sexual and clothing preference, are "concerned and confused and sincere," and all the characters in this novel are treated with compassion and mild humor.

As in many recent LGBTQ novels, characters often resist being placed in permanent identity categories. For example, Paul's old boyfriend, Kyle—who rejected him and said he was straight—tries to come up with an accurate description for what he is. He says he hates the word "bisexual" because it makes him feel "divided," when he's really "doubled." Paul suggests "ambisexual" or "duosexual," and Kyle asks why there has to be a word for it. "The world loves stupid labels," Paul thinks. "I wish we got to choose our own" (85). Kyle says he doesn't "know who I'm supposed to be," and Paul assures him that "nobody does" (86). This more flexible concept of identity, especially for young adults (gay and straight), is a common feature (as this study has shown) of more contemporary young adult fiction.

Although this is an unlikely high school with a cross-dressing football player and "a biker cheerleading team" (22), realistic love tangles and triangles ensue. Joni takes up with the male chauvinist Chuck after a breakup with a longtime boyfriend, Paul falls for Noah but then cheats on him with Kyle, and Infinite Darlene is in the middle of all of it. Joni and Paul fall out over her boyfriend, Chuck, whom Paul doesn't like. Paul takes his new love on a tour of their town, which has a "Veggie D's," a McDonalds taken over by vegetarian co-op (55) and "Joy Scouts," not Boy Scouts (who at the time the novel was written were not allowing gay boys to join) (66). At the park the boys visit, "the Old Queen and the Young Punk sit together and share memories of events that happened long before they were born" (69). Paul also shows Noah the "I Scream Parlor, which shows horror movies as you wait for your double dip [and] the Pink Floyd shrine in our local barber's backyard." Paul comments: "I know people always talk about living in the middle of nowhere.... But it's moments like this that I feel I live in the middle of somewhere. My somewhere" (69–70). This town, Paul's "somewhere" is very much like Oz, a place of eccentricity and joy (without the wicked witch or befuddled wizard).

In keeping with this utopian environment, Paul's family is completely accepting of his sexuality, "although I think they're always a little confused about who's my boyfriend and who is just a friend who happens to be a boy" (60). Paul friend (and not boyfriend) Tony's parents, on the other hand, "think that Tony's personality is simply a matter of switches, and that if they find the right one, they can turn off his attraction to other guys and put him back on the road to God" (70). Paul and Tony climb a mountain, and a friend of Tony's parents see them hugging.

Six. "What a wonderful world"

When they try to cut Tony off from Paul and his other friends, Paul's brother says it might be "time to send in the P-FLAG commandos" to talk to Tony's parents. In their town, P-FLAG is "as big a draw as the PTA" (115), Paul says. Eventually, Tony learns to stand up to his parents, and, while they don't exactly condone his behavior, they learn to respect his right to determine his own friends.

Tony tells Paul that at first he couldn't believe that Paul or his utopian town could exist. He thought he "would get up every morning with a secret and go to sleep every night with the same secret." When he met Paul, he says, "suddenly it was like this door had been opened." However, part of him wishes he had never glimpsed this other world (150–51). Paul tells him that he is brave, and Tony responds that it is becoming harder and harder to leave Paul's world and head back into his own (151). Tony insists that his parents love him, and Paul says that "part of love is letting a person be who they want to be" (152). When Tony's parents finally agree that he and Paul can see each other, Paul says, "It feels like wining. It feels like possibility" (158).

At the end of the novel, Tony's parents grudgingly allow him to go to the dance, and all of Paul's old and new friends, former and current lovers, and now-former enemies are there. "We are in the middle of somewhere and we are feeling everything," Paul thinks, looking around (184). Paul describes the nearly infinite variety of love at that moment, with Infinite Darlene dancing with a lesbian, two boys beginning their romance, his best friend slow dancing, and the object of his affection coming toward him with "a blessed smile on his lips" (185). The last lines of the book invoke Louis Armstrong: "And I think to myself. *What a wonderful world*" (185). This wonderful world is not completely without strife (both of the familial and the adolescent kind), but it is a world that allows Infinite Darlene, Tony, Paul, and Noah (and all their friends) to love whomever they choose.

Also by David Levithan, *Every Day* (2012) is a science fiction novel about a person who can be male or female, any race, any body size, any sexuality, and have any sort of ability or disability, depending on the day. This person, who thinks of itself as "A," falls in love with a girl, Rhiannon, and meets her in different bodies. It is also stalked by a fundamentalist boy whose body A inhabited one day. The bodies age as A does, and he/she is 16 when the novel opens. "Every day I am someone else," A says. "I am myself—I know I am myself—but I am also someone else" (1). This character—and this novel—are an interrogation of what it means to be human and sexual both within and transcending bodies. As A says about its peculiar state, "Knowledge is the only thing I take with me when I go" from body to body (7). The most important thing that A has learned is that people "all have about 98 percent in common with each other.... For whatever reason, we like to focus on the 2 percent that's different, and most of the conflict in the world comes from that" (77). Or, to put it another way, "when who you are changes every day— you get to touch the universal more" (107). Once again, Levithan insists that the "universal"—love, fear, human connection, empathy—transcends bodies and sexualities.

The object of A's affection is somewhat less sanguine about this situation, probably because she has not had 16 years to get used to the idea. When Rhiannon finds out who A is (he/she first met her in the body of her boyfriend and then contacted her surreptitiously in other bodies before A told her), she is somewhat accepting, although she says that "the outside matters, too" (131), even though A is the same on the inside. "In my experience, desire is desire, love is love," A tells her. "I have never fallen in love with a gender. I have fallen for individuals. I know this is hard for people to do, but I don't understand why it's so hard, when it's so obvious" (142). However, Rhiannon is "less affectionate" when A is in a girl's body, but he/she doesn't complain. "She's still with me, and she's still happy, and that's something" (225). Not surprisingly, Rhiannon and A don't stay together, but they (and readers) have learned something in the process about sexual attraction and its potential fluidity.

In one very interesting section of the novel, A awakens in the body of a trans male, Vic, and likes it there. Vic, A says, is "[l]iving within the definition of his own truth, just like me.... If you want to live within the definition of your own truth, you have to choose to go through the initially painful and ultimately comforting process of finding it" (253). A can identify with Vic because sometimes A would "resist some of the transitions.... There were days I felt like a girl and days I felt like a boy, and those days wouldn't always correspond with the body I was in. A had to learn "that when it came to gender, I was both and neither" (254). Still, A acknowledges the pain that Vic must feel, even though he currently has an accepting girlfriend. "It is an awful thing to be betrayed by your body. And it's lonely, because you feel you can't talk about it. You feel it's something between you and the body. You feel it's a battle you will never win ... and yet you fight it day after day, and it wears you down. Even if you try to ignore it, the energy it takes to ignore it will exhaust you" (254). Vic's girlfriend, however, sees Vic "exactly as he wanted to be seen" (256).

At the end of the novel, A meets someone who promises that he/she can control the changes, allowing him/her to stay in one body, and A decides to seek out that person. It isn't clear, however, whether A will choose to be a boy or a girl, or will instead to decide to move through the rest of life as all possible permutations of gender and desire. Levithan leaves his ending open, perhaps to allow readers to decide for themselves which option they might choose and why. Although this novel feels very much like a dystopia when A is trying to find Rhiannon or convince her to stay with him—or when trapped in a hostile or damaged body—the novel ends on an utopian note. A has the ability to choose not just his/her future or his/her future partner but his/her sexuality and gender.

The most recent Levithan novel discussed here, *Two Boys Kissing* (2013), is the story of Harry and Craig, who are attempting a marathon kissing session to get in the Guinness Book of World Records. They were once boyfriends but now are friends. Harry is out and Craig is not, although his parents find out during the kissing (and slowly start to accept his sexuality). It is also the story of transboy Avery and the object of his affection, Ryan, and of Cooper, who is outed by his online activity and thrown out of his house. What makes this contemporary story magical and utopian is that it is told by the choral voice of the gay ancestors, who died of AIDS, and who are watching over these young people. On the first page of the novel, the ancestors say to the young people, "We are a sprit-burden you carry, like that of your grandparents, or the friends from your childhood who at some point moved away" (1). They also say to these young people, "We resent you. You astonish us" (2). They introduce themselves to the boys (who never actually hear them but seem to feel their presence)—and to us:

> We are your shadow uncles, your angel godfathers, your mother's or your grandmother's best friend from college, the author of that book you found in the gay section of the library. We are characters in a Tony Kushner play, or names on a quilt that rarely gets taken out anymore. We are the ghosts of the remaining older generation. You know some of our songs [3].

The "shadow uncles" remind the boys that "things are not magical because they've been conjured for us by some outside force. They are magical because we create them, and then deem them so" (9). They also tell the young people that they, too, have "created our mix-and-match families, our homemade safety net" (86). These LGBTQ communities, born out of necessity and in trauma, are also ideal communities, chosen and constructed to provide the support and love not available to many gay men during the AIDS crisis (or to LGBTQ people, in general, for many years).

Late in the novel, Cooper attempts suicide, but he is stopped by a policeman at the last minute. "Cooper will live to meet his future self," the chorus says. "You should all live to meet your future selves" (195). The promise the elders make to the boys at the end of the novel is this: "There will come a time when you will have the same unalienable rights as your straightest friend," which has come closer to coming true in 2017, and, "if you play your cards right, the next generation will have so much more than you did" (195).[1] In this novel, most of the utopian element is in the supernatural world, in the world of the "uncles," but the juxtaposition between plot and chorus suggests that out of the tragedy of AIDS can come a community that supports (and even saves) its newest members.

Francesca Lia Block's Weetzie Bat novels resemble the utopias of Levithan, especially in *Boy Meets Boy*, but they are inflected much more strongly by popular culture and a Los Angeles aesthetic. Alleen and Don Nilsen say Block's works "start with something resembling normality followed by a period of chaos, which by the end rights itself to a kind of stasis," which indicates that these are essentially comic novels. However, Nilsen and Nilsen continue that "Block's tone is exaggerated and in keeping with her Hollywood setting" (37). Frequently, Block's characters seem to move through movie sets and float above the world like spirits. Jan Susina comments that Block "deftly weaves descriptions of real and imaginary places in her contemporary literary fairy tales set in a dreamy, mythical Los Angeles. Grounded in an urban landscape fueled by the entertainment industry, Block's stories celebrate the fantasy of Hollywood, while simultaneously examining the details of contemporary Los Angeles" (188). Block's regionalism, Susina says, "is not so much about a geographic sense of space, but a metaphorical sense of space: the silver screen. She shows how her Hollywood characters are unable to distinguish life from film" (194). I would argue that these cinematic and fantastical qualities are part of what makes these novels utopian.

Weetzie Bat (1990) is the first book in the series, which, according to

Six. "What a wonderful world"

Lobban and Clyde, could be read as "rich allegory, and modern fairy tale based on an ancient theme," or as a "shallow attempt to present a message in a heavy-handed, albeit trendy, way." Still, this book, like the others in the series, "provides a natural and accepting view of homosexuality" (15). Christine Jenkins notes, sardonically, that "[g]iven the gender-role restrictions, the prevalence of heterosexism and homophobia, and the perceived necessity of the closet, a YA novel in which, say, same-sex couples could freely walk hand in hand in public would hardly be considered a work of contemporary realism." However, Jenkins also remarks that in 1998, *Weetzie Bat*, "a story that employs magical realism to picture a closetless world with characters of various sexual orientations," was the only young adult novel portraying gay/lesbian people accurately and compassionately at that time (311). It seems that up until fairly recently, accurate and compassionate LGBTQ young adult novels needed to be set in utopia to be published—and purchased.

In spite of its groundbreaking status as a cheerful LGBTQ novel for young adults, *Weetzie Bat*, Jan Susina argues, is a "consumeristic paradise and they rarely look beyond the confines of their own rightly-appointed magic kingdom of wealthy white upper-class privilege" (198). It is true that worries about money or jobs or housing rarely plague Weetzie and her family, but the same could be said for the lives of many young adult protagonists, such as those in Levithan's novels. Susina does add, however, that Weetzie's "magical Shangri-L.A" is nevertheless "an eclectic, fragmentary, and contradictory postmodern landscape that is simultaneously fantastic and realistic" (199). Kaplan and Rabinowitz put it well, saying that Weetzie's family "forms a portrait by a queer Norman Rockwell outlined in glitter, an alternative American dream" (206).

The novel opens with Weetzie Bat in high school, travelling around this magical L.A. with her friend, and (to her mind) potential romantic partner Dirk. He soon tells her that he is gay, and they decide they now can go "Duck" hunting together, i.e., looking for guys (9). Weetzie finds a genie in a gift lamp from Grandma Fifi, and she asks for a Duck for Dirk, My Secret Agent Lover Man for her, and a house for them all to live in. All this happens, although sadly because of Dirk's grandmother's death. As Kaplan and Rabinowitz put it, "[t]he decidedly odd sexuality of Weetzie's little family only increases after she finds her own romantic partner" (205).

There is trouble in this sexual paradise, though, as Weetzie wants a baby and MSALM does not, so she has sex with Dirk and Duck (together) and gets pregnant. Kaplan and Rabinowitz say, rightly, that "there is nothing that the narrative voice finds wrong with the thoroughly queer sexual act of a heterosexual woman having intercourse with a pair of partnered gay men," and they call Weetzie's "triangle of het girl, gay boy, gay boy ... an overtly queer heterosexuality" (205). AIDS mars this world, however, and during this time, Dirk thinks that "love is a dangerous angel" (104), a phrase which becomes a poignant refrain for this series.

At the end of the novel, her entire family (including several "slinkster" dogs) are together again, and Weetzie thinks that "love and disease are both like electricity" because they are invisible. However, people "can choose to plug into the love current instead." She sees her constructed and biological family "lit up and golden like a wreath of lights. I don't know about happily ever after ... but I know about happily," she thinks (109). This ending seems very similar to the blissful prom scene at the end of *Boy Meets Bo*, and it is also reminiscent of the families described in *Two Boys Kissing*. Love may be a "dangerous angel," but in this Angelino utopia, it is also electric and powerful.

Witch Baby (1991) is the first of the sequels to *Weetzie Bat*, and Lobban and Clyde say that the novel "will appeal to Block's fans, while leaving the rest of us somewhat bewildered" (13), perhaps because of the complexity and unlikelihood of the plot. As Lobban and Clyde put it:

> A long-term homosexual relationship discovered and ultimately accommodated, mixed-race relationships, a child's search for her real parents, the treatment of illegal immigrants in the United States, the nature of talent and creativity, and the future of planet Earth—all this and much more amount to a lot of issues for just one book of 103 pages [14].

It's true that there's a lot going on in the novel, but it remains unified around the idea of family and belonging. Witch Baby, who, as Lobban and Clyde put it, was "conceived heterosexually but in anger" is "bitter, surreal, and depressive," unlike her half-sister Cherokee, the product of two gay men and their best friend, who is "lovely and lighthearted" (205). Gay reproduction leads to lightness and joy; straight reproduction to bitterness and anger. Her feelings of not belonging create a rift in the family that continues until nearly the end of the novel, but Witch Baby's sense of herself as an outsider allows her to identify with Dirk and Duck

Six. "What a wonderful world"

and support their relationship to Duck's homophobic family, saying that the two "are the most slinkster-cool team" (49). After various complicated plot developments, Witch Baby returns to Weetzie and their family and recognizes "that her own sadness was only a small piece of the puzzle of pain that made up the globe.... And there was a lot of happiness as well, a lot of love—so much that maybe, from somewhere, far away in the universe, the cottage shone like someone's globe lamp" (102-03). This novel ends much as the previous one did—with light, and warmth, and this strange and loving family back together.

Cherokee Bat and The Goat Guys (1992) is perhaps the darkest of the series, and one of the more supernatural. Weetzie and MSALM have left Cherokee and Witch Baby, who are teenagers, alone, and the youngsters decide to bring Witch Baby out of her ongoing depressing by forming a band, which seems to help. Things get weird, though, with magic talismans of wings, goat haunches, and a stolen horn, and the band members seem possessed and are partying too much. Before things get any worse, though, the girls' parents write that they are returning, and all is well at the end. In *Missing Angel Juan* (1993), Witch Baby goes to New York City, reconnects with her lover, and meets her father's ghost. Once again, things end strangely and peacefully.

Necklace of Kisses (2005) concludes the Weetzie Bat series. In it, Weetzie Bat is 45, and, after realizing that her relationship with Max (MSALM) has cooled, she moves to the Pink Hotel, which is filled with mermaids, fauns, an invisible cleaning woman, and a trans angel. There Weetzie learns about herself, gets back with Max, and scores a beautiful necklace.[2] Throughout all of these novels, Weetzie moves through a world only somewhat resembling our own, one filled with witch babies, goat guys, angels, slinkster dogs, and magic lamps. Even more fanciful, perhaps, is the accepting and loving nature of the main characters, for whom the entire spectrum of sexual and mythological identities causes little comment or disruption. Consequently, these utopias provide young readers with an imaginary world of tolerance and love that extends real-world values of empathy and hope.

Shifting from works set in an imaginary and supernatural Los Angeles to series of detective novels might at first seem like a movement from utopia to gritty reality, but the young detectives in Ruth Ann Simms's novels exist in a utopia of their own.[3] After reminding readers of the need for genre fiction like this to address the concerns of LGBTQ youth, Drewey Wayne Gunn says in the afterward to *Who Framed Lorenzo Garcia?* that this is "surprisingly underexplored territory" (115). Although they are not set in an ideal but non-existent present or a dystopian future, these gay and lesbian teen detectives have no counterparts in the real world (although they do resemble out-of-the closet gay and lesbian Nancy Drews and Hardy Boys).

In *Who Framed Lorenzo Garcia?* (1995), Ramon Torres is a 16-year-old gay kid who is being fostered by gay police sergeant Lorenzo Garcia because his parents threw him out when he told them he was gay. His newly acquired case worker is homophobic and doesn't want Lorenzo to be his adoptive parent. When Lorenzo is falsely accused of taking drugs from a crime scene, Ramon's friends at the LGBTQ youth center band together to solve the mystery. They name themselves the Pride Pack, and like the Nancy Drew or Hardy Boys series, they confront social issues, solve mysteries, and, unlike their earlier counterparts, they do it in a LGBTQ context. Day says that "Ramón and Lorenzo are a welcome addition to young adult literature which suffers from a scarcity of gay Latino characters. The members of the Pride Pack work together well, bravely tackling difficult situations" (33).

The Case of the Missing Mother (1995) features Becky Staley (15), who has two lesbian mothers. One of her mothers disappears, and the Pride Pack starts to look for her. It turns out that she has been kidnapped by a minister, who is opposed to both gay rights and abortion. He wants to frame her mother for arson, but he is eventually arrested by Ramon's father, and his plot is revealed by the Pride Pack. Becky is reconciled to her parents at the end, and the three women walk arm in arm "in a laughing, fumble-footed imitation of Dorothy and her friends on the yellow brick road to Oz" (117). It's interesting that both novels involve adults who have been framed for crimes because of their sexuality and their support of young people's sexuality. While these books often rely on stereotypical descriptions of homophobia and simplistic plots, they fill a gap in genre fiction for young LGBTQ readers.

More sophisticated and lighthearted than the Pride Pack books, Libba Bray's *Beauty Queens* (2011) is a satirical look at pageants, femininity, disability, sexuality, and gender identity (as well as deranged dictators and pirates) set on island where a group of beauty queen wannabes have been stranded after a plane crash. Bridgitte Barclay says that *Beauty Queens* "offers an honest discourse about multiple removals from power

Six. "What a wonderful world"

and satirizes dominant culture's norms to show the power of being, of indeterminacy, and of hybridity" (141). The novel, she argues, "is a dystopian vision that shows our own culture's trajectory by highlighting gender-normalizing pressure in our current world, using satire to exaggerate the absurdity of such pressures" (141). It "balances critique and hope" (142) and "uses laughter as a tool against a culture that dominates and 'others' women, a tool that points out absurdities, with a hope, in this case, that such exposure will elicit change for the better" (143). Although this could be called a dystopia, given that the girls are trapped on an island and in peril, it also can be seen as a utopia of acceptance and possibility, much as Jonathan Swift blended utopian and dystopian images in *Gulliver's Travels*.

The cast of characters on the island includes Petra West, a trans girl (and former member of a hit boy band) who dreams of playing Marlene Dietrich's role in *The Blue Angel* and whose favorite novel is Virginia Woolf's *Orlando* (38), and Jennifer Huberman, a working-class lesbian who wants to write graphic novels (59–61). When the other girls discover that Petra has a "wang-dang-doodle," she asks them, "Is that all that makes a guy a guy? What makes a girl a girl?" (99). The girls have no easy answer for that question. Petra's goal is to place in the pageant and then reveal herself as trans to cause people to "question everything they think about transgender people and about gender itself" (100). The girls accuse her of lying and demand that she drop out of the pageant, and she says, "Everybody lies about who they are. Name one person here who isn't doing that and I will drop out right now!" (108).

Another character, Mary Lou Novak, dreams of being a pirate and worries about revealing her family legacy of sexual voracity (161). Mary Lou discovers that "maybe girls *need* an island to find themselves. Maybe they need a place where no one's watching them so they can be who they really are" (177). At the end of the novel, the girls foil the evil dictator, Mary Lou takes up the life a pirate and encounters a man who is thrilled with her wildness, Jennifer becomes a writer of underground comics and finds a wife, and Petra marries one of the pirates (who likes to share her heels from time to time). In the last scene, during their completely revamped pageant on the island, the girls jump in the air: "As one, they leap, laughing, and that is where we leave them—mouths open, arms spread wide, fingers played to take in the whole world, bodies flying high in defiance of gravity, as if they will never fall" (390). The characters at the end of the novel, Barclay says, "are without blueprints, and the blueprints are made to seem ridiculous. This satire is potentially empowering to young adult readers as they consider their own identities in development" (143). This book seems especially important for young girls, as it suggests that they can take charge of their lives (and their sexualities) under the most adverse (if sometimes ridiculous) circumstances.

Far more serious in tone than *Beauty Queens*, *Proxy*, by Alex London (2013), is a dystopian novel set in a world where environmental disasters have reduced much of the United States to wasteland (jungles or deserts), and the primary city has become divided into the debtors and their lenders (known as "patrons"), who live in a protected high-tech enclave. Everyone below is in tremendous debt, and they often work off that debt by becoming "proxies" for the children of the rich, which means being punished in various ways for those children's misbehaviors. Main character Sidney Carton (all the orphan children are named after now-forgotten literary characters) is a proxy for Knox, but he has, of course, a secret identity, revealed by what he thinks is a birthmark at the back of his head. He turns out to be the savior of the world, Yovel, who has a program in his blood that will take down the system and eliminate debt—-and the power of the lenders. This novel has elements of *Feed*, and nearly every other kind of hero-oriented science fiction (and every orphan-finds-his true-identity story since Oedipus).

What makes this novel different is that Sidney is gay, or "Chapter 11" in the language of this world, which means that he is "bankrupt" reproductively (and perhaps morally), and also he is 1+1, attracted to the same sex. "Two of the same thing pressed together. The old way of saying it was homo" (24). Syd's best friend Egan doesn't care that Syd is Chapter 11 "as long as he was loyal" (25). This is fairly unusual in the resolutely hetero world of young adult science fiction, and even more unique because Syd's homosexuality is simply a fact of his identity and (not much) the object of scorn or oppression (except by some particularly unsavory characters). Still, this doesn't mean that Syd is free from self-loathing, which has been a prominent part of the LGBTQ experience. For example, although Syd knows that his feelings "weren't like other boys' feelings," he starts to believe that "his patron [Knox's] misdeeds were a reflection of his own dark thoughts." He goes back to his "childish belief that he deserved every punishment he received and that

Six. "What a wonderful world"

his particularly disobedient patron is his "cosmic punishment for his desires" (107–08).

The action in the novel takes off after Knox crashes a car, and kills a girl (Marie), and Syd, as his proxy, has to give his blood to save Knox. Facing 15 years imprisonment for Knox's accident, Syd escapes, and, while on the lam, he runs into Knox and takes him hostage, kissing him as a way of hiding from the guards that are searching for him (113). This is Syd's first kiss, and it is certainly one of the first boy/boy kisses in YA science fiction. A long chase sequence begins, with Knox and Sid, Marie (who turns out not to be dead), and Egan along for the ride. In the course of the long and dramatic escape to "Old Detroit," where the rebels are encamped, Syd begins to realize that although he and Knox (and everyone else, for that matter) begins as equals, the debtor/creditor proxy/patron relationship changes all that. However, "beneath it all, everyone bleeds" (233). He also discovers that, in spite of all the death on this trip, he's "just starting to feel alive" (251).

Although most of the novel is taken up with daring escapes and fighting, Syd's sexuality is a current running through the action. At one point, Knox suggests that Syd might be able to have sex with Marie, but Syd ignores him. Knox responds, "All right, you know what you like; that's fine" (258). Bandits capture them, and after killing Egan, one of them says, "Little Chapter Eleven coward, can't even take your revenge. I guess we know who was the man in your relationship. Guess you'll never bend over for Egan again" (288). Syd kills her, with relish. Marie tells Knox she doesn't think Syd is "looking to jump you in your sleep. Hard as that must be for you to imagine." Knox mentions the kiss (306). When Syd nearly drowns after a flash flood in the desert, Knox has to give him artificial resuscitation, and he calls it "our second kiss" (322). It seems that a romance, albeit reluctantly on Knox's part, is beginning here.

When they get to the rebel stronghold, it becomes clear that although Syd's blood is what can save the world, he will have to die to give it. Syd pauses. "It's not easy to throw your life away, even for a good reason, even when it's the right thing to do. It was simple enough. Debt or no: Syd did not want to die" (339). Knox tells him that "your life doesn't belong to me and it doesn't belong to them either. It's yours" (364). Knox decides to sacrifice himself in place of Syd (which works because he has Syd's blood in him). Right before he is going to die, Knox kisses Syd again. "At first, Syd flinched, then he relaxed and let his hands fall to Knox's side. The battle vanished around them, the violence, the debts owed and unredeemable, the world that was and the world that was to come, all disappears for one instant as their lips held on to each other" (375). One could argue that London is following a model laid down by earlier LGBTQ novels for young adults and killing off one of his gay characters before a happily-ever-after relationship can begin, but the sequel will offer a counter to that argument.

In *Guardian* (2014), the new debt-free world has been created, but all is not well in the socialist paradise. Knox's role is hidden, Syd is a revered leader, and from the first scene in the novel, he is watched over by Liam, his bodyguard. The guardians (genetically-modified protectors of the peace in the old days) are dying of a mysterious illness that begins to infect the rest of the population. It appears that without the old technological fixes in their blood, people begin to die. The leadership wants to let most of them die to build a new world with those who were never affected by technology, and Syd means to stop the destruction. In the midst of all this, Liam is in love with Syd, who is completely disillusioned about his role as figurehead. Liam offers to help Syd fix the problems in their society, and perhaps more. Syd responds: "I taught myself to be alone. I thought the whole bankrupt thing was about sex, but it wasn't. It was about ruin, about being the kind of guy who ruins whoever he touches" (149). In spite of Syd's sense of contagion Liam thinks, "I'd burn the world down if it would make you smile" (169), which they just about do.

Syd, Marie (who has reappeared in this novel as a dedicated supporter of the new regime), and Liam decide to go back to Mountain City (the setting of *Proxy*) to see if they can't rebuild the technology that might save people from the virus. Throughout all this, Syd and Liam's sexuality is secondary but nevertheless important to their relationship— and their identities. Liam, it appears, has something to teach Syd (and readers) about self-respect. For example, when a character mentions being a "Chapter 11" disparagingly, "Syd glanced at Liam, who didn't seem at all bothered by the insult. There were things Liam felt ashamed of in his life, but that wasn't one of them" (232).

Toward the end of the novel, Syd and Marie begin to feel sick from the virus, although Liam is immune (for reasons too complicated to detail here). At a crucial moment during various chases and escapes,

Six. "What a wonderful world"

Syd kisses Liam: "The kiss was no longer than a second, but in that second, any walls between them fell. Liam's body was Syd's body; Syd's mind was Liam's mind. Someone's eyelash tickled. Their lips drew apart" (304). This seems no different from the classic hetero kiss between hero and heroine in any high-action movie or film (think *Star Wars* or *Raiders of the Lost Ark*), except this is two boys kissing as the world burns around them. For mysterious reasons, the guardians start to spontaneously recover (saved by a kiss?), and they help save Syd, Liam, and Marie. Safe (if not exactly well yet) at the end, Syd is encouraged to sleep by Liam. The last words of the novel are "And Liam was still there" (340). Liam is watching over Syd as he did from the beginning, although they are no longer Yovel and his loyal bodyguard; they are two romantic partners at the beginning of a new world.

David Levithan, Francesca Lia Block, Ruth Simms, Libba Bray, and Alex London are just a few of the young adult writers who are imagining places in which sexuality is fluid, homosexuality is not stigmatized, and kids, whatever their sexual attractions, can save the planet. It may be a "wonderful world" for Levithan, a "happily," if not quite happily-ever-after world for Block, a Pride Pack bringing parents and children back together, beauty queens rescuing themselves, or two gay boys saving the world, but each writer is creating a home that they wish they could live in—one where two boys kissing is a celebration, not a shame, one where packs of LGBTQ kids solve mysteries, one where magic genies can start a family, and one where beauty queens can be tomboyish, feminine, cisgendered, or not. Each of these liminal spaces provide opportunities for young readers to see themselves—and the possibilities (fanciful and not) for their lives.

Conclusion
Why Read (or Teach) These Books, and Where Do We Go from Here?

Aside from the fact that the novels discussed in this study are enjoyable to read, reflective of young people's lives, and aware of their potential to initiate change in the minds of their readers, these works deserve further study because they offer hope for LGBTQ adolescents that the still-homophobic world in which they live might evolve. They also open up a space for empathy on the part of straight and questioning readers. Blackburn and Clark noted in 2011:

> The fluidity of reader identities promises more opportunity for change as it enables queer readers to talk about both the commonality across reading experiences with readers positioned as allies, as well as the discontinuities in experience. These opportunities enable the enactment of queer community within a group of readers, as well as allowing ally readers to hear and learn about queer experiences in ways that would inform and enable them to enact ally identities with greater insight in the future [161].

Through works such as these, classroom discussions can be enriched by the multiplicity of experiences, and out-of-class relationships between LGBTQ students and their straight classmates might be strengthened.

However, there are further steps to be taken. Thomas, Crisp, and Znezek say that LGBTQ texts for young adults "must continue to increase both in quantity and quality and that teachers must explicitly engage students in critical discussions of the ways in which texts work to construct for readers what it means and looks like to be gay" (77). However, it is important for teachers to keep in mind, the authors say, that "one text cannot carry the burden of representing a diverse population and our classrooms and bookshelves must reflect a range of LGBTQ identities" (79). New and even better young adult novels that

Conclusion

tell the LGBTQ story will offer readers a vision of a future that gets better but also affirm who some of them are right now.

A LGBTQ-inclusive discourse and reading materials, however, might not be enough, Blackburn, Clark, and Nemeth argue, as it tends to "insists that gay and lesbian people are just like straight people and thus erases significant differences." On the other hand, "a queer approach strives to suspend sexual and gender identifies rather than underscore them, interrogating heteronormativity by acknowledging a variety of genders, sexes, and desires, as well as foregrounding the sexual, thereby challenging the notion of what counts as normal among them" (12). Queer literature, they say, differs from LGBTQ-themed literature "in the way that it offers multiple and conflicting ideologies related to sexuality and gender" (24). Engaging with this kind of literature "may provide critical resources to young adult readers by countering the invisible ideologies of heterosexism, misogyny, and homophobia that circulate in their daily lives" (43). Perhaps even more importantly, looking at various representations of gender and sexual identity

> might free a student who has been tagged as a fag or a dyke, even for years, of the burden of homophobia, even if only in his or her English language arts class…. [E]xploring possibilities of sexual and gender identities that are multiple, variable, and fluid might alleviate some of the pressure of being or becoming someone who is socially acceptable and soothe the anxieties associated with being or becoming someone who is not [44].

Alleviating at least some of the pressure that young adults (especially LGBTQ young adults) feel is in itself a noble goal. In addition, for students from others times of non-traditional families, "complicating the notions of families and home can be a relief" (44). Very few families these days resemble the Dick-and-Jane white-two-straight-parent-middle class world of 1950s picture books, and young people in what is now the majority might like to see themselves—or someone equally "different"—represented in fiction. Finally, "for teachers and students, engaging with queer literature provides opportunities to exist and thrive in the realm of the queer, a space where multiple ideologies and conflicting ideologies around sexuality and gender can circulate and be considered, examined, embraced, or rejected by the reader, rendering the text more open and less settled, and the space of the classroom, as a whole, more queer" (45). A queerer classroom might well be a more open—and a more honest—classroom.

This "more queer" space seems a realizable dream these days, as established publishing houses such as Scholastic and Simon and Schuster publish an ever-increasing number of LGBTQ novels for young adults, and Alison Bechtel's *Fun Home* (an autobiographical graphic novel about growing up queer) makes its way to Broadway. Teachers, too, are becoming more comfortable introducing LGBTQ material in their language-arts classrooms, and censorship, while it hasn't entirely disappeared (just ask the American Library Association), seems less of an immediate threat, even in small-town America. However, complacency is ill-advised, even in the time of legalized same-sex marriage and the repeal of Don't Ask Don't Tell in the military. It's up to middle and high school teachers, media specialists, administrators, community librarians, and members of the general public with children and grandchildren to continue to bring home quality LGBTQ books for young adults—and to demand that they be taught in public schools. The universities have a role as well: to introduce future teachers to these books and encourage them to overcome their personal prejudices and fears about teaching them in their own classrooms.

Of course, books can't do everything. LGBTQ kids are still being harassed at school and in their neighborhoods, are bullied and abused by homophobic parents at home, and are vulnerable to much higher rates of suicide and other forms of self-harm than the general population of young people. Still, the safe spaces of the classroom and the library can provide a respite from the more hostile world outside and, one hopes, support for the voices calling for acceptance, empathy, recognition, and embrace. It may not yet be the "wonderful world" envisioned by David Levithan and others, but it could be.

Chapter Notes

Preface

1. Terminology matters—and is therefore contested. I have decided to use the abbreviation "LGBTQ" to describe these texts, as it seems the most the most descriptive of the types of fictions with which I am working. Especially with the most recent fiction, the "Q" (for "queer") best demonstrates the fluid and shifting sexualities and sexual identities of the characters.

Introduction

1. Before moving on to a discussion of queerness in literature, it is important to note an important voice for minority queer culture—José Esteban Muñoz. In his *Disidentifications: Queers of Color and the Performance of Politics* (1999), Muñoz says that "disidentificaiton is meant to be descriptive of the survival strategies the minority subject practices in order to negotiate a phobic majoritarian public sphere that continuously elides or punishes the existence of subjects who do not conform to the phantasm of normative citizenship" (4). He also offers a response to the Edelman debate, part of which was staged in *PMLA* in 2006: "It has been clear to many of us, for quite a while now," he says, "that the antirelational in queer studies was the gay white man's last stand" ("Thinking Beyond" 825).

Chapter One

1. Although *Patience and Sarah* appears seven years earlier, its protagonists are adults (or nearly so), and the audience was at the time of publication almost entirely adult.

Chapter Two

1. Because the novels are paired, the later novel will be discussed in this chapter out of chronological order.

Chapter Four

1. I have chosen the term "trans" to describe the teens in this chapter, although I acknowledge that I am including categories (including transvestism) that have often been treated as separate. Victoria Flanagan, on the other hand, prefers the term "cross-dressing" for these phenomena because she sees it as "a relatively neutral term that allows for multiple interpretive possibilities [that] linguistically marks a very simple act—the crossing of cultural boundaries related to the wearing of various articles of gender-specific clothing" (5). Anthropologist David Valentine argues that "the category transgender has come to be understood as a *collective* category of identity which incorporates a diverse array of male- and female-bodied gender varied people who had previous understating as distinct kinds of persons, including self-identified transsexuals and transvestites" (4). However, it seems to me, that the slightly newer term "trans" could encompass both "transsexuality" and "transvestism," without excluding one or the other, and many trans teens today often choose not to "cross dress," exactly, but to wear gender-neutral clothing and assume more ambiguous gender identities.

Chapter Five

1. Col. Cammermeyer was a 28-year veteran nurse in the Army and National

Chapter Notes

Guard. According to the Lambda Legal website:

> Among many other honors, she received a Bronze Star for her service in Vietnam and was selected as the Veterans Administration Nurse of the Year in 1985. After she was discharged based on her sexual orientation, Lambda Legal filed a lawsuit challenging the constitutionality of her discharge. Two years later, a federal district judge held that the military's pre–"Don't Ask, Don't Tell" ban violated the equal protection and due process guarantees of the U.S. Constitution and ordered the Army to reinstate Cammermeyer to the Washington National Guard. The government did not appeal Cammermeyer's right to be reinstated, but it asked the Ninth Circuit court of Appeals to strike the judge's ruling from the books. The ruling took issue with the old ban as well as "Don't Ask, Don't Tell." The Ninth Circuit denied this request and sent the case back to district court, which refused to strike its original judgment in favor of Cammermeyer. Cammermeyer has now retired.

Chapter Six

1. Although not strictly utopian novels, Levithan and Green's *Will Grayson, Will Grayson* (2010) and *Hold Me Closer: The Tiny Cooper Story* (2015), which are companion novels, do have their fanciful elements. Told in two narrative voices, *Will Grayson, Will Grayson* has two main characters who are both named Will Grayson, one gay and the other straight. It is mostly the story of Tiny Cooper and his search for love, but it is also about the friendship between straight Will Grayson and Tiny—and Tiny's romantic relationship with gay Will Grayson. This is primarily a realistic novel, but it is linked to *Hold Me Closer*, which is the script of the musical featured at the end of *Will Grayson, Will Grayson*. An introductory note says that the play "is meant to be true. (Except for the part where people keep bursting into song—that's only true sometimes.)" (1).

2. The Weetzie Bat series has two prequels, *Baby Be-Bop* and *Pink Smog*, which are out of chronological sequence with the rest of the novel and are less relevant to this study. They do participate in the same magical realism of the other works in the series, however. *Baby Be-Bop* (1995) tells the story of Dirk and his family (and some of the back story on Duck as well). The last part of the novel deals with Duck's story, from his leaving his hippy, surfer home in Santa Cruz (his father is dead, and he believes it would break his mother's heart if she found out gay) and going to L.A., where he discovers the gay scene, and gets a job in a surf shop. The last words of the novel are in Dirk's mind. "Stories are like genies, Dirk thought. They can carry us into and through our sorrows. Sometimes they burn, sometimes they dance, sometimes they weep, sometimes they sing. Like genies, everyone has one.... Our stories can set us free, Dirk thought. When we set them free" (106). According to Roberta Trites, *Baby Be-Bop* is "very Foucauldian in [its] tendency to privilege the discourse of homosexuality over the physical sexual acts of gay men, defining homosexuality more rhetorically than physically" (143). Dirk, she says, "like so many gay YA protagonists—feels far more pain that pleasure in this novel, although he never denies his knowledge of the pleasure he takes in his orientation" (148).

Pink Smog has a younger Weetzie living in Los Angeles with her alcoholic mother, and longing for her father, who has left them and moved to New York City. She starts getting mysterious messages, believes that she has a guardian angel named Winter, and is tortured by Winter's sister, who she believes to be a witch. At the end of the novel, Weetzie has a vision of the friends she will meet: "a tall, dark, handsome boy who looked scary but was really quite shy and gentle and a cute blonde surfer boy with a funny, snorty laugh and the easiest shoulders. I imagined a boy the dreadlocks and a girl with hair like flowers. And I thought of a boy in a fedora hat and trench coats, like a funny detective, like a secret agent man, with green eyes that were full of mystery and familiarity at the same time." She imagines that they "would all live together someday, in a sunny cottage like the one I lived in when I was born" (184). Her final message is that "the worse things get, the more you have to make yourself see the magic in order to survive" (185).

3. Out of print since 1995, the Pride Pack detective novels by Ruth Ann Simms (writing as R.J. Hamilton) have been reprinted, fortunately, by Cheyenne Publishing, after their original press was sold and the LGBTQ young adult line was discontinued. A third book in the series has recently been published, and the fourth book manuscript has gone missing.

Bibliography

Abate, Michelle. "From Cold War Lesbian Pulp to Contemporary Young Adult Novels: Vin Packer's *Spring Fire*, M.E. Kerr's *Deliver Us from Evie*, and Marijane Meaker's Fight Against Fifties Homophobia." *Children's Literature Association Quarterly* 32 (2007): 231-51. Project Muse.

Ahmed, Sara. *Queer Phenomenology: Orientations, Objects, Others*. Durham: Duke University Press, 2006. Book.

Archer, Bert. *The End of Gay: And the Death of Heterosexuality*. New York: Thunder's Mouth Press, 2002. Book.

Baccolini, Rafaella. "The Persistence of Hope in Dystopian Science Fiction." *PMLA* 119 (2004): 518-21.

Bacigalupi, Paolo. "The Invisible Dystopia." *Kirkus Reviews*. March 21, 2012. https://www.kirkusreviews.com/features/invisible-dystopias. January 27, 2016. Website.

_____. "Straight Laced Dystopias." *Kirkus Reviews*. April 4, 2012. https://www.kirkusreviews.com/features/straight-laced-dystopias/#continue_reading_post. January 27, 2016. Website.

Barclay, Bridgitte. "'Perpetually Waving to an Unseen Crowd': Satire and Process in *Beauty Queens*." *Female Rebellion in Young Adult Dystopian Fiction*. Ed. Sara K. Day, Marianda A. Green-Bartect, and Amy L. Montz. Burlington, VT: Ashgate, 2014. 141-53. Book.

Basu, Balaka, Katherine R. Broad, and Carrie Hintz. "Introduction." *Contemporary Dystopian Fiction for Young Adults: Brave New Teenagers*. New York: Routledge, 2013. 1-15. Book.

Beam, Cris. *I Am J*. New York: Little, Brown, 2012 (2011). Book.

Bergman, David. *Gaiety Transfigured: Gay Self-Representation in American Literature*. Madison: University of Wisconsin Press, 1991. Book.

Berlant, Lauren, and Michael Warner. "What Does Queer Theory Teach Us about X?" *PMLA* 110 (1995): 343-49. JSTOR.

Bersani, Leo. *Homos*. Cambridge: Harvard University Press, 1995. Book.

_____. "Is the Rectum a Grave?" *Is the Rectum a Grave? And Other Essays*. Chicago: University of Chicago Press, 2010. 3-30. Book.

Bess, Clayton. *Big Man and the Burn-out*. Boston: Houghton Mifflin, 1985. Book.

_____. http://webpages.csus.edu/~bobloc ke/bess/burnout.htm#. Website.

Blackburn, Mollie V., and J.F. Buckley. "Teaching Queer-Inclusive English Language Arts." *Journal of Adolescent and Adult Literacy* 48 (2005): 202-12. Ebsco.

_____, and Caroline T. Clark. "Becoming Readers of Literature with LGBT Themes." *Handbook of Research on Children's and Young Adult Literature*. Ed. Shelby A. Wolf, Karen Coates, Patricia Enciso, and Christine A. Jenkins. New York: Routledge, 2011. 148-63. Book.

_____, Caroline T. Clark, and Emily A. Nemeth. "Examining Queer Elements and Ideologies in LGBT-Themed Literature: What Queer Literature Can offer Young Adult Readers." *Journal of Literacy Research* 47 (2015): 11-48. SAGE.

Block, Francesca Lia. *Baby Be-Bop*. New York: HarperTeen, 1997 (1995). Book.

_____. *Cherokee Bat and the Goat Guys*. New York: HarperCollins, 1992. Book.

Bibliography

———. *Missing Angel Juan*. New York: HarperCollins, 1993. Book.

———. *Necklace of Kisses*. New York: HarperCollins, 2006 (2005). Book.

———. *Pink Smog: Becoming Weetzie Bat*. New York: HarperTeen, 2014 (2012). Book.

———. *Weetzie Bat*. New York HarperCollins, 1989. Book.

———. *Witch Baby*. New York: HarperCollins, 1991. Book.

Bornstein, Kate. *Gender Outlaw: On Men, Women, and the Rest of Us*. New York: Vintage, 1995 (1994). Book.

———. *A Queer and Pleasant Danger*. Boston: Beacon, 2012. Book.

Boylan, Jennifer Finney. *She's Not There: A Life in Two Genders*. New York: Broadway Paperbacks, 2013 (2003). Book.

Bradford, Clare, Kerry Mallan, John Stephens, and Robyn McCallum. *New World Orders in Contemporary Children's Literature*. New York: Palgrave, 2008. Book.

Braidotti, Rosi. "Becoming Woman: or Sexual Difference Revisited." *Theory, Culture & Society* 20 (2003): 43–64. Journal Article.

Bray Libba. *Beauty Queens*. New York: Scholastic, 2011. Book.

Brill, Stephanie, and Rachel Pepper. *The Transgender Child*. San Francisco: Cleis Press, 2008. Book.

Brooks, Peter. *Enigmas of Identity*. Princeton: Princeton University Press, 2011. Book.

Bruhm, Steven, and Natasha Hurley, eds. "Introduction." *Curiouser: On the Queerness of Children*. Minneapolis: University of Minnesota Press, 2004. ix–xxxviii. Book.

Butler, Christopher. *Pleasure and the Arts: Enjoying Literature, Painting, and Music*. Oxford: Oxford University Press, 2004. Book.

Butler, Judith. *Bodies That Matter: On the Discursive Limits of "Sex."* New York: Routledge, 1993. Book.

———. "The End of Sexual Difference?" *Undoing Gender*. New York: Routledge, 2004. 174–203. Book.

———. *Gender Trouble: Feminism and the Subversion of Identity*. New York: Routledge, 1990. Book.

———. *Undoing Gender*. New York: Routledge, 2004. Book.

Cammermeyer, Margarethe. "Foreword." In Howey and Samuels. xiii–xvi. Book.

Carlson, Shanna T. "Transgender Subjectivity and the Logic of Sexual Difference." *Differences* 21 (2010): 46–72. Ebsco.

Cart, Michael. "Annie…. Still on Our Minds." *Booklist*. Sept. 15, 1994. 127. Ebsco.

———, and Christine Jenkins. *The Heart Has Its Reasons: Young Adult Literature with Gay/Lesbian Queer Content: 1969–2004*. Metuchen, NJ: The Scarecrow Press, 2006. Book.

Castle, Terry. *The Apparitional Lesbian: Female Homosexuality and Modern Culture*. New York: Columbia University Press, 1992. Book

Charlton-Trujillo, E. E. *Fat Angie*. Somerville, MA: Candlewick, 2013. Book.

Chauncey, George. *Gay New York: Gender, Urban Culture, and the Making of the Gay Male World, 1890–1940*. New York: Basic Books, 1994. Book.

Clark, Kristin Elizabeth. *Freakboy*. New York: Farrar, Straus and Giroux, 2013. Book.

Cole, C.L., and Shannon L.C. Cate. "Compulsory Gender and Transgender Existence: Adrienne Rich's Queer Possibility." *Women's Studies Quarterly* 36 (2008): 279–87. Project Muse.

Collins, Carol Jones. "Finding the Way: Morality and Young Adult Literature." In Vandergrift, 157–83.

Connell, R. W., and James Messerschmidt. "Hegemonic Masculinity: Rethinking the Concept." *Gender and Society* 19 (2005): 829–59. JSTOR.

Crisp, Thomas. "From Romance to Magical Realism: Limits and possibilities in Gay Adolescent Fiction." *Children's Literature in Education* 40 (2009): 333–48. Ebsco.

———. "The Trouble with *Rainbow Boys*." *Children's Literature in Education* 39 (2008): 237–61.

Cronn-Mills, Kirsten. *Beautiful Music*

for Ugly Children. Woodbury, MN: Llewellyn, 2014 (2012). Book.

Cuseo, Allan A. *Homosexual Characters in YA Novels: A Literary Analysis, 1969–1982*. Metuchen, NJ: The Scarecrow Press, 1992. Book.

Day, Frances Ann. *Lesbian and Gay Voices: An Annotated Bibliography and Guide to Literature for Children and Young Adults*. Westport, CT: Greenwood Press, 2000.

Day, Sara K. "Docile Bodies, Dangerous Bodies: Sexual Awakening and Social Resistance in Young Adult Dystopian Novels." In Basu, et al., 75–93. Book.

Deran, Elisabeth. "Appendix." *Patience and Sarah*. Vancouver: Arsenal Pulp Press, 2005. 207–14. Book.

Donovan, John. *I'll Get There. It Better Be Worth the Trip*. Woodbury, MN: Flux, 2010 (1969). Book.

Donovan, Stacey. *Dive*. Kindle Edition, 2015 (2000).

Drabinski, Kate. "Incarnate Possibilities: Female to Male Transgender Narratives and the Making of Self." *Journal of Narrative Theory* 44 (2014): 304–29. Project Muse.

Duncan, Kaitlyn Tierney. "Hatchback." In Levithan and Merrell, 170–82.

Edelman, Lee. *No Future: Queer Theory and the Death Drive*. Durham: Duke University Press, 2004. Book.

Felski, Rita. *The Limits of Critique*. Chicago: University of Chicago Press, 2015. Book.

Fico, Eugenidies. "It's Not Confidential, I've Got Potential." In Levithan and Merrell, 12–20.

Flanagan, Victoria. *Into the Closet: Cross-Dressing and the Gendered Body in Children's Literature and Film*. New York: Routledge, 2008. Book.

Foucault, Michel. "The Gay Science." Trans. Nicolae Morar and Daniel W. Smith. *Critical Inquiry* 37 (2011): 385–403. Ebsco.

_____. *The History of Sexuality*. Vol. I. Trans. Robert Hurley. New York: Pantheon, 1978. Book.

_____. "Of Other Spaces." Trans. Jay Mikowiec. *Diacritics* 16 (1986): 22–27. JSTOR.

Fuoss, Kirk. "Portrait of the Adolescent as a Young Gay." *Queer Words Queer Images: Communication and the Construction of Homosexuality*. Ed. R. Jeffrey Ringer. New York: New York University Press, 1994. 159–74. Book.

Fuss, Diana. "Inside/Out." *Inside/Out: Lesbian Theories/Gay Theories*. Ed. Diana Fuss. New York: Routledge, 1991. Book.

Garber, Majorie. *Vested Interests: Cross-Dressing and Cultural Anxiety*. New York: Routledge, 1992. Book.

Garden, Nancy. *Annie on My Mind*. New York: Farrar, Straus and Giroux, 2007 (1982). Book.

Gillis, Bryan, and Joanna Simpson. *Sexual Content in Young Adult Literature: Reading Between the Sheets*. Lanham, MD: Rowman and Littlefield, 2015. Book.

Gold, Rachel. *Being Emily*. Tallahassee: Bella Books, 2012. Book.

Goodman, Jan. "Out of the Closet, But Paying the Price: Lesbian and Gay Characters in Children's Literature." *Interracial Books for Children Bulletin* 14 (1983): 13–15. Ebsco.

Gould, Sophia. "Nothing to Me." In Howey and Samuels, 1–13. Book.

Green, Jesse. *The Velveteen Father: An Unexpected Journey to Parenthood*. New York: Villard, 1999. Book.

Green, John, and David Levithan. *Will Grayson, Will Grayson*. New York: Penguin, 2011 (2010). Book.

Gross, Claire. "What Makes a Good Coming Out Book?" *The Horn Book*. http://www.hbook.com/2013/03/featured/what-makes-a-good-ya-coming-out-novel/#_26. March 2013. Website.

Gunn, Drewey Wayne. "Afterward." *Who Framed Lorenzo Garcia?* Camas, WA: Cheyenne, 2011 (1995). 115–16.

Guy, Rosa. *Ruby*. East Orange, NJ: Just Us Books, 2005 (1976). Book.

Halberstam, Judith. *In a Queer Time and Place: Transgender Bodies, Subcultural Lives*. New York: New York University Press. 2005. Book.

_____. "Oh Bondage Up Yours! Female Masculinity and the Tomboy." In *Curiouser*, 191–214. Book.

Hartinger, Brent. *Double Feature*. Create-

Bibliography

Space Independent Publishing Platform, 2007. Book.

———. *The Elephant of Surprise*. CreateSpace Independent Publishing Platform, 2013. Book.

———. *Geography Club*. New York: HarperTempest, 2004 (2003). Book.

———. *The Order of the Poison Oak*. CreateSpace Independent Publishing Platform, 2005. Book.

Herrmann, Anne. "Imitations of Marriage: Crossdressed Couples in Contemporary Lesbian Fiction." *Feminist Studies* 18 (1992): 609–24. Ebsco.

Hintz, Carrie, and Elaine Ostry, eds. *Utopian and Dystopian Writing for Children and Young Adults*. New York: Routledge, 2003. Book.

Holland, Isabelle. *The Man Without a Face*. New York: Harper Trophy, 1972.

Holmes, A.M. *Jack*. New York: Vintage, 1990 (1989). Book.

Horning, Kathleen. Interview with Nancy Garden. *Annie on My Mind*. New York: Farrar, Straus and Giroux, 2007. 239–63. Book.

Howey, Noell, and Ellen Samuels, eds. *Out of the Ordinary: Essays on Growing Up with Gay, Lesbian, and Transgender Parents*. New York: St. Martins, 2000.

Jenkins, Christine. "From Queer to Gay and Back Again: Young Adult Novels with Gay/Lesbian/Queer Content, 1969–1997." *Library Quarterly* 68 (1998): 298–334. Article.

Jensen, Cordelia. *Skyscraping*. New York: Philomel, 2015. Book.

Johnson, Maureen. *The Bermudez Triangle*. New York: Penguin, 2004. Book.

Juhasz, Suzanne. *Reading from the Heart: Women, Literature, and the Search for True Love*. New York: Viking, 1994. Book.

Kaplan, Deborah, and Rebecca Rabinowitz. "'Beautiful, or Thick, or Right, or Complicated': Queer Heterosexuality in the Young Adult Works of Cynthia Voigt and Francesca Lia Block." *Straight Writ Queer: Non-Normative Expressions of Heterosexuality in Literature*. Ed. Richard Fantina. Jefferson, NC: McFarland, 2006. 197–208. Book.

Katcher, Brian. *Almost Perfect*. New York: Random House, 2011 (2009). Book.

Katz, Jonathan. "Writing and Publishing *Patience and Sarah*: 'I Felt I Had Found My People.' Interview with Alma Routsong." *Gay American History: Lesbians and Gay Men in the U.S.A.* New York: Meridian, 1976. 433–43. Book.

Kenneally, Miranda. *Stealing Parker*. Naperville, IL: Sourcebooks, 2012. Book.

Kent, Kathryn R. "'No Trespassing': Girl Scout Camp and the Limits of the Counterpublic Sphere." In *Curiouser: On the Queerness of Children*. Minneapolis: University of Minnesota Press, 2004. 173–89. Book.

Kerr, M.E. *I'll Love You When You're More Like Me*. New York: Harper and Row, 1977. Book.

Kessler, Suzanne J. *Lessons from the Intersexed*. New Brunswick: Rutgers University Press, 2002 (1998). Book.

Kidd, Kenneth. "Introduction: Lesbian/Gay Literature for Children and Young Adults." *Children's Literature Association Quarterly* 23 (1998): 114–19. Project Muse.

———. "Queer Theory's Child and Children's Literature Studies." *PMLA* 126 (2011): 182–88.

Kimmell, Michael S. "Masculinity as Homophobia: Fear, Same, and Silence in the Construction of Gender Identity." *College Men and Masculinities: Theory, Research, and Implications for Practice*. Ed. Shaun R. Harper and Frank Harris III. San Francisco: Josey-Bass, 2010. 23–31. Book.

Koertge, Ron. *The Arizona Kid*. Cambridge, MA: Candlewick, 2005 (1988). Book.

Konigsburg, Bill. *Openly Straight*. New York: Scholastic, 2013. Book.

Kuklin, Susan. *Beyond Magenta: Transgender Teens Speak Out*. Sommerville, MA: Candlewick Press, 2014. Book.

Lambda Legal. http://www.lambdalegal.org/in-court/cases/cammermeyer-v-us-army. Website.

Lee, Vanessa Wayne. "'Unshelter Me': The Emerging Fictional Adolescent Lesbian." *Children's Literature Association Quarterly* 23 (1998): 152–59. Project Muse.

Bibliography

Levithan, David. *Boy Meets Boy*. New York: Knopf, 2005 (2003). Book.

_____. *Every Day*. New York: Random House, 2013 (2012). Book

_____. *Hold Me Closer: The Tiny Cooper Story*. New York: Penguin, 2015. Book.

_____. "Supporting Gay Teen Literature: An Advocate Speaks Out for Representation on Library Shelves." *School Library Journal* (2004): 44–45. Article.

_____. *Two Boys Kissing*. New York: Knopf, 2013. Book.

Levithan, David, and Billy Merrell, eds. *The Full Spectrum: A New Generation of Writing about Gay, Lesbian, Bisexual, Transgender, Questioning, and Other Identities*. New York: Knopf, 2006. Book.

Lobban, Marjorie, and Laura A. Clyde. *Out of the Closet and Into the Classroom: Homosexuality in Books for Young People*. 2nd Ed. Port Melbourne: D.W. Thorpe, 1996. Book.

London, Alex. *Guardians*. New York: Penguin, 2014. Book.

_____. *Proxy*. New York: Penguin, 2013. Book.

Love, Heather. *Feeling Backward: Loss and the Politics of Queer History*. Cambridge: Harvard University Press, 2007. Book.

McCallum, Robin. *Ideologies of Identity in Adolescent Fiction: The Dialogic Construction of Subjectivity*. New York: Routledge, 1999. Book.

Meyer, Carolyn. *Elliott and Win*. New York: Macmillan, 1990 (1986). Book.

Miller, Isabel. *Patience and Sarah*. Vancouver: Arsenal Pulp Press, 2005 (1969). Book.

Mills, Emily. "Bill on Transgender Students Doesn't Move Wisconsin Forward." *Milwaukee Journal-Sentinel*. 11 Oct. 2015. C1–2. Newspaper Article.

Morrison, Paul. *The Explanation for Everything: Essays on Sexual Subjectivity*. New York: New York University Press, 2001. Book.

Muñoz, José Esteban. *Disidentifications: Queers of Color and the Performance of Politics*. Minneapolis: University of Minnesota Press, 1999. Book.

_____. "Thinking Beyond Antirelationality and Antiutopianism in Queer Critique." *PMLA* 121 (2006): 825–26. JSTOR.

Murdock, Catherine Gilbert. *Dairy Queen*. Boston: Houghton Mifflin, 2006. Book.

Myracle, Lauren. *Kissing Kate*. New York: Penguin, 2007 (2003). Book.

Nealon, Christopher. *Foundlings: Lesbian and Gay Historical Emotion Before Stonewall*. Durham: Duke University Press, 2001. Book.

Nilsen, Alleen Pace, and Don L. F. Nilsen. *Names and Naming in Young Adult Literature*. Lanham, MD: The Scarecrow Press, 2007. Book.

Norton, Jody. "Transchildren and the Discipline of Children's Literature." *Over the Rainbow: Queer Children's and Young Adult Fiction*. Ed. Michelle Ann Abate and Kenneth Kidd. Ann Arbor: University of Michigan Press, 2011. 293–313. Book.

Norton, Terry L., and Jonathan W. Vare. "Literature of Today's Gay and lesbian Teens: Subverting the Culture of Silence." *English Journal* 94 (2004): 65–69. JSTOR.

Nutt, Amy Ellis. *Becoming Nicole: The Transformation of an American Family*. New York: Random House, 2015. Kindle Edition.

Owen, Gavrielle. "Young Adult Literature, Lesbian." *Encyclopedia of Contemporary LGBTQ Literature of the United States*. Ed. Emmanuel S. Nelson. Vol. II. Santa Barbara: Greenwood Press, 2009. 672–77. Book.

Patee, Amy S. "Sexual Fantasy: The Queer Utopia of David Levithan's *Boy Meets Boy*." *Children's Literature Association Quarterly* 33 (2008): 156–71. Project Muse.

Peck, Dale. *Sprout*. New York: Bloomsbury, 2009. Book.

Peters, Julie Anne. *Luna*. New York: Hachette, 2006 (2004). Book.

Polanski, Ami. *Gracefully Grayson*. Los Angeles: Hyperion, 2014. Book.

Prosser, Jay. *Second Skins: The Body Narratives of Transsexuality*. New York: Columbia University Press, 1998. Book.

Pugh, Tison. "Conclusion: Homosexuality and the End of Innocence in David

Bibliography

Levithan's *Boy Meets Boy.*" Innocence, Heterosexuality, and the Queerness of Children's Literature. New York: Routledge, 2011. 161–66. Book.

Rev. of *David and Jonathan.* https://www.kirkusreviews.com/book-reviews/cynthia-voigt/david-and-jonathan. Oct. 7, 2015. Website.

Rev. of *David and Jonathan.* http://www.publishersweekly.com/978-0-590-45165-9. Oct. 7, 2015. Website.

Rev. of *Geography Club. Kirkus Reviews.* https://www.kirkusreviews.com/book-reviews/brent-hartinger/geography-club. Oct. 7, 2015. Website.

Rev. of *Geography Club. Publishers Weekly* http://www.publishersweekly.com/978-0-06-001221-2. Oct. 7, 2015. Website.

Rev. of *The Method. Kirkus Reviews.* https://www.kirkusreviews.com/book-reviews/paul-robert-walker-4/the-method. Oct. 7, 2015. Website.

Rev. of *The Method. Publishers Weekly.* http://www.publishersweekly.com/978-0-15-200528-3. Oct. 7, 2015. Website.

Ripslinger, Jon. *How I Fell in Love and Learned to Shoot Free Throws.* Brookfield, CT: Roaring Brook Press, 2003. Book.

Ryan, P.E. *The Saints of Augustine.* New York: HarperTeen, 2007. Book.

Ryan, Sara. *Empress of the World.* New York: Viking, 2001. Book.

_____. *Rules for Hearts.* New York: Penguin, 2009 (2007). Book.

Sáenz, Benjamin Alire. *Aristotle and Dante Discover the Secrets of the Universe.* New York: Simon & Schuster, 2014 (2012). Book

St. Claire, Nancy. "Outside Looking In: Representations of Gay and Lesbian Experiences in the Young Adult Novel." *The ALAN Review* 23 (1995): 38–43.

St. James, James. *Freak Show.* New York: Penguin, 2008 (2007). Book.

Salat, Cristina. *Living in Secret.* Orinda, CA: Books MarcUs, 1999 (1993). Book.

Sambell, Kay. "Carnivalizing the Future: a New Approach to Theorizing Childhood and Adulthood in Science Fiction for Young Readers." *The Lion and the Unicorn* 28 (2004): 247–67. Project Muse.

_____. "Presenting the Case for Social Change: The Creative Dilemma of Dystopian Writing for Children." In Hintz and Ostry, 163–78. Book.

Sanchez, Alex. *Rainbow Boys.* New York: Simon & Schuster, 2001. Book.

_____. *Rainbow High.* New York: Simon & Schuster, 2005 (2003). Book.

_____. *Rainbow Road.* New York: Simon & Schuster, 2007 (2005). Book.

Sargent, Lyman Tower. "Afterward." In Hintz and Ostry, 232–34. Book.

Savage, Dan. *The Kid: What Happened After My Boyfriend and I Decided to Go Get Pregnant.* New York: Dutton, 1999. Book.

_____. "Preface." In Howey and Samuels, xi–xii. Book.

Scelsa, Kate. *Fans of the Impossible Life.* New York: Balzer + Bay, 2015. Book.

Schlichter, Annette. "Queer at Last? Straight Intellectuals and the Desire for Transgression." *GLQ* 10 (2004): 543–64. Project Muse.

Scoppettone, Sandra. *Happy Endings Are All Alike.* Brooklyn: Lizzie Skrunick Books, 2014 (1978). Book.

Sedgwick, Eve Kosofsky. *Epistemology of the Closet.* Berkeley: University of California Press, 1990.

_____. "How to Bring Your Kids Up Gay: The War on Effeminate Boys." In *Curiouser,* 139–49. Book.

_____. *Touching Feeling: Affect, Pedagogy, Performativity.* Durham: Duke University Press, 2003. Book.

Self, Jeffery. *Drag Teen.* New York: Scholastic (Push), 2016. Book.

Shimko, Bonnie. *Letters in the Attic.* Chicago: Academy, 2002. Book.

Simms, Ruth (writing as R.J. Hamilton). *The Case of the Missing Mother.* Camas, WA: Cheyenne, 2011 (1995). Book.

_____. *Who Framed Lorenzo Garcia?* Camas, WA: Cheyenne, 2011 (1995). Book.

Snediker, Michael. *Queer Optimism: Lyric Personhood and Other Felicitous Persuasions.* Minneapolis: University of Minnesota Press, 2009. Book.

Bibliography

Stephens, John. *Language and Ideology in Children's Fiction.* New York: Longman, 1992. Book.

Stimpson, Catharine. "Zero Degree Deviancy: The Lesbian Novel in English." *Critical Inquiry* 8 (1981): 363–79. JSTOR.

Stockton, Kathryn Bond. *The Queer Child: Or Growing Sideways in the Twentieth Century.* Durham: Duke University Press, 2009. Book.

Stryker, Susan. *Transgender History.* Berkeley: Seal Press, 2008. Book.

Susina, Jan. "The Rebirth of the Postmodern Flaneur: Notes on the Postmodern Landscape of Francesca Lia Block's *Weetzie Bat.*" *Marvels and Tales* 18 (2002): 188–200. Ebsco.

Thomas, Calvin. "Straight with a Twist: Queer Theory and the Subject of Heterosexuality." In *Straight with a Twist: Queer Theory and the Subject of Heterosexuality.* Ed. Calvin Thomas. Urbana: University of Illinois Press, 2000. 11–44. Book.

Thomas, P.L., Thomas Crisp, and Suzanne M. Knezek. "'Just Don't See Myself Here': Challenging Conversations about LGBTQ Adolescent Literature." *The English Journal* 99 (2010): 76–79. JSTOR.

Thompson, Dawn. "Prussic Acid with a Twist: *The Well of Loneliness*, M.E. Kerr, and Young Adult Readers." *Children's Literature Association Quarterly* 31 (2006): 282–99. JSTOR.

Totaro, Rebecca Carol Noël. "Suffering in Utopia: Testing the Limits in Young Adult Novels." In Hintz and Ostry, 127–38. Book.

Tribunella, Eric. *Melancholia and Maturation: The Use of Trauma in American Children's Literature.* Knoxville: University of Tennessee Press, 2010. Book.

Trites, Roberta. "Queer Discourse and the Young Adult Novel: Repression and Power in Gay Male Adolescent Literature." *Children's Literature Association Quarterly* 23 (1998): 143–51. Project Muse.

Valentine, David. *Imagining Transgender: An Ethnography of a Category.* Durham: Duke University Press, 2007. Book.

Vandergrift, Kay. "Introduction." *Mosaics of Meaning: Enhancing the Intellectual Life of Young Adults Through Story.* Ed. Kay Vandergrift. Lanham, MD: The Scarecrow Press, 1996. Book.

Verdi, Jessica. *My Life After Now.* Napierville, IL: Sourcebooks, 2013. Book.

Vicinus, Martha. "'They Wonder to Which Sex I Belong': The Historical Roots of the Modern Lesbian Identity." *Feminist Studies* 18 (1992): 467–98. JSTOR.

Voigt, Cynthia. *David and Jonathan.* New York: Scholastic, 1992. Book.

Walker, Paul Robert. *The Method.* New York: Harcourt, 1996 (1990). Book

Warner, Michael. "Introduction." *Fear of a Queer Planet: Queer Politics and Social Theory.* Ed. Michael Warner. Minneapolis: University of Minnesota Press, 1993. vii–xxxi. Book.

———. *The Trouble with Normal: Sex, Politics, and the Ethics of Queer life.* New York: The Free Press, 1990. Book.

Watts, Julia. *Finding H.F.* Tallahassee: Bella Books, 2011 (2001). Book.

Wickins, Corrine M. "Codes, Silences, and Homophobia: Challenging Normative Assumptions about Gender and Sexuality in Contemporary LGBTQ Young Adult Literature." *Children's Literature in Education* 42 (2011): 148–64. Ebsco.

Wittlinger, Ellen. *Heart on My Sleeve.* New York: Simon & Schuster, 2006 (2004). Book.

———. *Love and Lies: Marisol's Story.* New York: Simon & Schuster, 2010 (2008). Book.

———. *Parrotfish.* New York: Simon & Schuster, 2011 (2007). Book.

Wolf, Virginia L. "The Gay Family in Literature for Young People." *Children's Literature in Education* 29 (1989): 51–58. Ebsco.

Woodson, Jacqueline. *From the Notebooks of Melanin Sun.* Penguin, 2010 (1995). Book.

Zemser, Amy Bronwen. *Dear Julia.* New York: Greenwillow, 2008. Book.

Zimmerman, Bonnie. *The Safe Sea of Women: Lesbian Fiction—1969–1989.* Boston: Beacon Press, 1990. Book.

Zipes, Jack. "Foreword." In Hintz and Ostry, vii–xi. Book.

Index

Almost Perfect 121–23
Annie on My Mind 27, 37, 41–44, 49
Aristotle and Dante Discover the Secrets of the Universe 96–98
The Arizona Kid 139–40

Baby Be-Bop 186*ch6n*2
Beam, Chris 123–25; *I Am J* 123–25
Beautiful Music for Ugly Children 125–26
Beauty Queens 174–76
Becoming Nicole 112–14
Being Emily 127–28
The Bermudez Triangle 70–72
Bess, Clayton 44–47; *Big Man and the Burn-Out* 44–47
Big Man and the Burn-Out 44–47
Block, Francesca Lia 170–73; *Baby Be-Bop* 186*ch6n*2; *Cherokee Bat and the Goat Guys* 173; *Necklace of Kisses* 173; *Pink Smog* 186*ch6n*2; *Weetzie Bat* 170–72; *Witch Baby* 172–73
Boy Meets Boy 1, 162–64, 170, 171, 179, 183
Boylan, Jennifer Finney 110–11; *She's Not There* 110–11
Braidotti, Rosi 7–10
Bray, Libba 174–76; *Beauty Queens* 174–76
Butler, Judith 6–10, 11, 107

Cammermeyer, Col. Margarethe 134–35, 185–86*ch5n*1
Cart, Michael 3; and Christine Jenkins 18–19, 68
The Case of the Missing Mother 174
censorship 2, 14, 21, 22, 51, 183
Charlton-Trujillo, E.E. 60, 75–76; *Fat Angie* 75–76
Cherokee Bat and the Goat Guys 173
Clark, Kristin Elizabeth 128–30; *Freakboy* 128–30
Crisp, Thomas 19–20, 24, 78–79, 82, 88–89, 9, 93–96, 98, 163, 181
Cronn-Mills, Kirsten 125–26; *Beautiful Music for Ugly Children* 125–26

Dairy Queen 72–76
David and Jonathan 82–83
Dear Julia 151
Deliver Us from Evie 50, 51, 52, 55, 61, 72, 87
Dive 52–55, 66
Donovan, John 2, 18, 21, 24, 32–34, 48, 52, 66, 79; *I'll Get There. It Better Be Worth the Trip* 2, 18, 32–34, 52, 66
Donovan, Stacey 33, 60, 66; *Dive* 52–55, 66
Double Feature 86–88
Drag Teen 131–32
dystopias 157–79

The Elephant of Surprise 88–89
Elliott and Win 2, 47–48
Empress of the World 63–65
Every Day 167–69

families 134–56
Fans of the Impossible Life 155
Fat Angie 75–76
Finding H.F. 60–63
Freak Show 117–19
Freakboy 128–30
From the Notebooks of Melanin Sun 146–48
futurity 10–13

Garden, Nancy 16, 21, 24, 25, 35, 37, 38, 41–44, 48; *Annie on My Mind* 27, 37, 41–44, 49
gender performativity 6–10
Geography Club 82–85
Gold, Rachel 127–28; *Being Emily* 127–28
Gracefully Grayson 130–31
Green, Jesse 136–37; *The Velveteen Father* 136–37
Guardian 178–79
Guy, Rosa 24, 34–36; *Ruby* 34–36

Hard Love 55–57
Hartinger, Brett 82–88; *Double Feature* 86–88; *The Elephant of Surprise* 88–89; *Geography Club* 82–85; *The Order of the Poison Oak* 85–86

Index

Heart on My Sleeve 69–70
Hold Me Closer: The Tiny Cooper Story 186ch6n1
Holmes, A.M. 140–42; *Jack* 140–43
How I Fell in Love and Learned to Shoot Free Throws 148–49

I Am J 123–25
I'll Get There. It Better Be Worth the Trip 2, 18, 32–34, 37, 49, 52, 54, 66

Jack 140–43
Jenkins, Christine 18, 23, 171; and Michael Cart 18–19, 68
Jensen, Cordelia 154–55; *Skyscraping* 154–55
Johnson, Maureen 60, 70–72; *The Bermudez Triangle* 70–72

Katcher, Brian 121–23; *Almost Perfect* 121–23
Kenneally, Miranda 152–53; *Stealing Parker* 152–53
Kerr, M.E. 24, 36–37, 51, 55, 60, 87; *Deliver Us from Evie* 51, 55, 87; *I'll Love You When You're More Like Me* 36–37
The Kid 137–38
Kissing Kate 67–69
Koertge, Ron 139–40; *The Arizona Kid* 139–40
Konigsberg, Bill 98–100; *Openly Straight* 98–100

Letters in the Attic 66–67
Levithan, David 20, 24, 49, 79, 87, 109; *Boy Meets Boy* 1, 162–64, 170, 171, 179, 183; *Every Day* 167–69; *Hold Me Closer: The Tiny Cooper Story* 186ch6n1; *Two Boys Kissing* 169–70; *Will Grayson Will Grayson* 186ch6n1
Living in Secret 143–46
London, Alex 176–79; *Guardian* 178–79; *Proxy* 176–78
Love and Lies: Marisol's Story 57–60
Luna 115–17

The Method 80–82
Meyer, Carolyn 2, 24, 47–48; *Elliott and Win* 2, 47–48
Miller, Isabel 2, 24, 25–32; *Patience and Sarah* 2, 25–32, 35, 37, 39, 43–44, 49, 62, 185ch1n1
Murdock 72–76, 60; *Dairy Queen* 72–76
My Life After Now 153–54
Myracle, Lauren 60, 67–69; *Kissing Kate* 67–69

Necklace of Kisses 173
Nutt, Amy Ellis 112–14; *Becoming Nicole* 112–14

Openly Straight 98–100
The Order of the Poison Oak 85–86

Parrotfish 119–121
Patience and Sarah 2, 25–32, 37, 39, 43–44, 49, 62, 185ch1n1
Peck, Dale 95–96; *Sprout* 95–96
Peters, Julie Ann 115–17; *Luna* 115–17
Pink Smog 186ch6n2
Polonski, Amy 130–31; *Gracefully Grayson* 130–31
Pride Pack 174, 186ch6n3
Proxy 176–78

queer adolescent sexualities in literature 13–22
queer theory 3–6

Rainbow Boys 89–91
Rainbow High 91–92
Rainbow Road 92–94
Ripslinger, Jon 148–49; *How I Fell in Love and Learned to Shoot Free Throws* 148–49
Ruby 34–36
The Rules for Hearts 65–66
Ryan, P.E. 150–51; *The Saints of Augustine* 150–51
Ryan, Sarah 60, 63–66; *Empress of the World* 63–65; *The Rules for Hearts* 65–66

Sáenz, Benjamin Alire 96–98; *Aristotle and Dante Discover the Secrets of the Universe* 96–98
St. James, James 117–19; *Freak Show* 117–19
The Saints of Augustine 150–51
Salat, Christine 143–46; *Living in Secret* 143–46
Sanchez, Alex 88–95; *Rainbow Boys* 89–91; *Rainbow High* 91–92; *Rainbow Road* 92–94
Savage, Dan 137–38; *The Kid* 137–38
Scelsa, Kate 155; *Fans of the Impossible Life* 155
Scoppettone, Sandra 37–41; *All Happy Endings Are Alike* 37–41
Self, Jeffrey 131–32; *Drag Teen* 131–32
She's Not There 110–11
Shimko, Bonnie 60, 66–67; *Letters in the Attic* 66–67
Simms, Ruth Ann 173–74; *The Case of the Missing Mother* 174; *Pride Pack* 174,

Index

186*ch*6*n*3; *Who Framed Lorenzo Garcia?* 174
Skyscraping 154–55
Sprout 95–96
Stealing Parker 152–53

teaching LGBTQ young adult literature 181–83
trans 1, 2, 9, 14, 16, 19, 20, 25, 49, 88, 93, 101, 102–33, 134, 139, 151, 156, 162, 168–69, 173, 175, 185*ch*4*n*1
Trites, Roberta 78–79, 82, 186*ch*6*n*2
Two Boys Kissing 169–70

utopias 157–79

The Velveteen Father 136–37
Verdi, Jessica 153–54; *My Life After Now* 153–54

Voigt, Cynthia 82–83; *David and Jonathan* 82–83

Walker, Robert Paul 80–82 ;*The Method* 80–82
Watts, Julie 60–63; *Finding H.F.* 60–63
Weetzie Bat 170–72
Who Framed Lorenzo Garcia? 174
Will Grayson Will Grayson 186*ch*6*n*1
Witch Baby 172–73
Wittlinger, Ellen 24, 49, 57–60, 64, 69–70, 119–121, 155; *Hard Love* 55–57; *Heart on My Sleeve* 69–70; *Love and Lies: Marisol's Story* 57–60; *Parrotfish* 119–121
Woodson, Jacqueline 146–48; *From the Notebooks of Melanin Sun* 146–48

Zemser, Amy Bronwen 151; *Dear Julia* 151

197

www.ingramcontent.com/pod-product-compliance
Lightning Source LLC
Chambersburg PA
CBHW032100300426
44116CB00007B/832